To my wife
Jennie Noren Hobson

THE FIRST YALE BASKETBALL TEAM

Pioneers of college basketball (1896–97), this team played the first game of college basketball with five men on a side, defeating the University of Pennsylvania by 32–10 on March 20, 1897. Notice the padded trousers, long stockings, and low-cut shoes.

Front row: Moore, Sanford. *Back row:* H. Peck, Clark, Beard, W. Peck (Captain), Sharpe, Rockwell, and Marshall. *(Photo courtesy of Henry W. Peck, Webster, New York, and William H. Peck, Glen Ridge, New Jersey.)*

Scientific Basketball

For COACHES, PLAYERS, OFFICIALS
SPECTATORS and SPORTSWRITERS

SECOND
EDITION

Howard A. Hobson

HEAD BASKETBALL COACH
YALE UNIVERSITY

New York
1955

PRENTICE-HALL, Inc.

Preface to the
Second Edition

SINCE THE PUBLICATION OF THE FIRST EDITION OF THIS BOOK, progress in the development of basketball has been evident. Techniques and skills have improved greatly, better equipment and facilities are available, rules have been subject to study and have been changed to make the game better—but, most important of all, basketball has continued to grow, both as a spectator sport and in the number of participants, not only in the United States but throughout the world. Even a tragic series of scandals in college basketball during this period has failed to have lasting detrimental effects on our great game.

Yet, in spite of the progress evident, the game is still in its infancy with its major development still in the future.

The purpose of the second edition of this book is to add reports of the available improved performances of the past few years in a way that we hope will be valuable to all concerned with the game. We hope that our findings and comments may help to increase the enjoyment of each individual through a greater, more enlightened, and wider participation in the sport.

Twenty-six new tables have been added to this second edition, and many new interpretations of the results of our studies have been given. Our own study (referred to in the book as the "control group") is supplemented by material not previously available that has been gathered from statistics of many other college, high school, and professional games.

The author wishes to express his deep appreciation to the following persons for their assistance in the preparation of the second edition:

Mr. Homer Cooke and Mr. Stephen Boda of the National Collegiate Athletic Association Bureau;

Mr. H. V. Porter of the National Federation of State High School Athletic Associations;

The many high school athletic association officers who kindly contributed valuable data;

Our bursary boys, student managers, and players at Yale University, whose combined efforts were invaluable in the study of our control group.

HOWARD A. HOBSON

Preface to the
First Edition

BASKETBALL IS NOW RECOGNIZED AS OUR MOST POPULAR winter sport. In spite of this fact, the game in many ways is still in its infancy. It is much younger than our other major sports, such as football and baseball. Probably for this reason, the rules of basketball have been changed rather frequently, and the game is still in the process of development. Very little has been done to analyze the game from a technical point of view. This is more true from the standpoint of scouting than from that of playing techniques. Most coaches today are well versed in the fundamentals of the game, and great strides have been made in developing offensive and defensive systems. However, in the execution of the various plays used, there have been very few standards by which to measure the exact success or failure of these plays and exact player and team performance. In a general sense, of course, we know when a team wins and when it loses; but measurement of the factors that contribute to the victory or the loss is not well established.

This entire situation might well be compared to our oldest game, baseball. In baseball a batter who has a .300 average is a good batter, and if he is able to do an average job of fielding, he will have a place on the team. This is known because thousands of cases have been studied, and a .300 average is accepted as a criterion of performance. By the same standard it follows that if a player is only able to bat .100 he cannot expect to play on a team because his defensive play cannot possibly compensate for such a great weakness in his batting. In the same manner, fielding averages, pitchers' averages, and many other baseball statistics have been worked out so that standards of performance for a baseball player are well known.

Now let us compare this with basketball. It has been the practice, and it still exists in most situations, to credit the individual and the team merely with the number of points scored by goals from the field and from the free-throw line. About the only factors of the game that have been universally recorded, other than total points, have been personal fouls and, in some cases, free-throw attempts. An individual player may score twenty points in a game and yet shoot very poorly, depending on the type and number of shots that he attempts. The same may be true for the entire team. It also follows that a player who scores points may not be a great asset to his team if he does not contribute in other ways. For example, little attention has been paid to the number of times a player or a team loses the ball during a game through bad passes, violations, or poor ball-handling. Little attention has been paid to the number of interceptions that a player or team makes in a game, or to the number of times that a player retrieves a ball or a rebound from the backboard.

It is the author's intention that the material contained in this book show that the above-mentioned factors and others may be objectively measured, and that it will be possible to establish, by analysis, a relationship between these factors of performance and the success or failure of the individual player and of the team. The standards thus produced will be of importance to coach or player in connection with his own team and his opponent's.

The information on scouting of basketball is basic to the material in the chapters for the player, official and sportswriter.

The author wishes to express deep appreciation to the following people for their assistance in making this book possible:

Players, coaches, student managers, and sportswriters throughout the country who have assisted in supplying data;

Dr. Harry A. Scott, Dr. C. L. Brownell, and Dr. E. S. Evenden of Columbia University for their invaluable suggestions, advice, and assistance during the entire preparation of the book;

Dr. Irving Lorge, Dr. Helen Walker, and Dr. W. L. Hughes of Columbia University, and Mr. Ned Irish of Madison Square Garden for valuable consultation and assistance;

Miss Ethel M. Feagley, Columbia University librarian, for assistance in preparing the annotated bibliography.

HOWARD A. HOBSON

Contents

xiii

Tables and Illustrations

Tables

Tables (cont.)

Tables (*cont.*)

Forms

Forms (cont.)

Photographs (between pages 76 and 77)

Introduction

IT IS THE PURPOSE OF THIS BOOK TO PRESENT THE RESULTS OF our studies of college basketball games, supplemented by similar available data from other college, high school, and professional games. Our original study reported in the first edition covered 460 college games over a 13-year period from 1936–37 through 1948–49. Most of the tables of this study are now included in Appendix A where they may be referred to for comparative and historical purposes. This second edition adds results of a study of 132 games during the last five years, 1949–50 through 1953–54. Altogether, our studies cover a total of 592 college games over an 18-year period. The teams and players in our study might be referred to as a "control group" with the other available material classed as supplementary. Many of the factors included, however, are available only from results of our study.

Individual and team shooting is emphasized but all other measurable factors that can be accurately recorded during the progress of a game are also included.

It is hoped that certain standards of performance are resulting from an analysis of this information and that coaches will receive helpful suggestions on how intelligently to scout and analyze their own players and teams as well as their individual and team opponents.

The findings appear to be equally adaptable to all levels —from junior high and high school to the top professional teams.

"Scouting" is defined as "the observing, analyzing, and recording of all performances of both teams, the individual players, and the officials during the progress of the game." The values of these observations, analyses, and records for coaches, players, officials, sportswriters, and spectators are discussed fully. In addition, examples of scout reports and methods of scouting as well as complete forms and charts for analysis of scouting material are included.

Tables are used to list the results of the game reports. The reader is urged to give careful attention to these tables from which yearly, periodical and total findings are available for all objective factors of the game.

1

The Game—
Its History and Future

BASKETBALL IS AMERICA'S GREATEST CONTRIBUTION TO THE sports field. It is the only major sport that is entirely American in origin. Basketball was invented in 1891 at Springfield College, Springfield, Massachusetts by the late Dr. James Naismith. Little did the inventor realize at that time that the game would develop to its present position in the field of national sports. It was his intention to introduce a game that could be played indoors with a minimum amount of equipment, to fill in between the major sports seasons of football and baseball. It was also his intention to eliminate bodily contact so far as possible, and thereby lessen the risk of injury prevalent in football.

Peach baskets were first used as goals and since there were no openings in the bottoms, the ball had to be retrieved by the use of ladders after each goal. Originally, there were nine players on each side but because of the congestion caused when eighteen players moved rapidly over a small area, the number was reduced to seven and finally to five.

Yale University really pioneered the five-man game. The

first college game with five men on a team was played at Yale University between Yale and the University of Pennsylvania on March 20, 1897.   Yale won the game 32-10 (see frontis-piece).

The development of basketball since that time has produced other major rule changes that have greatly improved the game.   At one time it was customary for the winning team to hold the ball in the back court to "stall out" the remaining time.   To eliminate this the ten-second rule was introduced, making it necessary for a team to advance the ball across the center line within ten seconds, or relinquish the ball to their opponents.   This change did much to speed up the game and gave the trailing team a better chance. Another major change that noticeably affected the game was the elimination of the center jump during the seasons from 1936 until 1938.   Up to that time it was the practice to have a tip-off between the two centers after each free-throw goal or field goal.   The scoring team now relinquishes the ball to its opponents after each goal, with a few exceptions when the ball is dead following a goal.   This change has popularized the fast break and has greatly increased scoring.   It also means that tall men, previously used mainly to secure the tip-off, had to be better all-round players to earn a place on the team.

Another major change prohibits any offensive player from standing in the free-throw lane for more than three seconds. This opens up the area under the basket and also prevents tall men from standing directly under the basket where they formerly scored by "dunking" the ball into the basket.

These and other rule changes have made the game a five-man shooting contest.   For example, one player formerly shot all the free throws for his team.   Now, the fouled player shoots the free throw and all have an opportunity to score free-throw points.   The changes that have speeded up the game and brought the fast break into prominence have also made it possible for all the players to participate in the scoring. This has added great interest to the game, for both players and spectators.

There will no doubt be further changes which will improve the game as basketball is still very much in the developmental stage. Although the game has been played since 1891, it was in the mid-thirties that it became a prominent major sport in most parts of the country.

Interest in basketball has been particularly great since Mr. Ned Irish conceived the idea of bringing college basketball into Madison Square Garden in 1934–35. The tremendous publicity given to these New York games, the intersectional interest, the All-America selections, and the National Tournaments, effected a country-wide growth and interest in basketball. Even the college basketball scandals of thrown games uncovered in 1950, while a saddening blow, failed permanently to affect the game and present interest is greater than ever. It is now estimated that well over 20 million people play basketball each year in the United States. Over 318 million fans bought tickets to their favorite sports events in 1949. Of these, 105 million or 33 per cent were for basketball games.[1] Basketball far surpasses any of our other major sports in both participation and spectator attendance.

Basketball has become a major part of all physical education programs and is played by many boys and girls recreationally on a non-competitive basis; it is one of the leading intramural sports in school programs; and it is played on a highly competitive basis by high school, college, amateur, and professional teams throughout the country. The game was also one of the chief conditioning and recreational sports used by our Armed forces during World War II. For example, in 1944 there were more than 2,000 American service teams playing basketball in Great Britain and approximately 1,500 in Italy.

---

[1] Figures through the courtesy of Ray Bethers and *This Week* magazine.

Hundreds of service teams have more recently played in Germany, Japan, Korea, and other countries in which we have had military bases. As a result, interest in the game increased greatly throughout the world. In the 1948 and 1952 Olympics many countries looked to America for coaches and leaders to help them with the game. A number of recent Olympic teams of other nations have been coached by Americans. It is quite possible that in the near future basketball will be the leading international sport.

The future of basketball is truly great. Improvements in transportation are making intersectional and international games possible for many teams. For example, in 1946–47 the University of Oregon team played two games in New York and were away from school only five days, missing only two days of classes. In 1948–49 the Yale University team played two games in San Francisco during vacation and made the trip in six days. Both trips, of course, were made by air, and many teams are making similar trips now. In the summer of 1953, the Yale University team played 30 games in eight countries in South America in less than two months. College teams have toured Europe and Pacific Coast teams fly to Honolulu for games every year.

The widespread interest in the game has caused many large structures to be built to accommodate large crowds. At the present time construction is underway for many buildings which will seat up to 20,000 spectators each. This will rival the already customary attendance at Madison Square Garden. Montevideo, Uruguay, has an arena that will seat over 30,000 and Luna Park in Buenos Aires accommodates 25,000. Out-of-doors facilities are also being developed rapidly and the game is becoming a year-round sport in many sections.

This great future that is predicted for basketball, including intersectional and international competition, is important to all interested in the game. It certainly indicates the need for greater study in order that the game's fullest possibilities may be realized.

Value of scouting

"Scouting" is a term that is used in athletics with various meanings. Using this term in a broad sense, we have defined basketball scouting as the observing, analyzing, and recording of all performances of both teams, the individual players and the officials during the progress of the game. The results of scouting include objective data that are recordable and productive of averages and percentages. They also include subjective observations on styles of play or similar factors. These cannot be as accurately measured or reported as the objective factors but are probably of equal importance. Scouting also includes observations regarding one's own team as well as the opponents.

The information received about a thoroughly scouted game should be of value to all interested in and connected with basketball in, of course, different ways. Some of these values are as follows:

Values for the coach

First, let us consider the values of objective observations in scouting an individual player. Among the factors of the game that can be measured objectively are field-goal attempts and field goals from various locations; free-throw attempts and free-throw goals; recoveries such as offensive and defensive rebounds; recovered jump balls and interceptions; losses-of-ball due to bad passes, violations, and poor ball-handling; personal fouls.

The field-goal data alone are of great value to the coach. If his players are shooting below the accepted average some change may be necessary in their fundamental work. If an opponent is able to score only from certain areas or to score only certain types of shots, this fact has valuable implications as to how to play against that opponent. For example, if an opponent has a big center and the charts indicate that he can score only in the short area close to the basket, the defensive center may run back to the keyhole and wait for him, knowing probably that he will not take a long shot. If the scout report shows his style of shooting and he shoots only with his right hand, he may be played accordingly. The scouting data may indicate that a star guard on the opposing team is very fast and takes shots under the basket but cannot shoot from a long distance. The defensive player, therefore, can play him loose and prevent him from using his speed. If, on the other hand, reports indicate that a player is a good long shot he will have to be played accordingly. Often scout reports indicate that a player does all or most of his shooting from one side of the court. Knowing this is an aid to the defensive player in getting back to a proper position and also in playing the offensive man on a particular side.

Objective free-throw data are valuable mainly for instructional purposes. An analysis of free-throw percentages is a necessity for intelligent correction or suggestions.

Rebound data are particularly valuable for indicating the strong rebounders on your own and the opposing team. The use of such data is the only way to know what your own players are doing and it will lead to better instruction. Knowing the strong rebounders on the opposing team will enable a coach to devise means of screening out these men and making them less effective.

Information on other recoveries such as jump balls retrieved and interceptions is also of value. This information helps the coach to combat the opponents' strong retrievers and to strengthen his own players in this particular department. Retrieving a jump ball toward the end of a close game is worth a little time and effort. It may set up the winning goal.

Loss-of-ball data are extremely important for instructional

purposes.   A player who constantly travels with the ball or makes bad passes will more readily correct his errors if the number of times this occurred during a game can be pointed out to him.   Advantages may also be gained by knowing of opponents who have bad habits in this regard.   For example, an uncertain passer may be pressed by the defense, causing him to lose the ball more frequently.

Personal foul data are commonly utilized by coaches for instructional purposes.   It is also of value for a coach to know which opponents foul most frequently so that strategy may be planned accordingly.   Naturally, offensive threats should be directed toward defensive weaknesses.   A player who fouls repeatedly on defense may be a key offensive man.   If so, the offense should be directed toward him.   Under the present rules, if a key player has three or four fouls, a smart opponent will put him on the spot, running plays at him repeatedly until he fouls out.   Personal foul data are an important part of any scout report and much strategy may result from it.

Objective team data may be obtained by computing the totals of individual records.   For the coach's own team, the total picture will show not only the team average but whether the team in general is failing to drive in for the basket, is taking bad shots, or is failing to take advantage of known defensive weaknesses in certain areas.   In many games we reviewed the charts at the half and discovered that our team had taken only three or four shots the entire half in the short area. Naturally, this means that the team was not taking advantage of plays going into the basket, or that they were not feeding the post man properly, or possibly that the offensive rebounding was off.

There is nothing more valuable in planning an attack against an opposing team than knowledge of that team's general shooting ability and styles of performance.   Charting a team will indicate whether it is a free-shooting, or a conservative "percentage" shooting team.   Some teams have shot at the basket as few as 18 times in a game, while others have shot as many as 132 times.   In the first example, a coach would naturally play a pressing defense, if behind, in order to make the other team shoot and play ball.   In the second example, a team could safely play loose away from the ball, knowing that shots would be taken without much encouragement. When a team is shooting freely at the basket it is probably employing a fast break, which means that the defensive team may wish to sacrifice offensive rebounds and get the defensive men back fast.   An example may be used to illustrate these points.

Several years ago, one of the University of Utah's fine teams played the University of Oregon.   Not having seen them play previously, Oregon knew little about their offense. At the half, the charts indicated that they took only one-hand shots, and that very few shots were taken in the long-shot area.   With a slight lead, Oregon played a keyhole defense the second half, resulting in a 51 to 15 victory for Oregon. The strategy was entirely guided by information on the opposing team's shooting pattern taken from the first-half shooting charts.   Usually, charting an opposing team several times will present a good picture as to its general performance in shooting.

Now let us consider the values of subjective scouting observations.   A report should be made on each player, and it should include such factors as size, speed, aggressiveness, competitive ability, endurance, temperament, and defensive ability.   These observations are just as valuable as the objective ones in coaching individual players and planning the play against individual opponents.

Subjective *team* observations are of course one of the foundations for coaching a basketball team and for planning the attack against opponents.   Certainly the coach must be able to observe his plan of offensive and defensive team plays and organization.   He must be able to decide which are functioning and what adjustments need to be made during the progress of the game. He must also be able to take from this subjective scout report information that will be helpful in future games. Shall a fast break be used for the entire game? Shall a pressing man-to-man defense or a zone defense be used? Are the out-of-bound plays being utilized? Is the team rebound organization functioning? These observations and many others are accurate only if scout reports and records are kept.

Subjective observations about the opposing team are of equal importance. What offensive plays and tactics do the opponents use? What measures shall be employed by the defensive team to stop them? Do the opponents use a man-to-man, zone, or combination defense, and how do they use it? What offensive plan will best attack the opponents' defense? Obviously these subjective team observations are invaluable to any coach.

Still other phases of both objective and subjective scouting include the performance of individuals and teams on home courts as compared to visiting courts, during the first half as compared to second half which involves endurance, for example, or performance in practice games as compared to major games. Information of this kind is extremely valuable in the conditioning of both players and teams and in the psychology of coaching.

Value for players, officials, sportswriters, spectators

The players

In one sense, the player is the ultimate recipient of all scouting information. Scouting is conducted chiefly for the purpose of improving individual and team play. Aside from this, however, it has unique values for the player. First, the player benefits from all objective scouting data because the information may help him to improve his game offensively and to play more scientifically against his opponent defensively.   Before scouting was thought of in basketball, it was the rule for a player to analyze his opponent during the early part of a game so that he could play accordingly.   Objective scouting merely eliminates the guess work.   Second, the player benefits from subjective scouting data through conferences with the coach and through an analysis of this part of his game.   Third, the player benefits through self-testing and rating which is a form of scouting.   There are many factors that contribute to making a successful basketball player. An analysis of these factors by the player himself, as well as by his teammates and the coach, will be invaluable.

The officials

Scouting an official is comparatively new in basketball, but it is important.   Because of the unique position of the basketball official as compared to officials of other sports, it is essential that the work of the official during a game be recorded, analyzed, and rated.   The results through proper follow-up work should be valuable to every official.   This scouting and rating may be done by representatives from official bureaus or associations, or other competent observers.

The sportswriters

Basketball owes much of its popularity to the publicity that has been given to the game through channels such as the press, radio, and TV.   Sportswriters have not had a great deal of objective data to report to the public.   Many have expressed a desire to have more of this information.   Certain parts of the scout reports which may be kept conveniently by sportswriters or reporters themselves such as field-goal attempts, losses, and recoveries, will be of great value in reporting games to the public.

The spectators

Similarly, objective data will give spectators a better appreciation of the game.   Scouting information will make it possible for spectators who like to keep score at games to do so more intelligently, and forms may be made available to them so that other data may be tabulated if desired. Actually this is of benefit to many fans because it relieves unnecessary nervous tension during games.

2

A Complete Game Scout Report

THE SCOUT REPORT ILLUSTRATED IN FORM A, PAGES 16–22,
gives a complete picture of the objective and subjective observations during a complete game.   On the front of Form A all
of the objective data are reported.   The back of the form
gives all subjective observations during the game.   These
minimum essentials are included:

1. *Objective Data (Individual)*
   (a) Long field-goal attempts and goals scored
   (b) Medium field-goal attempts and goals scored
   (c) Short field-goal attempts and goals scored
   (d) Total field-goal attempts and goals scored
   (e) Free-throw attempts and goals scored
   (f) Loss of ball
       1) through violations
       2) through poor ball handling
       3) through poor passing
   (g) Interceptions
   (h) Tie-ups
   (i) Jump-ball recoveries

14

(j) Offensive rebound recoveries
(k) Defensive rebound recoveries
(l) Assists
(m) Personal fouls
(n) Points-responsible-for
(o) Total points

2. *Objective Data (Team)*

(a) Team totals for each of the individual items (*a*) to (*o*) listed above

(b) Team shooting percentages and averages for long, medium, and short shots, and free throws

(c) The running score

In regard to objective information, some coaches will wish to include more extensive material, such as style of shots attempted and scored; first and second half divisions, or possibly in quarter divisions; shots taken and scored as a result of certain styles of play such as the fast break or set plays. Additions of this kind may be easily kept by using symbols.

Tie-ups, assists, points-responsible-for, and running score are not a part of this study but are mentioned and described briefly because they are recognized as a part of a complete scout report. All other items included in Form A are treated thoroughly later.

A tie-up occurs when a player causes a held ball to be called by gaining partial possession of the ball while it is in the control of an opponent.

An assist may be credited to a player when he makes a pass that contributes directly to a field goal. Since this is a matter of judgment, the assist is not entirely an objective item.

Points-responsible-for are charged to the defensive player when his man scores a field goal or when a player fouls an opponent and the latter scores from the free-throw line.

The running score gives valuable information. A diagonal line is drawn through the proper number each time a score

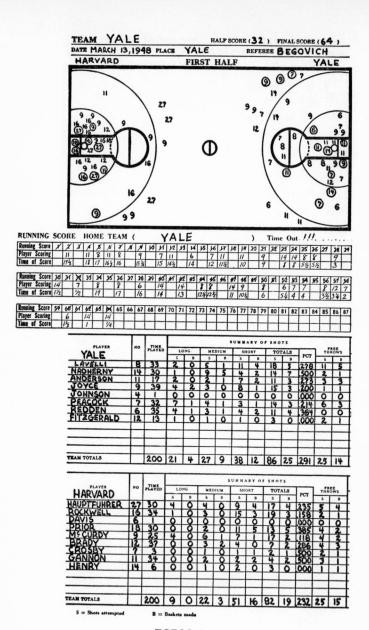

TEAM YALE HALF SCORE (**32**) FINAL SCORE (**64**)

DATE MARCH 13, 1948 PLACE YALE REFEREE BEGOVICH

HARVARD FIRST HALF YALE

RUNNING SCORE HOME TEAM (YALE) Time Out ///

Running Score	1	2	3	4	5	6	7	8	9	10	11	12	13	14	15	16	17	18	19	20	21	22	23	24	25	26	27	28	29
Player Scoring	11		11	8	11	8		9		7	11		6		7	11		11		9		14	14	8	8		9		
Time of Score	19½		18	17	16½	16		15¾		15	14½		14		12	11½		10		9		8	8	5½	5½		3		

Running Score	30	31	32	33	34	35	36	37	38	39	40	41	42	43	44	45	46	47	48	49	50	51	52	53	54	55	56	57	58
Player Scoring	14		7		8		8		6		14	14			8	8		14	9		8		6	7	7			8	12	7
Time of Score	1½		½		19		17		16		14		13		12½	12½		11	10¼		6		5¼	4	4			3½	3½	2

Running Score	59	60	61	62	63	64	65	66	67	68	69	70	71	72	73	74	75	76	77	78	79	80	81	82	83	84	85	86	87
Player Scoring	6		14		14																								
Time of Score	1½		1		¼																								

PLAYER YALE	NO	TIME PLAYED	LONG S	LONG B	MEDIUM S	MEDIUM B	SHORT S	SHORT B	TOTALS S	TOTALS B	PCT	FREE THROWS S	FREE THROWS B
LAVELLI	8	33	2	0	5	1	11	4	18	5	.278	11	5
NADHERNY	14	30	1	0	9	5	4	2	14	7	.500	2	1
ANDERSON	11	17	2	0	2	1	7	2	11	3	.273	3	3
JOYCE	9	39	4	2	3	0	8	1	15	3	.200	1	1
JOHNSON	4	1	0	0	0	0	0	0	0	0	.000	0	0
PEACOCK	7	32	7	1	4		3		14	3	.214	6	3
REDDEN	6	35	4	1	3	1	4	2	11	4	.364	0	0
FITZGERALD	12	13	1	0	1	0	1	0	3	0	.000	2	1
TEAM TOTALS		200	21	4	27	9	38	12	86	25	.291	25	14

PLAYER HARVARD	NO	TIME PLAYED	LONG S	LONG B	MEDIUM S	MEDIUM B	SHORT S	SHORT B	TOTALS S	TOTALS B	PCT	FREE THROWS S	FREE THROWS B
HAUPTFUHRER	27	30	4	0	4	0	9	4	17	4	.235	5	4
ROCKWELL	16	34	1	0	3	0	15	3	19	3	.158	2	1
DAVIS	6	1	0	0	0	0	0	0	0	0	.000	0	0
PRIOR	18	30	0	0	2	0	11	5	13	5	.385	4	2
McCURDY	9	25	4	0	6	1	7	1	17	2	.118	4	2
BRADY	12	37	0	0	3	2	4	0	7	2	.286	4	3
CROSBY	7	3	0	0	1	0	1	1	2	1	.500	0	0
GANNON	11	34	0	0	2	0	2	2	4	2	.500	5	3
HENRY	14	6	0	0	1	0	2	0	3	0	.000	1	1
TEAM TOTALS		200	9	0	22	3	51	16	82	19	.232	25	15

S = Shots attempted B = Baskets made

FORM A

A COMPLETE GAME SCOUT REPORT

16

UMPIRE **SCHOENFELD**   TIMER **DESMOND**   SCORER **ARNOLD**

YALE	SECOND HALF	HARVARD

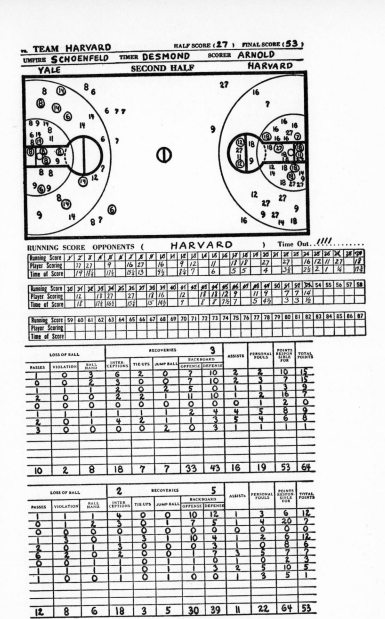

RUNNING SCORE   OPPONENTS (**HARVARD**   )   Time Out ..////........

Running Score	1	2	3	4	5	6	7	8	9	10	11	12	13	14	15	16	17	18	19	20	21	22	23	24	25	26	27	28	29
Player Scoring	27	27		9		16	27		16		9	12		11		18	18		27		27		16	12	11	27		18	
Time of Score	19	18½		17½		15½	13		9½		8½	7		6		5	5		4		3½		2½	2	1	¼		17½	

Running Score	30	31	32	33	34	35	36	37	38	39	40	41	42	43	44	45	46	47	48	49	50	51	52	53	54	55	56	57	58
Player Scoring	12		18	27		27		18	16		12		18	18	12	9		11	9		7	7	14						
Time of Score	18		17½	16½		15½		15	14½		9		8	8	7½	7		5	4½		3	3	½						

Running Score	59	60	61	62	63	64	65	66	67	68	69	70	71	72	73	74	75	76	77	78	79	80	81	82	83	84	85	86	87
Player Scoring																													
Time of Score																													

LOSS OF BALL			RECOVERIES			3		ASSISTS	PERSONAL FOULS	POINTS RESPONSIBLE FOR	TOTAL POINTS
PASSES	VIOLATION	BALL HAND.	INTERCEPTIONS	TIE-UPS	JUMP BALL	BACKBOARD OFFENSE	DEFENSE				
1	0	3	6	2	0	7	10	2	2	10	15
0	0	2	3	0	0	7	10	2	3	7	15
1	1	1	2	0	2	5	0	1	1	3	9
2	0	0	2	0	1	11	10	1	2	16	7
0	0	0	0	0	0	0	0	0	1	2	0
1	0	1	1	1	1	2	4	4	5	8	8
2	0	1	4	2	1	0	3	5	4	6	8
3	0	0	0	0	2	0	3	1	1		1
10	2	8	18	7	7	33	43	16	19	53	64

LOSS OF BALL			RECOVERIES	2		5		ASSISTS	PERSONAL FOULS	POINTS RESPONSIBLE FOR	TOTAL POINTS
PASSES	VIOLATION	BALL HAND.	INTERCEPTIONS	TIE-UPS	JUMP BALL	BACKBOARD OFFENSE	DEFENSE				
1	1	1	4	0	0	10	12	1	3	6	12
0	1	2	3	0	0	7	5		4	20	7
0	0	0	0	0	0	0	0	0	0	0	0
1	3	0	3	0	0	10	4		2	6	12
2	0	1	3	0	0	0	3	1	5	8	6
6	2	0	2	0	0	0	7	3	5	7	7
0	0	0	1	0	0	0	0	2	5	2	3
1	1	0	0	0	1	3	3		5	10	5
1	0	0	0	0	1	0	0	1	3	5	1
12	8	6	18	3	5	30	39	11	22	64	53

FORM A

A COMPLETE GAME SCOUT REPORT

(*cont.*)

HARVARD OFFENSE — YALE DEFENSE

Harvard started their three big men so we played a man to man pressing defense all over the court at the start of the game. However, all five men did not do this so much of the effectiveness was lost. Later in the first half we played a standard man to man defense and dropped a man back to take care of Rockwell who was breaking down fast for them. They did not use a regular five man fast break but sent Rockwell and Gannon down ahead fast and used long passes. They always bring the ball up the court fairly fast so it is really not necessary to press them in order to make them play a fast game. Harvard scored very little on the fast break and depended mainly on their set play attacks. Against our man to man defense they used a single pivot but did not use the same man in the pivot all the time. Prior started in this position and later Hauptfuhrer and Rockwell played the position. They used standard plays off of this formation and like to screen away from the ball. We played loose and changed men on this particular play which was quite effective. However, they did score off these plays some and particularly on rebounds. They had far too many close shots at the basket in this game. For this reason, we should have changed to our zone defense at the half, as they were taking very few long shots, and not making any of them. When they continued to get too many short shots in the second half we finally did change to a zone in the middle of the half, and it was quite effective. They used two methods of attacking the zone. The first was to break a man into the key as indicated in Diagram 1. Later they put a man on the key and tried to pass the zone out of position, as indicated in Diagram 2. When they did this, we shifted into a loose man to man defense. Harvard is a dangerous team in close and our individual defense was poor. We made many unnecessary fouls and should work on this part of our game. Harvard hit a very poor average from the field or they would have made the game much closer.

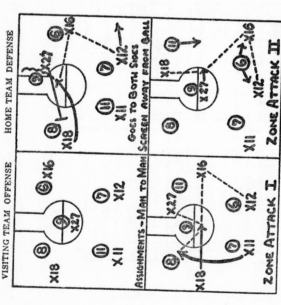

VISITING TEAM OFFENSE

HOME TEAM DEFENSE

ASSIGNMENTS — MAN TO MAN

GOES TO BOTH SIDES
SCREEN AWAY FROM BALL

ZONE ATTACK I

ZONE ATTACK II

FORM A

REVERSE SIDE

(Part 1)

18

YALE OFFENSE — HARVARD DEFENSE

Harvard used a man to man defense the entire game. In their assignment there was one major difference since the last game. This meant that Hauptfuhrer played opposite Lavelli in the bucket. They played Gannon against Lavelli in the bucket. This meant that Hauptfuhrer played opposite Peacock and Peacock was able to drive in for several scores. Harvard played a tighter defense also and did not drop off away from the ball as much. This made our center attack good. We used a standard fast break most of the game. We stressed driving hard and having Anderson and later Nadherny hitting the end line and breaking back out to meet the ball. Of the 32 points we scored in the first half, at least 20 were made on the fast break. We would have made more had we hit a higher average. We had 43 attempts but made only 12 baskets. Harvard recovered better to stop our fast break than they did in the first game, but we were still able to get a number of two on one and three on two situations. On the set plays we used the single pivot the entire game, except the last four minutes when we went into a ball control game to protect our lead. No. 1 was our best scoring play and we used it to both sides effectively. The second cutter is usually open when we split the post. In the ball control game we scored two baskets on No. 4 down the center. We also used the same play to the other side but Gannon loosened to the center and stopped it, and Lavelli did not cut for the basket. We still do not use the proper option on our set plays and depend too much on the fast break. Harvard pressed down the court on the defense in the second half some. We used the long pass game effectively when they did this. A mediocre performance in shooting from the field and also from the free throw line prevented us from making a higher score.

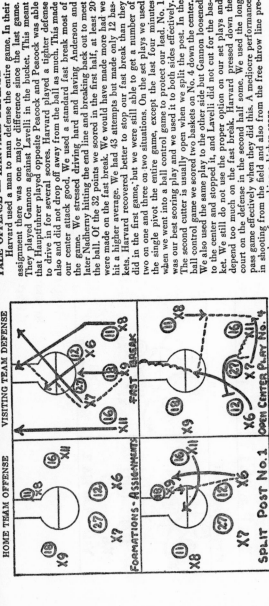

HOME TEAM OFFENSE   VISITING TEAM DEFENSE

FORMATIONS - ASSIGNMENTS

FAST BREAK

OPEN CENTER PLAY No. 4

SPLIT POST No. 1

✕ = Offensive Player

◯ = Defensive Player

------ = Pass

〜〜〜 = Dribble

⟶ = Path of Player

⊤ = Screen

FORM A

REVERSE SIDE

(Part 2)

19

JUMP-BALL PLAYS

When we were in scoring territory and controlled the tip we used No. 1 twice and later No. 3. We scored directly on No. 3. On most of the jump balls Harvard controlled the tip because of superior height. Against this we rotated three men keeping a safety man back. Harvard used no apparent jump-ball plays, but usually tipped to the right side. We were able to gain a slight advantage on all jump balls 7 to 5.

REBOUND ORGANIZATION

Harvard rebounded all three of their big men on the offensive board and they did this very well. They did no obvious cross screening but got position very well and particularly Hauptfuhrer and Prior hurt us in this department. Harvard rebounded all five men defensively but did not attempt to screen out our big men. Our rebound organization was standard. We rebounded 3 men offensively and at times four. However, later in the game we had to drop men back to stop their break and at times rebounded only Lavelli and Joyce. Defensively, we did a poor job in screening out their big men. Our guards did not do a good job in this department.

FREE-THROW ORGANIZATION

Harvard used a long pass break after free throws that caught us twice. We should have two men back. They rebound very well on missed free throws with their big men. They made three baskets in this manner and we will need to correct this in the next game.

OUT-OF-BOUNDS PLAYS

We used No. 2 and No. 5 twice each and scored once on No. 5. We used no side out of bounds plays, as they did not play us tight. Harvard did not use any apparent out of bounds plays. We zoned the area under the basket which may have discouraged them using the plays they used against us before.

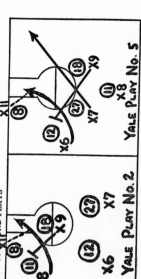

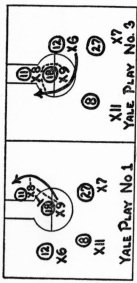

JUMP-BALL PLAYS

YALE PLAY No. 1

YALE PLAY No. 3

OUT-OF-BOUND PLAYS

YALE PLAY No. 2

YALE PLAY No. 5

FORM A

REVERSE SIDE

(Part 3)

20

PERSONNEL — YALE: LAVELLI

A bad first half. Was off on his shooting and not aggressive on the boards. However, did play a very fine second half, finishing with fifteen points, playing a good defensive game and getting at least half of our rebounds. Had worst game of season but getting throw line but finished season with 80%. Still needs to work on individual defense but much improved.

ANDERSON

Still handicapped because of wrist injury. Played aggressive game but had trouble with Gannon defensively. Is slow in recovering on defense.

NADHERNEY

Played a fine second half. Hit baskets when they counted. Is fine competitor. Floor game must improve as well as defense.

JOYCE

Needs to concentrate on shooting. Must practice this a great deal to be a consistent scorer. Played better on boards and is improving.

PEACOCK

Played a good first half. Then took shots he didn't have in second half. Fouled out by committing unnecessary fouls. Goes after ball on dribble when there is no chance.

REDDEN

A fine defensive game. Needs to have more confidence in shooting. Called time-outs at proper time and did a good job in leading team.

FITZGERALD

Not confident enough in shooting and needs to develop drive. Can be a fine player.

JOHNSON

Only in the game one minute. Committed a foul by weak defense. Could be a good player with hard work.

PERSONNEL — HARVARD: HAUPTFUHRER

Six feet, five inches, 210, good man on both boards, good defensively for big man. Will shoot out in second area but not in third area. Shoots mostly with right hand. Has good fakes.

ROCKWELL

Fast. Leads fast break. Six feet, 3 inches, 190, left-handed. Shoots mostly with left and goes to left. However, will shoot from outside as well as inside; only fair defensively. Very dangerous offensive player.

PRIOR

Six feet, 6 inches, 220, very effective on both boards. Very aggressive. Offensively, a threat mainly in first area. Fair defensively for big man.

BRADY

Five feet, 10 inches, 170, very aggressive and fair defensive player. Fouled out mainly because of aggressiveness. Shoots mainly from second area. Seems to be sparkplug of team.

GANNON

Six feet, 1 inch, 180, football player. Very aggressive. Fast. Left-handed. Uses left-handed hook shot. Played pivot man defensively and plays to the side and in front. Did fairly good job on Lavelli.

HENRY

Six feet, 170, replaced Gannon. Played pivot man defensively. Aggressive but not as good defensively as Gannon. Fouls easily.

CROSBY

Five feet, 10 inches, 160. Replaced Brady. Is good shot from foul area. Fairly fast. Fair on defense.

DAVIS

Six feet, three inches, 180. Replaced Hauptfuhrer. Played in

(*Continued on next page*)

FORM A

REVERSE SIDE

(Part 4)

pivot. Shoots with either hand. Did not appear to be rugged on boards or strong defensively.

McCURDY

Six feet, 160. Shoots from in and out. Good set shot, off in this game. Shoots very freely. Always dangerous. Fair defensive player.

OFFICIALS — BEGOVICH

Excellent game. Followed ball well and used good judgment. Called plays quickly and decisively.

SCHOENFELD

A good game except interpretation on travelling. Did not allow shooter to lift pivot foot in shooting. In the main, however, used good judgment and game under control at all times.

GENERAL COMMENTS —
SUGGESTIONS FOR FUTURE GAMES

Harvard is big and aggressive. Condition is an important factor and we did not keep up a fast pace all the way in this game. Mentally, we were keyed too high for this game—not necessary against a traditional opponent. Players seemed nervous and over anxious entire first half—settled down in second half. Harvard may zone more next game with big men—be ready for this. Against man to man we need to develop better side attack against them as they concentrate defense in key area. Defensively assigned man to man seems best but we must play it much tighter next game. They are a free shooting team and must be picked up clear out to center of court.

In this game we coasted with 12 point lead in second half and they caught us. Harvard has hard fighting team and do not give up easily. Can't let up against them.

FORM A

REVERSE SIDE

(Part 4, *cont.*)

is made. The jersey number of the scoring player is placed beneath the score number. The time remaining in the half is placed beneath the number of the player scoring. This information will show which team is leading at any time during the game. It also indicates consistency in scoring by players and teams.

3. *Subjective Observations*

(a) Team offense and opponent's defense

It is suggested that these two major items be scouted and recorded together. This includes offensive formations, positions of players, methods of bringing the ball down the court, and all set-play patterns. It also includes the manner in which the defensive team gets back to position and the opponent's styles of team defense.

(b) Team defense and opponent's team offense. This is the reverse of (a).

(c) Jump-ball plays (both teams)

(d) Rebound organization (both teams)

This includes team rebound organization by both teams on the offense and on the defense. It also includes any particular rebound strategy or plays that may be used.

(e) Free-throw organization

Observations should be recorded on free-throw information of both teams on offense and defense. Any plays or strategy employed following free throws should also be recorded.

(f) Out-of-bounds plays (both teams)

This includes both the offense and defense on all out-of-bounds situations; team organization and plays of both teams; situations where the ball is taken out-of-bounds under a team's own basket, under the opponent's basket, or on the sides of the court.

(g) Personnel (both teams)

If it is not already known, this should include the height, weight, class, and age of each player; and all individual observations of the player in this particular game, such as speed, defensive ability, and offensive ability. A good personnel report is as valuable as any part of the scouting report in basketball.

(h) Officials

A brief report regarding the work of the officials in the game should be included.

(i) General comments—suggestions for future games

This may include any observations not covered in any other items, such as condition of the court, lighting conditions, psychological factors, general observations of different stages of the game, and "pep" talk reactions.

Since the report includes all information found in a score book, it may be used as an official score record. But the official score book should also be kept to minimize possibilities of error.

A more detailed explanation of the procedure used in obtaining these data follows. This type of report and the following procedure were used in securing the data for the 592 college games upon which many of the suggested scouting principles in the book are based.

3

Scouting Methods Employed

Objective data are obtained through the use of charts kept by expert observers. There are several plans which may be used, but it is best if three trained observers are used to keep the records during a game. Student managers or others familiar with the game may easily do the observing since it is an entirely objective process.

It is suggested that one observer record all field-goal attempts and field goals for both teams. This may be done by using a chart as illustrated in Form B on pp. 26–27. It will be noted that the scoring area is divided into three parts: the short area includes shots out to a radius of twelve feet from the basket; the second, or medium area, includes shots from a radius of twelve to twenty-four feet from the basket; the third, or long area, includes shots farther than a radius of twenty-four feet from the basket. Other areas may be included, such as right and left side of the court. The techniques are simple. If a player takes a shot at the basket, merely record his number on the chart at the position from which the shot was taken. Tip-ups and blocked shots count

TEAM				HALF SCORE ( ) FINAL SCORE ( )
DATE		PLACE		REFEREE

FIRST HALF

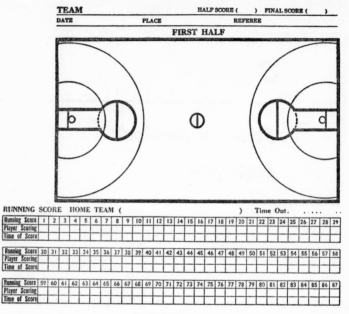

RUNNING SCORE   HOME TEAM (   )   Time Out. . . . .

Running Score	1	2	3	4	5	6	7	8	9	10	11	12	13	14	15	16	17	18	19	20	21	22	23	24	25	26	27	28	29
Player Scoring																													
Time of Score																													

Running Score	30	31	32	33	34	35	36	37	38	39	40	41	42	43	44	45	46	47	48	49	50	51	52	53	54	55	56	57	58
Player Scoring																													
Time of Score																													

Running Score	59	60	61	62	63	64	65	66	67	68	69	70	71	72	73	74	75	76	77	78	79	80	81	82	83	84	85	86	87
Player Scoring																													
Time of Score																													

FORM B

BASKETBALL SCORING FORM

(To be kept by first observer.)

as attempts.   If the shot is successful, the number is encircled.
If more detailed data are desired, such as the style of shot or a
shot resulting from a certain style of play, additional symbols
may be used.   The shot observer may also keep the running
score for both teams.

The second observer should tabulate rebounds for individual players of both teams.   This again is a simple procedure.   Form C on page 28 is suggested.   The observer
merely records a tally each time a player retrieves an offensive
or defensive rebound.   An offensive rebound is one which
is retrieved from a player's own basket.   A defensive rebound
is one that is retrieved from the opponents' basket.   An observer may check the accuracy of his figures, since the total

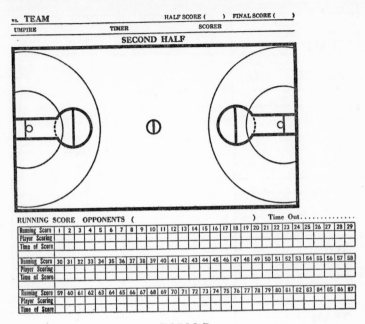

vs. TEAM   HALF SCORE (   )   FINAL SCORE (   )

UMPIRE   TIMER   SCORER

SECOND HALF

RUNNING SCORE   OPPONENTS (   )   Time Out..............

Running Score	1	2	3	4	5	6	7	8	9	10	11	12	13	14	15	16	17	18	19	20	21	22	23	24	25	26	27	28	29
Player Scoring																													
Time of Score																													

Running Score	30	31	32	33	34	35	36	37	38	39	40	41	42	43	44	45	46	47	48	49	50	51	52	53	54	55	56	57	58
Player Scoring																													
Time of Score																													

Running Score	59	60	61	62	63	64	65	66	67	68	69	70	71	72	73	74	75	76	77	78	79	80	81	82	83	84	85	86	87
Player Scoring																													
Time of Score																													

FORM B

BASKETBALL SCORING FORM

(cont.)

number of rebounds should be approximately equal to the number of missed field-goal attempts and missed free throws less missed free throws when the ball is dead following the attempt. For example, if team A shoots at the basket 60 times and succeeds 15 times, there will be 45 rebounds at that basket from field-goal attempts alone. If team A attempts 20 free throws and makes 10, there could be an additional 10 rebounds, or a total of approximately 55 offensive and defensive rebounds at that basket.

Occasionally a missed free throw is a dead ball and there is no rebound. This may occur, for example, on the first free throw when two are awarded or on a missed free throw awarded for a technical or double foul. Records indicate

	OFFENSIVE	DEFENSIVE
TEAM		
PLAYER NO.		
TOTALS		

	OFFENSIVE	DEFENSIVE
TEAM		
PLAYER NO.		
TOTALS		

FORM C

REBOUND FORM

(To be kept by second observer.)

28

	LOSSES			RECOVERIES		
	Passes	Vio-lation	Ball Hand.	Inter-ceptions	Tie-Ups	Jump Ball
TEAM						
PLAYER NO.						
TOTALS						

	LOSSES			RECOVERIES		
	Passes	Vio-lation	Ball Hand.	Inter-ceptions	Tie-Ups	Jump Ball
TEAM						
PLAYER NO.						
TOTALS						

FORM D

LOSSES-OF-BALL AND RECOVERIES (EXCEPT REBOUNDS)
(To be kept by third observer.)

that examples of this kind averaged less than three a game except in 1952–53 and 1953–54 when the "one-one" free throw rule raised the average to about 14 a game.

All missed shots when the ball remains "live" or in play result in rebounds.

When a rebound results in a held ball, the *team* finally retrieving the jump ball should be given a rebound recovery. In case a shot goes out-of-bounds without hitting the backboard the opposing *team* is credited with a rebound. In these latter two cases they are recorded as *team* rebounds rather than individual.

The third observer should record losses-of-ball by players of both teams and recoveries other than rebounds (see Form D, page 29). It will be noted that losses are divided into three divisions, namely bad passes, violations, and ball-handling. Occasionally a player will be guilty of losing the ball when it is obviously not the passer's fault: for example, not cutting properly to meet a pass. In this case the offender should be charged with a loss under ball-handling.

Interceptions are credited to a player who gains possession of the ball from the other team in general floor play. If a player throws the ball out-of-bounds a *team* interception is credited to the opponent. The observer may check his accuracy since the number of interceptions should equal the number of losses due to bad passes and poor ball-handling. Jump-ball recoveries are credited to the player retrieving the jump ball. This observer may also keep tie-ups if desired. If assists and points-responsible-for are to be kept, either the second or third observer may keep them by adding the necessary columns to Form C or D.

The procedure in recording losses and recoveries is to mark a tally opposite the player's name in the proper column.

The observers may total the results and have the records available to the coach at half time. After the game they should be recorded on the complete scout report sheet and percentages computed.   Everything shown on the front page of the game scout record, Form A, may be derived from Forms B, C, and D and the score book.   The transfer to the permanent sheet (Form A) may be done in less than one hour.   It is suggested that the coach do this so that he may analyze the performances of the players and team during the game.

The subjective part of the report is a matter of observation *by an expert,* usually the head coach.   An assistant coach, or some other qualified observer, may record plays and notes on forms during the game.   However, this cannot be done by a casual observer.   It is suggested that immediately following the game or during the next day, the coach record his subjective observations on the back of Form A.   If a secretary is available, much of the subjective report may be dictated and typed on the form.   If other scouts are available a collaborated report may be given.   Completing the objective and subjective report should not take more than two to three hours of a coach's time and the permanent record with its future values will repay his effort.

Other scouting methods

Individual charts

Many coaches may prefer to secure objective data through the use of individual charts, as illustrated in Form E, page 32. In this method, the starting player in each position is No. 1. The first substitute in a position is No. 2, the second substitute is No. 3.   If a shot is successful the number is encircled. Second-half shots may be underlined to distinguish them from first-half shots.   This is the most simple method of charting shots on individual charts.   If more detailed information is desired, various symbols may be used.   Some coaches desire the following information (in each case special symbols may be used):

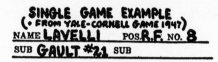

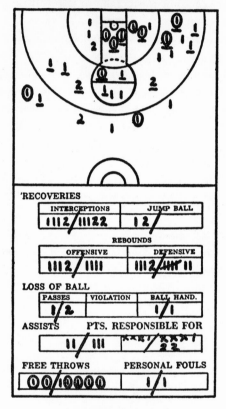

FORM E

Individual Chart

1. Bad shots as distinguished from good shots. This requires an expert observer with knowledge of the game.

2. The type of shot taken, whether it be a one-hand shot, a two-hand shot, a hook shot, an under-hand shot, or an overhead shot. If types of shots are recorded, one method is

to use numbers for each type of shot. For example, 1—set shot; 2—right-hand shot; 3—left-hand shot; 4—lay-up shot; 5—rebound shot.

3. Whether the shot was taken as the result of a rebound, a fast break, or a set play.

It is suggested that coaches avoid complicating the charts with a mass of data which will not be of actual value. Most coaches will find it sufficient merely to chart the shots attempted and the shots made from the proper location.

The other objective data should be recorded by using the same method. No. 1 is used for the starting player, No. 2 for the first substitute, etc. A diagonal line separates the two halves.

In the points-responsible-for box an *x* indicates two points (field goal) and the number *1* indicates one point (free

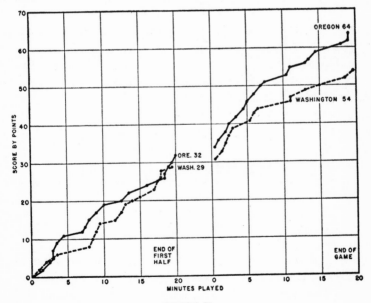

FORM F

GRAPH OF A BASKETBALL GAME

throw). If a second player is playing in the position, use number 2 below the symbol (see example).

One advantage of the individual chart method is that it gives the coach the complete picture of each player's achievement at a glance. This type of record has often been used along with the team forms. The results may easily be recorded on a permanent scout report like Form A. In other words the individual chart gives the same information as that obtained from Forms B, C, and D.

Graphs

Some coaches prefer the use of graphs in keeping game records. Form F, page 33, illustrates how a graph may be used to show the progress of teams during a game. A glance at the graph will indicate when each team scored and the game situation at any minute during the game.

Graphs may also be used for individual and team shooting and scoring records but they are more complicated and less desirable than the plans already described.

The individual-chart method and the graph method refer, of course, to objective scouting. Subjective observations are always the same in procedure.

4

Using Scout Reports for the Future

EACH SCOUT REPORT, IF CAREFULLY STUDIED, SHOULD LEAD to recommendations for the next game, even though it be with another opponent. In any event, the parts of the report that have to do with one's own team may be utilized. Prior to playing the next game, possibly on the Monday following a week-end game, the scout report may be taken up with the squad and plans made for the game to come.

It has been found that reviewing scout reports over a period of years helps in planning to meet a known opponent. A sample of notes taken from scout reports to meet a situation of this kind follows:

Yale vs. Pennsylvania, 1954 (Notes taken from scout reports of last two seasons)

1. Keep out of corners on fast break with the ball.
2. Trailer man is open around the sides of the court.
3. At least one man play the ball down court; two if possible.
4. With lead make them come out; they prefer to play loose.
5. Drive in on them individually. They will foul. Pass to open man when they take over.

6. They use a long-pass fast break. Two defensive men must be back at all times.

7. Analyze their personnel. Leach and Heylmun are key veterans.

8. No. 3 on Heylmun's side of floor was good last year. See where he plays and run plays at him.

9. Wide attack is good. Screen for side set shots.

10. They slap rebounds back. Guards play to intercept these.

11. Screen out Leach and Sturgis on boards.

12. Diagram their jump-ball play. It scored for them last year.

13. All five Pennsylvania men can score. They must all be guarded tightly.

14. Have Demcak shoot from sides. They will play him loose.

15. Watch man who loosens to tie up the post man. His man should cut for basket.

16. Don't throw to forwards down the side. They watch for this and will intercept.

17. No. 5 man can drive into foul area and down sides.

18. On defense guards must go through on the No. 3 play. They fake to the outside and go to the inside.

19. The out-of-bounds play to the left side going into the basket was good last year.

20. On jump balls tip away from Heylmun. He is their ball hawk.

21. Their center jumps in front of the post man. Pass over him.

22. The screen on sides is easy for set shots.

23. Force play early and as much as possible. Tie up their guards.

24. They had three men on the offensive board but do not press down court; they drop back fast. If forwards take their guards to the sides, our guards can drive in.

25. Free-throw arrangement must be reviewed. They use rebound plays.

26. Take over fast on defense. Make them shoot from outside.

27. Drive all the way to the end of the court. They stop their defense half way.

28. They rebound harder offensively when trailing.

29. They alternate post men—don't let Sturgis or Leach get ball in close scoring position.

30. Roll ball into the pivot. On defense they play hard on the sides.

31. Set up plays early in the game. Increase tempo later.

32. Go over the defense for their No. 3 play. Sliding defense will be best.

33. Cross the forwards on the fast break.

34. One guard can rebound offensively early in game. Get the lead.

35. The left side plays are good. They expect us to work to the right.

Additional uses of scout reports

Another valuable way to use scout reports of your games in the future is to keep permanent records of the performance of each player and of the team during the season. These records are easily obtainable from the game reports. Forms G and H on pages 38–39 and 43 illustrate how a player's complete record for the season may be kept. In this particular example, the player's record is for conference games only. For example, the first game listed is Yale vs. University of Pennsylvania. It is very simple to examine the scout report for this game and take the individual player's record from it.

On the shooting chart in Form G, the shot attempts and goals scored by each player are given for each game. The numbers used correspond to the game number as indicated in the Game Number column. For example, *1* indicates games with the University of Pennsylvania. If the shot attempt is successful, it is encircled.

The example in Form G divides the shooting chart into games played away from home and games played at home, since this particular information was desired. It also shows results for the first-half shooting compared to the second half. Other plans may be used depending on the coach's or player's needs.

Much information may be gained from studying this report. The over-all picture shows that this player made twelve field goals in sixty-six attempts in the long area for a percentage of .182. He made eleven goals in forty-three attempts

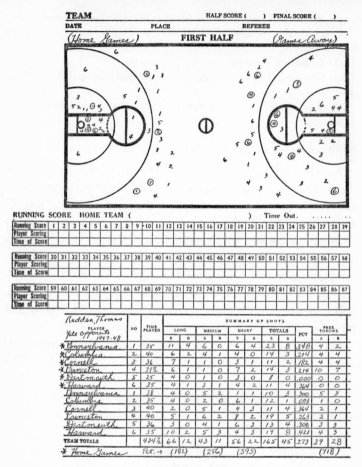

FORM G

PLAYER'S SEASON RECORD

(Form 1)

PLAYER Yale opponents 1947-48	NO	TIME PLAYED	LONG		MEDIUM		SHORT		TOTALS		PCT	FREE THROWS	
			S	B	S	B	S	B	S	B		S	B
* Pennsylvania	1	35	11	4	6	0	6	4	23	8	.348	4	2
* Columbia	2	40	6	2	4	1	4	0	14	3	.214	4	4
* Cornell	3	36	7	1	1	0	3	1	11	2	.182	4	4
* Princeton	4	37½	6	1	1	0	7	2	14	3	.214	10	7
* Dartmouth	5	25	4	0	1	0	3	0	8	0	.000	0	0
* Harvard	6	35	4	1	3	1	4	2	11	4	.364	0	0
Pennsylvania	1	38	4	0	5	2	1	1	10	3	.300	5	3
Columbia	2	35	4	0	2	0	6	1	12	1	.093	1	0
Cornell	3	40	2	0	5	1	4	3	11	4	.364	2	1
Princeton	4	40	5	1	6	2	8	2	19	5	.263	2	1
Dartmouth	5	36	3	0	4	1	6	3	13	4	.308	3	3
Harvard	6	35	10	2	5	3	4	3	19	8	.421	4	3
TEAM TOTALS		434½	66	12	43	11	56	22	165	45	.273	39	28
* Home Games		Pct. →	(182)		(256)		(393)					(718)	

in the medium area for a percentage of .256. He made twenty-two goals in fifty-six attempts in the short area for a percentage of .393. His total performance was forty-five field goals in one hundred and sixty-five attempts for a .273 percentage. This player was a much more accurate shooter

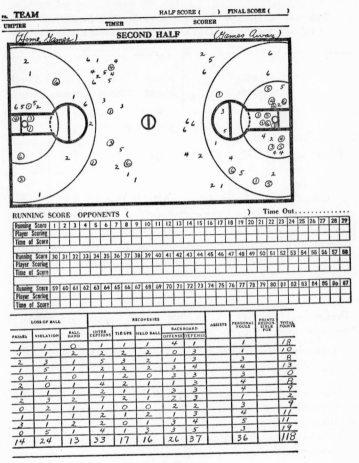

| n. TEAM | | | HALF SCORE ( ) | FINAL SCORE ( ) |

| UMPIRE | TIMER | SCORER |

(Home Games) **SECOND HALF** (Games Away)

RUNNING SCORE OPPONENTS ( ) Time Out..............

Running Score	1	2	3	4	5	6	7	8	9	10	11	12	13	14	15	16	17	18	19	20	21	22	23	24	25	26	27	28	29
Player Scoring																													
Time of Score																													

Running Score	30	31	32	33	34	35	36	37	38	39	40	41	42	43	44	45	46	47	48	49	50	51	52	53	54	55	56	57	58
Player Scoring																													
Time of Score																													

Running Score	59	60	61	62	63	64	65	66	67	68	69	70	71	72	73	74	75	76	77	78	79	80	81	82	83	84	85	86	87
Player Scoring																													
Time of Score																													

LOSS OF BALL			RECOVERIES					ASSISTS	PERSONAL FOULS	POINTS RESPONSIBLE FOR	TOTAL POINTS
PASSES	VIOLATION	BALL HAND	INTER CEPTIONS	TIE-UPS	HELD BALL	BACKBOARD OFFENSE	DEFENSE				
1	1	0	1	1	1	4	1		1		18
·1	1	2	2	2	2	0	3		1		10
2	3	1	5	3	2	1	3		3		8
1	5	1	2	2	2	3	4		4		13
0	1	0	1	2	0	3	3		3		0
2	0	1	4	2	1	1	3		4		8
1	1	1	2	1	1	3	3		4		9
2	3	2	7	2	1	2	3		1		2
0	2	1	1	0	0	2	2		3		9
1	1	1	2	1	2	1	3		4		11
3	1	2	2	0	1	3	4		5		11
0	5	1	4	1	3	3	5		3		19
14	24	13	33	17	16	26	37		36		118

FORM G

Player's Season Record

(cont.)

in the second half. First-half totals show that he **made**
only seventeen field goals in eighty-seven attempts—a .195
shooting percentage. In the second half, however, he made
twenty-eight field goals in seventy-eight attempts—a .359
percentage. This indicates that the player is in good condi-

THOMAS REDDEN—1947–48—OFF-SEASON SUGGESTIONS
1947–48 SHOOTING DATA (12 CONFERENCE GAMES)

	Long Shots	Medium Shots	Short Shots	Total Shots	Free Throws	Total Points
	66-12	43-11	56-22	165-45	39-28	118
Percentage	.182	.256	.393	.273	.718	
*Av. Per Game	6-1	4-1	5-2	15-4	4-3	11

	At Home Shooting	Away Shooting	1st Half Shooting	2nd Half Shooting
	81-20	84-25	87-17	78-28
Percentage	.247	.298	.195	.359

* Based on time played: 434½ min. (approximately equal to 11 40-min. games).

Your record also shows 51 losses-of-ball (nearly 5 per game); 63 rebounds (6 per game); 66 other recoveries (6 per game) and 36 fouls (3 per game).

You can be considered a good college basketball player. You have aggressiveness, determination and are a good competitor. However, you still have some rough spots in your game that could be improved. If you will work hard during the off-season you will have a much better season next year. Work on the following fundamentals:

Footwork:

You are too stiff in your actions and this is one reason you lose the ball as much as you do. Practice stops, starts and pivots that we have covered. Defensively, you also need to improve on footwork, get down lower, and learn to move backward faster. But, your defense this year was probably better than that of most of the other players.

Dribbling, Passing and Ball-Handling:

Your dribble is too high (another reason for your frequent loss of the ball this year). You need to get down over the ball, be able to dribble fast with either hand and also develop a change of pace in your dribble. You also need to practice quick ball-handling and passing which will be used a great deal more with a moving offense next year.

Shooting:

This should demand a major part of your off-season practice time. Your short shooting was not up to a winning average. You need to practice driving in hard and shooting with either hand and high jumping rather than broad jumping. You also need much practice shooting about eight feet out from the basket. In the middle area, work hard on the right-hand shot. You can also use the set shot in this area. Practice both of these a great deal. You do not hit a high average in these shots.

Individual Defense:

Get an opponent whenever possible and keep practicing your individual defense. Do the same thing on rebounds. You could do better defensive rebounding and practicing this will make you more conscious of it. Each time you go on the court, end your practice with running for conditioning. Finish with some good sprints and also some backward sprints. This will build up your endurance for the coming season. Please keep in touch with me during the summer.

---

tion and a good second-half competitor. However, the first-half record is so low that it must be brought up to par. Perhaps a longer warm-up period is necessary for him or he may be unusually nervous before a game. The report also shows that this player was a more accurate shooter away from than at home. He made twenty-five field goals in eighty-four attempts (a .298 percentage) away from home as compared to twenty field goals in eighty-one attempts (a .247 percentage) at home. This is rather unusual but it again indicates that the player is a good competitor and is not bothered by unfamiliar surroundings. Poor home-court lighting may have been a factor.

The report also shows free-throw results. This same man made twenty-eight free-throw goals in thirty-nine attempts, a .718 percentage. It also shows all of the other objective findings such as rebounds and losses-of-all. Since the total number of minutes played are given, it is possible to determine how many forty minute periods each player plays and arrive at the average number of attempts, goals, rebounds, and losses per game, if desired.

A typical example of suggestions to the player that may be recorded on the back of Form G is given on pages 40–41. These, of course, are based on the season record and any subjective observations noted during the season. *A copy of this report should be given to the player so that he can improve his game accordingly.* Similar records are possible for players on opposing teams if enough data are available.

Form H, below, shows how an individual-chart form may be used for a player's season record. Again, the results are taken from the game reports. The report is not broken down into first and second halves or games at home and away from home. Neither is it broken down for the different games. It merely shows field-goal attempts by a vertical line and the line is encircled if the goal was made. Notice that this particular player did most of his shooting from the center or right side of the court.

The team's record for a complete season may be kept in the same manner. Form I on pages 44–45 gives an example. Again, this record is for conference games only. Since each individual game report shows the field-goal attempts and goals on the game charts, it is not necessary to duplicate this on the season record charts. The recordings on the season charts merely indicate by a vertical line the spot from which a field-goal attempt is taken. If the line is crossed, it indicates that

SEASON SUMMARY EXAMPLE

NAME **PEACOCK**   POS. **LG**   NO. **7**

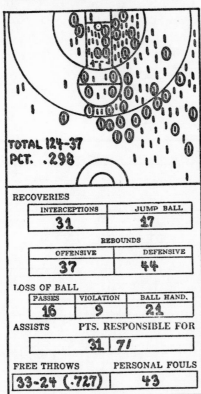

FORM H

PLAYER'S SEASON RECORD

(Form 2)

the attempt was successful. This record, at a glance, gives the shooting percentages of the team from all areas; the free-throw percentage; and the other objective information. Percentages and averages per game may be worked out.

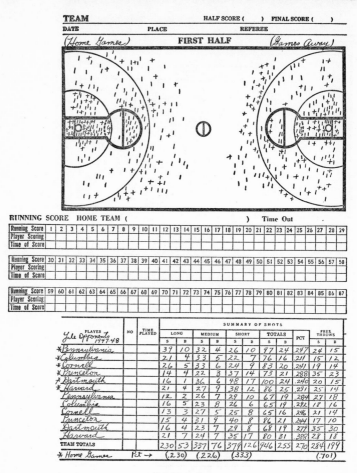

TEAM _____ HALF SCORE ( ) FINAL SCORE ( )
DATE _____ PLACE _____ REFEREE _____

(Home Games)   **FIRST HALF**   (Games Away)

RUNNING SCORE   HOME TEAM (   )   Time Out

Running Score	1	2	3	4	5	6	7	8	9	10	11	12	13	14	15	16	17	18	19	20	21	22	23	24	25	26	27	28	29
Player Scoring																													
Time of Score																													

Running Score	30	31	32	33	34	35	36	37	38	39	40	41	42	43	44	45	46	47	48	49	50	51	52	53	54	55	56	57	58
Player Scoring																													
Time of Score																													

Running Score	59	60	61	62	63	64	65	66	67	68	69	70	71	72	73	74	75	76	77	78	79	80	81	82	83	84	85	86	87
Player Scoring																													
Time of Score																													

PLAYER Yale Opponents 1947-48	NO	TIME PLAYED	LONG S	B	MEDIUM S	B	SHORT S	B	TOTALS S	B	PCT	FREE THROWS S	B
*Pennsylvania			39	10	32	4	26	10	97	24	.247	24	15
*Columbia			21	4	33	5	22	7	76	16	.211	15	12
*Cornell			26	5	33	6	24	9	83	20	.241	19	14
*Princeton			14	4	22	3	37	14	73	21	.288	35	23
*Dartmouth			16	1	36	6	48	17	100	24	.240	20	15
*Harvard			21	4	27	9	38	12	86	25	.291	25	14
Pennsylvania			12	2	26	7	29	10	67	19	.284	27	18
Columbia			16	5	23	8	26	6	65	19	.292	18	16
Cornell			13	3	27	5	25	8	65	16	.246	21	14
Princeton			15	4	31	9	40	8	86	21	.244	17	10
Dartmouth			16	4	23	7	29	8	68	19	.279	35	30
Harvard			21	7	24	7	35	17	80	31	.388	28	18
TEAM TOTALS			230	53	337	76	379	126	946	255	270	.284	199
* Home Games Pct →			(.230)		(.226)		(.333)					(.701)	

FORM I

TEAM'S SEASON RECORD

In a similar manner, the same information may be recorded
about the opposing team during the season. This is very important if your team's achievements are to be compared with
those of the opponents'.

It is interesting to note that in this season report, the team
had a shooting average of .249 at home and .295 away from

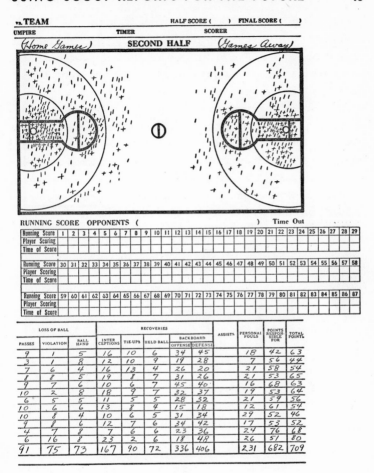

FORM I

TEAM'S SEASON RECORD

(*cont.*)

| LOSS OF BALL | | | RECOVERIES | | | | | ASSISTS | PERSONAL FOULS | POINTS RESPONSIBLE FOR | TOTAL POINTS |
PASSES	VIOLATION	BALL HAND	INTERCEPTIONS	TIE-UPS	HELD BALL	BACKBOARD OFFENSE	DEFENSE				
9	1	5	16	10	6	34	45		18	42	63
3	1	8	12	10	9	19	28		7	56	44
7	6	4	16	13	4	26	20		21	58	54
8	8	5	19	8	7	31	26		21	53	65
9	7	6	10	6	7	45	40		16	68	63
10	2	8	18	9	7	32	37		19	53	64
6	5	5	11	5	5	28	32		21	59	56
10	6	6	13	8	4	15	18		12	61	54
10	8	4	10	6	5	31	34		29	52	46
9	8	6	12	7	6	34	42		17	53	52
4	7	8	7	6	6	23	36		24	76	68
6	16	8	23	2	6	18	48		26	51	80
91	75	73	167	90	72	336	406		231	682	709

home. Perhaps it was partly psychological, but the players complained that the lighting on the home court was very poor. Using these records as a selling point, an improvement was made before the next season. The shooting average of the team in 1948–49 improved from .270 to .319 and the home shooting average improved accordingly. This indicates that these reports have many uses besides being coaching aids. Whether it was due to improved lighting or psychological factors, shooting did improve.

It has been my experience that such information about individual players and the team is invaluable in planning for the next season. Each game must be planned carefully, based on findings of previous games. Similarly, a coach should plan the coming season in the light of the past season's experiences.

The following is an example of information that may be included for future reference on the back of Form I.

SEASON SUMMARY—YALE—1947–48

Suggestions for Next Year

At Home Shooting	Away Shooting	1st Half Shooting	2nd Half Shooting
515-128 .249	431-127 .295	460-116 .252	486-139 .286

(For Other Shooting Records, see Form H)

AVERAGES PER GAME

	Shots	Goals
Long Shots	19	4+
Medium Shots	28	6+
Short Shots	32—	11—
Total Shots	79	21
Free Throws	24	17

Loss-of-Ball........	20
Rebounds..........	62
Other Recoveries....	27
Personal Fouls......	19
Total Points........	59
Opponents Points...	57

Shooting was up to par only in the long area. The record in the medium area should be much higher and the short area at .333 was extremely low. We also had fewer short shots at the basket than our opponents. Lack of adequate shooting practice early in the season must be corrected next year. The fact that we were a better shooting team away from home bears out the point that lighting on the home court is very poor. It must be improved next season.

Each player must have individual instruction in shooting and this must be emphasized in off-season practice.

Next to shooting, our biggest weakness was poor rebounding. Although we retrieved an average of sixty-two rebounds a game, we were weak in this department against the top teams. Individual work and team rebound organization must be improved next year.

Defensively, every player on the squad should improve. The opponents averaged fifty-seven points a game which is far too many. We must pay more attention to individual defense in early season practice.

The fact that we committed nineteen personal fouls a game indicates that our footwork and general individual defense is below par.

Losses-of-ball totaled 239 for 12 games, an average of 20 per game. This may give the other team 20 points every ball game. Much of this was due to learning a new, fast-break system but it must be cut down materially next year.

Generally speaking, the squad was very cooperative and had a very good attitude. The fact that the squad was learning a new system and got a late start contributed very much to a mediocre season.

In addition to emphasizing fundamentals and team play, we must stress better physical condition next year. We were not a strong second-half team during the past season. We should also make more effort to have the entire squad available daily for practice.

5

Basketball Shooting and Its Implications

THE ONLY WAY TO SCORE IN A BASKETBALL GAME IS TO
"shoot a basket." (See photo, Shooting a Basket, in illustrated section.) And, as the rule book states: "The purpose
of a basketball team is to throw the ball into its own basket
and to prevent the other team from securing the ball and scoring." [1] Therefore to "shoot a basket" becomes the main
objective. Various fundamentals, techniques, systems, and
styles of play are all directed to this end. The fact that all
players can shoot at the basket is a chief reason for wide
participation in the game. Shooting is obviously the most
important factor in the game. In view of this fact, it is sur-
prising that so little attention has been paid to shooting percentages and to an analysis of the areas from which shots are
taken.

Shooting averages in basketball are just as important as batting averages in baseball. We should have some standard by
which to measure the shooting ability of a player. If a good
baseball batting average is .300, what is a good basketball

---

[1] Technically, a team's "own basket" is the one *at which* they are shooting.

shooting average?   How much shooting ability should be expected from a basketball player?   Since shots are taken from various parts of the court, we must also know what shooting performance to expect at various distances from the basket.

By compiling the results of many college basketball games it is possible to arrive at certain results.   The games include the original study of 460 college games over a 13-year period starting in 1936–37 and now supplemented by 132 additional college games through 1953–54.   These games are very representative of average college basketball as they include many intersectional games, teams employing every style of play and teams of all levels of ability.   Tabulations of field-goal attempts and field goals have been made in various areas.   Free-throw attempts and free-throw goals were also recorded.

Comparisons are made between first- and second-half performances, winning and losing teams, home and visiting teams, major and minor games, conference and non-conference games.   Intra-squad scrimmages and practice shots are also used for comparison purposes.   The results of this survey are given in this chapter, along with other supplementary material.

Available records from the National Collegiate Athletic Bureau, National Federation (high schools) and the National Basketball Association (professional) are also given.   Although these records are not complete, it is gratifying to see the trend toward the keeping of shooting and other objective records by these bureaus.

Basketball scoring

There has been a long, steady trend toward higher scoring in both college and high school basketball during the last two decades.   The professional game in the National Basketball Association also shows an increase in scoring since records were made available during the 1947–48 season.

In all three divisions, however, there were slight decreases in scoring between the 1952–53 season and the 1953–54 season which may indicate that the saturation point has finally been reached.

Part of the increase in scoring has been due to rule changes that have lengthened the actual playing time. Also the elimination of the center jump and the trend toward a faster, free-shooting game has increased scoring. The present college average is approximately 138 points a game for both teams or 69 points a game for each team. The high school average is approximately 115 points a game for both teams or about 58 points a game for each team. The professionals naturally would score more points due to greater accuracy and their present record shows approximately 159 points per game for both teams or nearly 80 points a game for each team.

The four tables (pages 51, 52, 53, and 54) show the records for the control group used in the writer's college study, the N.C.A.A. records, the high school records, and the professional records. Averages are given in all divisions for the last five years.

The high scoring game that we have today in basketball means that special attention must be given to shooting and shooting percentages.

Basketball shooting percentages in college games

Note: A field-goal attempt occurs when a player shoots, throws or taps the ball at the basket; when in the opinion of the scorer, he is attempting to score a goal (except when he is fouled in the act of shooting and the goal is not made). Tip-ups and blocked shots count as field-goal attempts. A shooting percentage is determined by dividing the number of field-goal attempts into the number of field goals made.

Accuracy in field-goal shooting in college games has increased greatly during the last seven years or so, but the ceiling has not been reached. The first known study on basket-

TABLE I

ALL GAMES SCORING (control group)

Season	Number of Games	Score	Average Score per Game
1949–50	26	2918	112.2
1950–51	27	3392	125.6
1951–52	28	3604	128.7
1952–53	25	3293	131.7
1953–54	26	3637	139.9

5-year totals 1949–50—1953–54 inclusive

	Number of Games	Score	Average Score per Game
Game totals (both teams)	132	16844	127.6
First Half (both teams)	132	7980	60.5
Second Half (both teams)	132	8864	67.2
Winning Team	132	9207	69.8
Losing Team	132	7637	57.9
Home Team	132	8636	65.4
Visiting Team	132	8208	62.2
Major Games (one team)	97	5966	61.5
Minor Games (one team)	35	2456	70.2
Conference Games (one team)	62	3753	60.5
Non-conference Games (one team)	70	4669	66.7
Scrimmages (one team)	100	7307	73.1

This table shows total scores and average scores per game for both teams by seasons for 132 games in the college study. Similar information is given for first- and second-half performances for both teams and for winning and losing teams, home and visiting teams, major and minor games, conference and non-conference games, and for scrimmages.

For the college study of 460 games between 1936–37 and 1948–49 see Table I-A in Appendix A.

51

ball shooting percentages to be made public was started in the 1936–37 season. It included 460 college games, beginning that year and extending through the 1948–49 season. The original table showing the results of this study may be found in Table II-A in Appendix A.

TABLE II

ALL GAMES SCORING—N.C.A.A.
(both teams)

Season	Number of Teams	Number of Games	Average Score per Game (both teams)
1947–48	160	3945	106.5
1948–49	149	3737	109.5
1949–50	145	3659	115.1
1950–51	153	3974	121.4
1951–52	156	4009	126.6
1952–53	158	3754	138.0
1953–54	160	3933	137.8
5-year totals 1949–50–1953–54 inclusive	772	19329	127.8

This table shows the average score per game for both teams by seasons for college games reported to the N.C.A.A. Bureau.

In midseason of 1944–45 the results of this study up to that time were given to the New York sports writers and coaches. As a result, for possibly the first time national publicity was given to basketball shooting percentages.* In 1947–48, the National Collegiate Athletic Association started to compile reports from records of the college games. Shooting percentages have increased steadily since that time. Some

---

* Of course, many coaches had kept shooting charts and records prior to this, but very few had made the results public.

have been slow to see the value in keeping shooting percentages, either because of the detail involved or because they feel players will not do as well when conscious of their averages.

TABLE III
ALL GAMES SCORING—HIGH SCHOOL
(both teams)

Season	Number of Games	Average Score per Game (both teams)
1938–39	1000	56.9
1942–43	1000	69.9
1944–45	1000	83.9
1946–47	1000	87.2
1947–48	1000	93.0
1948–49	1000	90.1
1949–50	1000	91.0
1950–51	1000	103.6
1951–52	1000	108.3
1952–53	1000	118.6
1953–54	1000	115.1
5-year totals 1949–50–1953–54 inclusive	5000	107.3

This table shows average scores per game for both teams by seasons for 1,000 games each season as reported to the National Federation Bureau.

The results, however, show the opposite to be the case. Calling the attention of shooting percentages to the player will cause him to take better shots at the basket, and will help eliminate carelessness. Players must be taught the elements of competition and they must know the results of their efforts. There will always be players who play to protect their averages, just as some do in baseball, but these players do not get very far. It is indeed gratifying to see the trend toward keeping shooting percentages and the great improvement in accuracy that has resulted from this practice. Roughly, the average college player makes one-third of his attempts now compared to a little more than one-fourth several years ago.

TABLE IV

ALL GAMES SCORING—PROFESSIONAL (N.B.A.)
(both teams)

Season	Number of Games	Average Score per Game (both teams)
1946–47	331	135.6
1947–48	192	145.4
1948–49	360	160.2
1949–50	561	160.0
1950–51	354	168.2
1951–52	330	167.4
1952–53	352	165.0
1953–54	324	159.1
5-year totals 1949–50–1953–54 inclusive	1921	163.9

This table shows average scores per game for both teams by seasons for professional games in the National Basketball Association.

Table V on page 55 gives the continuation of the college study for the last five years. Note that while the shooting percentage has increased substantially during this period, the average number of field-goal attempts per game has not increased. This again indicates that the players are going to be more careful in the shots that they take and concentrate on making a higher percentage. A complete study of Table V should give some idea of what can be expected from individuals and teams in various game situations.

Table VI on page 56 gives the shooting percentages as reported to the N.C.A.A. Bureau. It will be noted that the same increase in shooting accuracy appears in this report.

TABLE V

TOTAL SHOTS (control group)

Season	No. of Games	Field-Goal Attempts	Field Goals	Per-cent-age	Average per Game	
					Attempts	Goals
1949–50	26	3942	1106	.281	151.6	42.5
1950–51	27	4216	1229	.292	156.1	45.5
1951–52	28	4132	1306	.316	147.6	46.6
1952–53	25	3237	1077	.333	129.5	43.1
1953–54	26	3764	1241	.330	144.8	47.7

5-year totals 1949–50–1953–54 inclusive

	No. of Games	Field-Goal Attempts	Field Goals	Per-cent-age	Attempts	Goals
Game totals (both teams)	132	19291	5959	.309	146.1	45.1
First Half (both teams)	132	9662	2882	.298	73.2	21.8
Second Half (both teams)	132	9629	3077	.320	72.9	23.3
Winning Team	132	9561	3277	.343	72.4	24.8
Losing Team	132	9730	2682	.276	73.7	20.3
Home Team	132	9725	3042	.313	73.7	23.0
Visiting Team	132	9566	2917	.305	72.5	22.1
Major Games (one team)	97	6789	2076	.306	70.0	21.4
Minor Games (one team)	35	2792	903	.323	79.8	25.8
Conference Games (one team)	62	4262	1285	.302	68.7	20.7
Non-conference Games (one team)	70	5319	1694	.318	76.0	24.2
Scrimmages (one team)	100	8319	2917	.351	83.2	29.2
Practice Shots		33945	18071	.532		

This table shows field-goal attempts and field goals by both teams, by seasons, for 132 games; percentage of attempts scored and average number of attempts and goals per game. It gives similar information for first- and second-half performances, winning and losing teams, home and visiting teams, major and minor games, conference and non-conference games; also a sampling from intra-squad scrimmages and practice shots without defense.

However, the shooting percentages are considerably higher than the ones given in Table V. Reasons for this are two-fold. First, it is likely that the better shooting teams reported the results while the weaker teams did not.   For example, in 1953–54 only 160 teams reported; which is only about one-fifth of the college basketball teams in the country.   The second reason for the higher percentage no doubt lies in the fact that many recorders do not count tip-ups and blocked shots as attempts.   There is still a lack of uniformity in this regard.

TABLE VI

TOTAL SHOTS—N.C.A.A.
(both teams)

Season	No. of Teams	No. of Games	Average Field-Goal Attempts per Game	Average Field Goals per Game	Percentage
1947–48	160	3945	138.7	40.6	.293
1948–49	149	3737	134.7	41.4	.307
1949–50	145	3659	136.8	43.2	.316
1950–51	153	3974	137.8	45.6	.331
1951–52	156	4009	140.6	47.5	.338
1952–53	158	3754	138.1	48.0	.348
1953–54	160	3933	135.4	48.0	.355
5-year totals 1949–50– 1953–54 inclusive	772	19329	137.8	46.5	.337

This table shows field-goal attempts and field goals by both teams, by seasons, with percentages and averages per game as reported to the N.C.A.A. Bureau.

From the two reports, we should try to arrive at the present probable average shooting percentage for college basketball. A good estimate would place the present college basketball shooting percentage average at about .340, certainly no higher than that.   As more teams keep proper recordings and report them to the N.C.A.A. Bureau, it is predicted that the college average will reach .400 within the next few years.

Basketball shooting percentages in high school games

Unfortunately, nation-wide high school records are not available at present on shooting percentages.   Secretaries of the 48 states were contacted as well as the National Federation

TABLE VII

TOTAL SHOTS—HIGH SCHOOL

(both teams)

Season	No. of Games	Average per Game		Percentage
		Attempts	Goals	
*1938–39	1000	101.3	22.0	.217
*1942–43	1000	106.2	27.0	.254
*1944–45	1000	114.5	31.5	.275
*1945–46	1000	102.9	31.5	.306
*1946–47	1000	115.5	33.8	.293
*1947–48	1000	110.9	32.5	.293
*1948–49	1000	119.4	36.3	.304
*1949–50	1000	128.0	37.3	.291
**1949–50	15	150.2	48.7	.324
**1950–51	15	147.9	45.0	.304
**1951–52	16	147.1	44.6	.303
**1952–53	15	146.5	48.4	.330
†1952–53	26	124.7	39.0	.313
**1953–54	15	130.7	46.0	.352
††1953–54	6	119.5	41.3	.346

Attempts and Goals are approximate.
  * Number of attempts and goals are computed by adding one-hand and two-hand attempts as recorded by National Federation.   Tip-ups are not included.
** From Kentucky State Finals Tournament Records.
  † From Oregon State Tournament Records (all games).
†† From Ohio State Finals Tournament Records (A & B).
  This table shows an estimated number of field-goal attempts and field goals per game and shooting percentages based on figures from the National Federation. It also includes similar information from high school tournaments in Kentucky, Ohio, and Oregon.

Bureau but very few reported that this kind of data were on record.   Table VII shows the information that is available. The reports through 1949–50 were compiled by taking the figures of a study that was made during those years on the one-hand compared to the two-hand style of shooting so that even in those years, records were not kept for the purpose of determining shooting percentages. The figures that were recorded during the last five years are from isolated state tournaments and do not give a sufficient sampling to draw any conclusions. The information that is available seems to indicate that the high school teams have not enjoyed the same improvement in accuracy that has been apparent in the college game; due, probably, to the lack of attention to shooting percentages. Undoubtedly there are many individual teams and districts that keep these records, but they are urged to make them public so that all can benefit from their experience.

TABLE VIII

TOTAL SHOTS—Professional (N.B.A.)

Season	No. of Games	Average per Game		Percentage
		Attempts	Goals	
1946–47	331	185.8	51.8	.279
1947–48	192	192.0	54.4	.283
1948–49	360	177.4	58.0	.327
1949–50	561	166.2	56.4	.339
1950–51	354	167.2	59.8	.358
1951–52	330	161.6	59.2	.366
1952–53	352	153.8	56.8	.369
1953–54	324	150.8	56.2	.373
5-year totals 1949–50–1953–54 inclusive	1921	159.9	57.7	.361

This table shows the average number of field-goal attempts and field goals per game, with percentages of attempts scored for both teams, by seasons, for professional games as reported to the N.B.A.

Present shooting averages in high school appear to be above the .300 mark, but the nation-wide estimate would be impossible at the present time. The shooting percentages should be as high as the college percentages because the level of competition would be affected by defense as well as offense. In the same way a baseball player in high school is as easily able to bat .300 as is a college or professional player.

Basketball shooting percentages in professional games

Table VIII gives the available data on professional basketball games in the National Basketball Association for the seasons 1946–47 through 1953–54. Again, the noticeable increase in shooting accuracy is apparent with shooting percentages going from .279 in 1946–47 to .372 during the 1953–54 season. There has been some increase every year the records have been kept. No player is more conscious of his objective achievements than is the professional. He is paid partly as the result of his record; yet he cannot afford to sacrifice the winning of games or good teamwork to maintain a high individual average or percentage. The professional managers are quick to seize on the opportunity to keep and publicize shooting percentages, so that the players and the public will be conscious of them. As a result, the professional has improved faster than the high school or college player in this regard. They have also, as a result, given the spectators a better game to watch with more scoring and better shooting.

Shooting percentages in various areas

Shooting percentages on total shots, however, are not sufficient to give a true and accurate picture. A player who plays in the bucket near the basket and takes most of his shots from that area, should naturally make a higher percentage of his shots than a player who shoots mostly from the outside areas. A team that is able to work in for many close shots will naturally make a higher percentage than a team that takes more shots from the medium or long area. It is essential, therefore, to record the shot attempts and determine percentages from various areas on the floor. Our college study divides the scoring area into three divisions and the following pages give the results from the so-called short, medium, and long areas.

The short shot

(See photos in illustrated section)

A "short shot" is a shot taken within a radius of 12 feet from the basket. The 12-foot radius is stipulated because this is the accepted area for the lay-up or cripple shot. These are predominantly shots taken with one hand and, in many cases, are backboard shots. It is, of course, a shot that players and teams try to use most frequently because the accuracy is and should be higher in this area.

The recent five-year college study indicates that 42 per cent of all field-goal attempts are taken in the short area and that 51 per cent of all field goals are scored in this area. Obviously great attention on the part of the coach and player should be devoted to the shooting techniques and practices of the short shot. Percentages are still much lower than they should be as may be indicated from the fact that players consistently score nearly three-fourths of their attempts in practice in this area without defense. The present college percentage for the short shot appears to be approximately .397 with the average for the past five years at .376. Table IX on page 61 gives the complete figures.

Again, it is unfortunate that more records are not available from high school for shooting and scoring in the various areas. One state, however, has reported this kind of information for its state tournaments and the Kentucky five-year record is offered. One report is not a sufficient sampling from which to draw conclusions. It is hoped that in the future other high school data will be available. Table X on page 62 gives the Kentucky high school report.

Why are averages in this area not higher? A tighter defense is partly responsible for this fact but it is also due to

taking poor shots at the basket.   Players who get in as close
as this are inclined to take a shot at the basket, whether they
are in a position for a good shot or not.   This is particularly

TABLE IX

SHORT AREA SHOOTING * (control group)

Season	No. of Games	Field-Goal Attempts	Field Goals	Per-cent-age	Average per Game	
					Attempts	Goals
1949–50	26	1669	576	.345	64.2	22.2
1950–51	27	1645	581	.353	60.9	21.5
1951–52	28	1642	645	.393	58.6	23.0
1952–53	25	1330	526	.396	53.2	21.0
1953–54	26	1839	730	.397	70.7	28.1
5-year totals 1949–50–1953–54 inclusive						
Game totals (both teams)	132	8125	3058	.376	61.6	23.2
Winning Team	132	4450	1794	.403	33.7	13.6
Losing Team	132	3675	1264	.344	27.8	9.6
Major Games (one team)	97	2872	1061	.369	29.6	10.9
Minor Games (one team)	35	1235	491	.398	35.3	14.0
Conference Games (one team)	62	1821	667	.366	29.4	10.8
Non-conference Games (one team)	70	2286	885	.387	32.7	12.6
Scrimmages (one team)	100	3997	1722	.431	40.0	17.2
Practice shots		5955	4391	.737		

This table shows total shots with percentages and averages as in Table V, but
for short shots only. First- and second-half performances, however, are not
included.

* Short shots are those taken within a radius of 12 feet from the basket.

true after retrieving rebounds.   The coach who insists that
only *fundamentally sound* shots be taken at the basket will
be well repaid.   It might even be reasonable to improve the
shooting average for the short shot to .500.   It is also suggested that players first ground themselves properly in the

fundamentals of the short shot and follow this with constant practice. A player who will drive toward the basket at full speed and shoot each time until ten successive goals have been made will be surprised at the improvement made. The area eight or ten feet from beneath the basket should receive special attention from all players since many players neglect to practice shooting in this area.

TABLE X

SHORT AREA SHOOTING—HIGH SCHOOL
(both teams)

Season	No. of Teams	No. of Games	Field-Goal Attempts	Field Goals	Per-cent-age	Average per Game	
						Attempts	Goals
1949–50	16	15	1409	504	.358	93.9	33.6
1950–51	16	15	1359	466	.343	90.6	31.1
1951–52	16	15	1134	393	.347	75.6	26.2
1952–53	16	15	1103	431	.391	73.5	28.7
1953–54	16	15	951	370	.389	63.4	24.7
5-year totals 1949–50– 1953–54 inclusive	80	75	5956	2164	.363	79.4	28.9

This table shows field-goal attempts, field goals, percentages and averages per game, for both teams, by seasons for short area shots as reported from the state tournaments of Kentucky including the seasons 1949–50 through 1953–54.

The medium shot

(See photos in illustrated section)

A "medium shot" is a shot taken between a radius of 12 feet and a radius of 24 feet from the basket. This particular area was selected for the medium-distance shot because it is considered the half-way mark for shooting from the floor. Very few shots are attempted beyond the 36-foot mark. Therefore, the medium shot is midway between the short- and long-shot areas. Probably the most helpful information is found when examining statistics on this "abused" area in basketball.   Table XI, page 64 gives complete facts about this area.

Our recent college study shows that 42 per cent of all field-goal attempts are taken in the medium area; which is just about the same as in the short area.   However, the field goals scored in this area only represent about 36 per cent of the total because the shooting percentage falls down considerably in this area.   A fairly satisfactory increase has been made in the shooting percentage.   The original study to 1949 (see Table IV-A in Appendix A) shows a percentage of .222 while the average for the last five years is .267.   However, the shooting average in this area should be up around 40 per cent.

Players seem to take a great variety of shots from this area. The two-hand set shot from the chest is used a great deal in the East.   In other sections the one-hand set shot is favored. And, where one-hand shooting predominates, there is much shooting on-the-run.   Pivot shots, jump shots, and hook shots are also taken frequently from the medium or middle area. Players from some other sections use an overhead shot from this area, either from a standing position or using a jump.

Most coaches have become rather lenient in their views on shooting in recent years, as is indicated by the increase in total shots attempted by the average team during a game.   As a result, players shoot very freely from this area and take poor shots in many cases.   As was suggested in discussing the short-shot area, shots should be taken that are earned. Coaches should observe closely the type of shot taken from this medium area and eliminate the poor-risk shots.   This does not mean that all players must use the same type of shot, but they must have one that they can make, one on which they can depend.   The following story will illustrate this point.

Tony Lavelli is probably the greatest hook shot the game has ever seen.   See photo in illustrated section.   In the first prac-

tice session with Tony, I was rather disappointed to learn that
the hook shot was the one that he depended on in the medium
area.   Most coaches do not consider the hook shot an orthodox

TABLE XI

MEDIUM AREA SHOOTING * (control group)

Season	No. of Games	Field-Goal Attempts	Field Goals	Percentage	Average per Game	
					Attempts	Goals
1949–50	26	1422	338	.238	54.7	13.0
1950–51	27	1677	432	.258	62.1	16.0
1951–52	28	2001	548	.274	71.5	19.6
1952–53	25	1559	459	.294	62.4	18.4
1953–54	26	1386	369	.266	53.3	14.2

5-year totals 1949–50–1953–54 inclusive

Game totals (both teams)	132	8045	2146	.267	60.9	16.3
Winning Team	132	3850	1152	.299	29.2	8.7
Losing Team	132	4195	994	.237	31.8	7.5
Major Games (one team)	97	3025	821	.271	31.2	8.5
Minor Games (one team)	35	1236	341	.276	35.3	9.7
Conference Games (one team)	62	1864	491	.263	30.1	7.9
Non-conference Games (one team)	70	2397	671	.280	34.2	9.6
Scrimmages (one team)	100	3485	963	.276	34.9	9.6
Practice Shots		15715	8445	.537		

* Medium shots are those shots taken between a radius of 12 feet and a radius of 24 feet from the basket.
This table shows total shots with percentages and averages as in Table IX, but for medium shots only.

shot and it is not a dependable one for most players.   Tony
was asked to shoot twenty of these highly specialized shots
from a distance of approximately fifteen feet.   He obliged
and made eighteen out of the twenty.   He moved out a little

farther and nearly duplicated the performance.   The next request was for Tony to try the shot with his left hand.   He
then took twenty hook shots at a distance of fifteen feet and

TABLE XII

Medium Area Shooting—High School
(both teams)

Season	No. of Teams	No. of Games	Field-Goal Attempts	Field Goals	Per-cent-age	Average per Game	
						Attempts	Goals
1949–50	16	15	712	194	.272	47.5	12.9
1950–51	16	15	758	185	.244	50.5	12.3
1951–52	16	15	824	219	.266	54.9	14.6
1952–53	16	15	762	194	.255	50.8	12.9
1953–54	16	15	714	224	.314	47.6	14.9
5-year totals 1949–50– 1953–54 inclusive	80	75	3770	1016	.269	50.3	13.5

This table shows total shots with percentages and averages as in Table X, but
for medium shots only.

Table XII gives the available information from the state tournaments of Kentucky for the high school medium area shooting between the years 1949–50 and
1953–54.   Please note that even in this very sparse sampling the percentage drops
from .363 in the short area to .269 in the medium area for the five-year average.

made sixteen.   Always the gentleman, Tony asked, "What
suggestions do you have?   Do you think I should change the
shot?"   The coach's reply was, "My boy, if you can drop-
kick the ball through the basket and make that percentage,
it's all right with me."

This great player did not master the hook shot by ac-
cident.   It was only mastered after many hours of daily practice through the years.   Of course, any shot must be fundamentally sound if it is to be consistently accurate.   Tony had
a perfect follow-through with his hook shot and perfect wrist
and finger action.   Yet, even this phenomenal shooter improved his shooting percentage nearly twenty points in his last

college year through a prescribed practice-shooting program.

There is no reason for the shooting average to drop from .376 in the short area to .267 in this medium area. Practice shooting with no defense in this area shows that players make an average of .537. Why then should it drop so markedly in games? Certainly the fatigue and mental factors could not make this difference. One reason for poor shooting averages from this area, and from all areas, is the fact that most players do not have their attempts and shots recorded, so that they are not conscious of the fact that their averages are low. Naturally, in these cases there is not the incentive to improve. By insistence on good shot attempts from this area, there is reason to believe that the shooting average might be increased to as high as .400 in major competition. A team should strive to succeed in two-fifths of its attempts in this area.

Either the one-hand or two-hand shot may be accurate in this area. If the shot is sound, one is as good as the other. Purely from observation, however, it seems that the one-hand shot causes most of the abuses. Players who are in motion are more inclined to take poor shots while going away from the basket. It is suggested that teachers of the one-hand shot pay particular attention to the elimination of poor shots.

The long shot

(See photo, The Two-Hand Shot, in illustrated section)

A "long shot" is a shot taken outside a radius of 24 feet from the basket. The distance for the long shot was set at 24 feet when the court was divided into three scoring areas, since there are few shots taken beyond the 36-foot mark. Hence, each area has a 12-foot length.

Only about 16 per cent of all field-goal attempts are taken in the long area and about 11 per cent of field goals are scored in this area. These are the figures taken from the last five years in college basketball in our study. It is interesting to note that the original 13-year study gives 22 per cent of field-goal attempts in the long area and 16 per cent of field goals scored. This would indicate even a further trend toward less shooting from the outer areas, no doubt due to a de-emphasis of teaching the two-hand set shot. It is true, however, that the shooting percentage shows about one-fourth of shot attempts to be successful in the long area now as compared to one-fifth in the original study; so progress in accuracy is evident.

Here the two-hand set shot taken from the chest predominates. The one-hand set shot is also used in the inner part of this long shooting area. Table XIII, Long-Area Shooting, page 68 gives complete findings. The shooting average in this area could not be expected to compare favorably with the shooting in the short area. However, poor shooting in this area has had many detrimental effects on the game in recent years. This is mainly because the one-hand shot has come into use in many sections of the country to the extent that the two-hand set shot is actually not used at all. From a coaching standpoint, this has encouraged the use of the zone defense and types of defense that call for playing loose away from the ball and congesting the keyhole area.

Suppose that a team is ten points ahead in the middle of a game. The other team cannot shoot long shots well. Why then would not the leading team play a keyhole defense whether it is zone, switching, loose away from the ball, or some similar defense? What chance does a trailing team have to work the ball in if they cannot draw the defense out with at least an occasional long shot? Unless the trailing team can score on a fast break or has an unusually strong re-bounding team, they do not have a chance. This type of game is not only unsatisfactory from a coaching standpoint, but it also ruins spectator interest. The answer is to teach boys a good set shot that they can use out to the forty-foot mark. It is one of the oldest stratagems of the game that a player shoots long to draw his opponent to him so that he can drive in to the basket.   This is becoming somewhat rare in basketball.

Because of these facts, coaches are strongly urged to teach the long shot, starting with the *beginner* in basketball.   No

TABLE XIII

LONG AREA SHOOTING * (control group)

Season	No. of Games	Field-Goal Attempts	Field Goals	Per-cent-age	Average per Game	
					Attempts	Goals
1949–50	26	851	192	.226	32.7	7.4
1950–51	27	894	216	.242	33.1	8.0
1951–52	28	489	113	.231	17.5	4.0
1952–53	25	348	92	.264	13.9	3.7
1953–54	26	539	142	.264	20.7	5.5
5-year totals 1949–50–1953–54 inclusive						
Game totals (both teams)	132	3121	755	.242	23.6	5.7
Winning Team	132	1261	331	.262	9.6	2.5
Losing Team	132	1860	424	.227	14.1	3.2
Major Games (one team)	97	892	194	.217	9.2	2.0
Minor Games (one team)	35	321	71	.221	9.2	2.0
Conference Games (one team)	62	577	127	.220	9.3	2.0
Non-conference Games (one team)	70	636	138	.217	9.1	2.0
Scrimmages (one team)	100	837	232	.277	8.4	2.3
Practice Shots		12275	5235	.426		

* Long shots are those taken beyond a radius of 24 feet from the basket.

Table XIII shows total shots with percentages and averages as in Tables IX and XI, but for long shots only.

shot has more player and spectator appeal, or is more helpful to the entire offensive plan in any style of play.

College coaches in many sections are faced with the problem of players who report to them never having learned a two-hand set shot. At Yale, for example, boys come from all sections of the country. At least 70 per cent of those who report have never used a two-hand set shot for their long shots

TABLE XIV

Long Area Shooting—High School
(both teams)

Season	No. of Teams	No. of Games	Field-Goal Attempts	Field Goals	Per-cent-age	Average per Game	
						Attempts	Goals
1949–50	16	15	132	32	.242	8.8	2.1
1950–51	16	15	101	24	.238	6.7	1.6
1951–52	16	15	248	57	.230	16.5	3.8
1952–53	16	15	333	101	.303	22.2	6.7
1953–54	16	15	296	96	.324	19.7	6.4
5-year totals 1949–50– 1953–54 inclusive	80	75	1110	310	.279	14.8	4.1

This table shows total shots with percentages and averages as in Tables X and XII, but for long shots only.

and most of them cannot shoot accurately from the long area at all. Although it is possible, it is still difficult to teach a player of college age to learn new shots. Players should learn the technique of the two-hand set shot while in Junior High School or even earlier. The shot should be mastered first in areas close to the basket. By the time a player is in college, he should be able to hit the two-hand set shot from as far as 35 or 40 feet.

The long two-hand set shot is a "must" in professional basketball, and many excellent prospects have failed in the professional ranks because they have failed to master it.

The high school report, inconclusive as it is, does substantiate the college report. Only 10 per cent of all attempts in the last five high school tournaments in Kentucky were taken in the long area, and less than 9 per cent of the goals scored were in that area.   Just think what would happen if a team took one-fourth of its attempts from the long area and could hit 40 per cent or better.   Such an achievement is possible because practice shooting with no defense shows better than a 40 per cent average.   The players are either not permitted or do not have the confidence to use these shots in games.

Players and coaches should make careful study of shooting from the various areas.   Naturally, all teams try to work in for as many close shots as possible; but it is very important to be able to score well from all areas and time allotted to practice should be decided somewhat by the number of attempts and the field-goals scored in the various areas.   To point up this part of the study Table XV is added which shows the percentage of total field-goal attempts and field goals scored in the various areas.   In the short area, for example, more than 40 per cent of the attempts are taken and over half of the points are scored (see Table XV, page 71).

Styles of field-goal shooting

This book does not include a complete study of skills or techniques.   However, the one-hand and two-hand shots have caused so much controversy that a sampling of games was used to study them.   Table XVI, Styles of Field-Goal Shooting, pages 72–73, gives the results in seventy-seven major games.

This report is from the original study of games prior to the year 1949–50 as no recent data are available.   However close observations would indicate that the following suggestions are still valid.

The two-hand set shot is considered best for use in the long-shot area.   While the results indicate that the one-hand shot is a bit more accurate from a long distance (the average is .186 as compared to .177 for the two-hand shot), it should be pointed out that most of the one-hand shooting was done just outside the twenty-four foot mark.   The accuracy of

TABLE XV

PERCENTAGES OF TOTALS OF FIELD-GOAL ATTEMPTS TAKEN AND FIELD GOALS SCORED IN AREAS (control group)

	Short Area Shots		Medium Area Shots		Long Area Shots	
	Percentage of All Field-Goal Attempts Taken	Percentage of All Field Goals Made	Percentage of All Field-Goal Attempts Taken	Percentage of All Field Goals Made	Percentage of All Field-Goal Attempts Taken	Percentage of All Field Goals Made
5 years 1936–37– 1940–41 inclusive	.296	.432	.453	.388	.251	.180
5 years 1941–42– 1945–46 inclusive	.375	.514	.416	.334	.209	.152
3 years 1946–47– 1948–49 inclusive	.439	.557	.376	.297	.185	.146
1949–50	.423	.521	.361	.306	.216	.174
1950–51	.390	.473	.398	.352	.212	.176
1951–52	.397	.494	.484	.420	.118	.087
1952–53	.411	.488	.482	.426	.108	.085
1953–54	.489	.588	.368	.297	.143	.114
5-year average 1949–50– 1953–54 inclusive	.421	.513	.417	.360	.162	.127
Five-Year High School Average Kentucky Tournaments 1949–50– 1953–54 Inclusive	.550	.620	.348	.291	.102	.089

This table must be studied with caution. Percentages *ARE NOT* of attempts scored as in other tables. This table shows the percentage of the total of field-goal attempts *TAKEN* and the percentage of total field goals that are scored in each of the short, medium, and long areas. The table has nothing to do with shooting percentages as to accuracy.

71

TABLE XVI

STYLES OF FIELD-GOAL SHOOTING
(both teams)

The Long Shot

	No. of Games	One-Hand Attempts	Baskets	Percentage	Two-Hand Attempts	Baskets	Percentage
1st Half	77	343	52	.152	982	170	.173
2nd Half	77	344	76	.221	911	166	.182
Total		687	128	.186	1893	336	.177

The Medium Shot

	No. of Games	One-Hand Attempts	Baskets	Percentage	Two-Hand Attempts	Baskets	Percentage
1st Half	77	1644	362	.220	426	95	.223
2nd Half	77	1669	342	.205	394	83	.211
Total		3313	704	.212	820	178	.217

The Short Shot

	No. of Games	One-Hand Attempts	Baskets	Percentage	Two-Hand Attempts	Baskets	Percentage
1st Half	77	2132	734	.344	88	27	.307
2nd Half	77	2321	813	.350	90	25	.278
Total		4453	1547	.347	178	52	.292

TABLE XVI (Cont.)

Total Shots

	No. of Games	Attempts	Baskets	Percentage
1st Half	77	5615	1440	.256
2nd Half	77	5729	1505	.263
Total		11344	2945	.260

This table shows a comparison of one-hand and two-hand shooting in seventy-seven games. Number of attempts, goals scored, percentage of attempts scored and totals, in long, medium and short areas and in first and second halves, are given; also totals for both types of shots, with percentages, in first and second halves. The report is for both teams.

this type of shot dropped considerably from a greater distance. The study included 51 games in Madison Square Garden (mostly intersectional games), one other New York game, and twenty-five games from western areas where the one-hand shooting is used to a greater extent. It is significant that the one-hand shot average in the long area was only .135 in the Garden games, while it was .203 for the other games. Another significant fact is that less than five one-hand attempts were made by both teams per game, so that possibly not enough shooting was attempted to form any definite conclusion.

In the medium area it will be noted that there was very little difference between the accuracy of the one-hand and two-hand shot. However, the one-hand shot was used more than four times as much as the two-hand shot. This was true of both eastern and western teams.

The short shot is almost entirely a one-hand shot in all sections.

TABLE XVII

STYLES OF FIELD-GOAL SHOOTING—High School
(both teams)

Season	No. of Games	One-Hand			Two-Hand			Totals		
		Attempts per Game	Goals per Game	Pct.	Attempts per Game	Goals per Game	Pct.	Attempts per Game	Goals per Game	Pct.
1938–39	1000	52.4	12.4	.237	48.9	9.6	.197	101.3	22.0	.217
1942–43	1000	74.1	19.8	.267	32.1	7.2	.224	106.2	27.0	.254
1944–45	1000	92.1	26.0	.282	22.4	5.5	.244	114.5	31.5	.275
1945–46	1000	84.9	26.7	.314	18.0	4.8	.267	102.9	31.5	.306
1946–47	1000	97.8	28.9	.295	17.7	4.9	.275	115.5	33.8	.293
1947–48	1000	93.6	28.2	.301	17.3	4.3	.251	110.9	32.5	.293
1948–49	1000	95.0	29.5	.310	24.4	6.8	.278	119.4	36.3	.304
1949–50	1000	110.0	33.0	.300	18.0	4.3	.240	128.0	37.3	.291

This table shows average number of one-hand, two-hand, and total attempts, goals and success percentages for both teams, by seasons, as reported to the National Federation. The totals are the product of the one-hand and two-hand columns and do not include tip-ups.

Conclusions are that the one-hand shot is as good, or better, in the first two areas; the two-hand set shot is still recommended in the long area.

Styles of field-goal shooting in high school

A study was made by the National Federation for a number of years through the season 1949–50 to determine the number of one-hand shots compared to the number of two-hand shots taken, and the percentage of these that were successful. Table XVII gives the result of parts of this study. The reader must bear in mind, however, that this study does not take into consideration the areas from which the shots were taken; this is a very important factor. The study does show the trend from a two-hand style of shooting to the one-hand style in general shooting practice. For example, the 1949–50 season shows a .300 percentage for the one-hand shot as compared to a .240 percentage for the two-hand shot. It is quite likely, however, that the two-hand attempts may have been taken from the outer area whereas the one-hand attempts may have been taken in the short or medium areas.

The free throw

Championships are won at the free-throw line. Our study shows that nearly one-fourth of all games played are decided by four points or less. In each of these games a perfect free-throw record by the losing team would have made it the winner.

For example, in the 1949–50 season, Yale lost five conference games and four of these were by three points or less. Better free throwing would have won each of the four games lost and any two of those games would have meant the championship. Basketball coaches know that they lose enough games at the free-throw lines each year to make the difference in winning and losing a championship race.

Recent rule changes have made free throwing even more

important.   The new 1954–55 rule, for example, that awards an extra free throw on certain occasions if the first one is successful, will mean more concentration on this type of shooting.

Records in all divisions show a marked increase in free-throwing accuracy in recent years.   This has been due partly to improvement in equipment and facilities (better balls and baskets and improved lighting conditions) and partly to in-struction and practice; yet the average is still much lower than might be expected.

Free throwing in college games

Our recent college study shows the five-year average of .645 with the 1953–54 average at .648 as compared to our original study of earlier years which show the percentage of .592.   Recent N.C.A.A. averages, which of course include many more games, show the five-year average at .633 with the 1953–54 average of .650; whereas in 1949 the N.C.A.A. Bureau reported the percentage of .617.   From these figures we may assume that the present college average is approxi-mately 64 per cent.   Tables XVIII and XIX on pages 77 and 78 give complete results of free throwing on the college level for recent years.

It should be kept in mind that the free throw is one type of shot that is exactly the same under game conditions as in practice, as far as the actual physical performance is con-cerned.   No one is guarding the shooter as when a player attempts a field goal.   Table XVIII shows that our practice shot percentage over a five-year period is. 766.   What then makes the difference during a game?

A study of 132 games indicates that, in the first half, the free-throw percentage was .655 while in the second half it dropped to .636.   This difference indicates that the element of fatigue may enter into the situation.   It is therefore sug-gested that after the technique of the free throw is mastered,

1951—Yale's basketball team arrives for a series of games in Puerto Rico. *(Photo courtesy Pan American World Airways System.)*

PAZ, BOLIVIA, [1953]—Yale's basket-[bal]l team before a [ga]me played in a [bul]lfight ring in [fro]nt of 5,000 spec-[tat]ors. Yale's team [wa]s the first from [th]e U. S. to play in [Bo]livia (see page [3]). *(Photo cour-[tes]y "Foto Linares.")*

SHOOTING A BASKET. The ball finds its mark. The ultimate goal of basketball (see page 48)

THE ONE-HAND SHOT. Perfect follow through is illustrated in this one-hand shot. (*Photo courtesy Warren Teter.*)

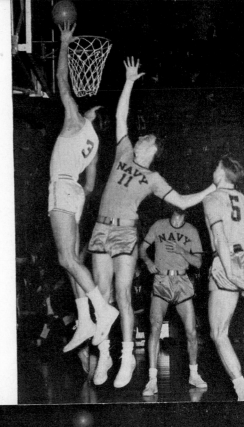

THE SHORT SHOT. Ted Anderson, former Yale star, goes high into the air for a short "lay-up" shot in a Yale–Navy game (see page 60). *(Photo courtesy The Yale Daily News.)*

THE MEDIUM SHOT. Tony avelli illustrates a shot from e medium area in a Yale–olumbia game, using his left-nd hook style (see page 62). *Photo courtesy The Yale Daily ews.)*

THE JUMP SHOT. Dave Hobson,
Yale guard and captain, in the start
of the now-popular jump shot (see
page 63).

THE TALL MAN IN BAS-
KETBALL. George Mikan,
6'9" former Minneapolis
Laker and All America
DePaul player, uses his
height to tip in a goal under rather adverse condi-
tions (see page 144).
(World Wide Photos.)

THE TWO-HAND SET
SHOT. Dick Joyce, for-
mer Yale captain, shows
the starting position of the
two-hand set shot (see
page 66.) *(Photo cour-
tesy The Yale Daily
News.)*

THE ONE-HAND FREE
THROW. Tony Lavelli, Yale's
All America and modern collegiate free-throw champion
sets a new major college scoring record (his 1871st point)
in Yale–Harvard game. No-
tice his perfect follow through
(see page 84). *(Photo courtesy The New Haven Register.)*

THE REBOUND. Paul Arizin of the Philadelphia Warriors gives a good illustration of rebound technique in a game with Baltimore (see page 87). *(International News Photo.)*

THE HOOK SHOT. Tony Lavelli demonstrates excellent form and follow through in this hook shot (see page 63). *(Photo courtesy The Yale Daily News.)*

THE CENTER JUMP. Yale's Dick
Joyce jumps high to gain the tip (see
page 91). *(Photo courtesy The Yale
Daily News.)*

THE HELD BALL. Nothing for the
referee to do in this situation but to
call a held ball and let the players
jump for it (see page 106).

THE PERSONAL FOUL. A defensive
man goes under the jumper to commit a
personal foul in a DePaul–N.Y.U. game
(see page 102).

THE FORDHAM–COLUMBIA EXPERIMENTAL GAME. Notice the white markings indicating the widened free-throw lane, and the large outside arc that divides the court into two scoring areas (see page 155).

players practice free throws during and following strenuous
practice sessions. Of course, proper physical condition that
will carry a player through an entire game is an even better

TABLE XVIII

FREE THROWS

Season	No. of Games	Free-Throw Attempts	Free-Throw Goals	Per-cent-age	Average per Game	
					Attempts	Goals
1949–50	26	1137	706	.621	43.7	27.2
1950–51	27	1497	934	.624	55.4	34.6
1951–52	28	1493	992	.664	53.3	35.4
1952–53	25	1732	1139	.658	69.3	45.6
1953–54	26	1783	1155	.648	68.6	44.4
5-year totals 1949–50–1953–54 inclusive						
Game Totals (both teams)	132	7642	4926	.645	57.9	37.3
First Half (both teams)	132	3381	2216	.655	25.6	16.8
Second Half (both teams)	132	4261	2710	.636	32.3	20.5
Winning Team	132	4046	2653	.656	30.7	20.1
Losing Team	132	3596	2273	.632	27.2	17.2
Home Team	132	3932	2552	.649	29.8	19.3
Visiting Team	132	3710	2374	.640	28.1	18.0
Major Games (one team)	97	2790	1814	.650	28.8	18.7
Minor Games (one team)	35	963	650	.675	27.5	18.6
Conference Games (one team)	62	1818	1183	.651	29.3	19.1
Non-conference Games (one team)	70	1935	1281	.662	27.6	18.3
Scrimmages (one team)	100	2384	1473	.618	23.8	14.7
* Practice shots		29048	22264	.766		

* Two in succession only.

This table shows total free-throw attempts and free-throw goals, percentage of
attempts scored, and average number of attempts and goals per game, by seasons,
for 132 games. The table also gives similar information for first and second
halves, winning and losing teams, home and visiting teams, major and minor
games, conference and non-conference games, scrimmages and practice shots without defense.

answer.   Research also indicates that the winning team made a percentage of .656 while the losing team made an average of .632.   This may indicate that the winning team was more skillful in free-throw shooting but it also indicates a probable decrease in the fatigue factor.   There was no great difference noted in the free-throw performance at home and on visiting courts; the percentage for home games was .649 and for games away from home was .640.   These trends were all similar in the original thirteen year study prior to 1950. (See Table VI-A in Appendix A.)

TABLE XIX

FREE THROWS—N.C.A.A.
(both teams)

Season	No. of Teams	No. of Games	Average per Game		Percentage
			Attempts	Goals	
1947–48	160	3945	42.2	25.3	.600
1948–49	149	3737	43.3	26.7	.617
1949–50	145	3659	46.5	28.7	.617
1950–51	153	3974	48.1	30.1	.626
1951–52	156	4009	50.5	31.5	.624
1952–53	158	3754	65.8	42.1	.640
1953–54	160	3933	64.3	41.8	.650
5-year totals 1949–50– 1953–54 inclusive	772	19329	55.0	34.8	.633

This table shows the average number of free-throw attempts and goals per game, percentage scored, for both teams, by seasons, as reported to the N.C.A.A. Bureau.

Another factor that affects the player in free-throw shots and probably reduces his efficiency even more than fatigue is his mental state.   Players who are affected by spectators, the importance of the game or of the situation in the game, and who allow themselves to think of other things except making the free throws, are no doubt the rule rather than the exception.

A typical example of this occurred a number of years ago in a game between Oregon and Washington State College. As the gun sounded ending the game, a foul was called that gave an Oregon guard two free throws at the basket. Oregon was one point behind—needing one free-throw goal to tie the score and two to win. Unfortunately, the player missed both free throws. The usual "hard luck" consolation remarks went around the dressing room but later in the eveing, after things had cooled off, the boy was asked what he was thinking of when he toed the free-throw line. It was necessary to know what outside factors entered the picture, since the player was an expert at free-throw shots and consistently made 90 per cent of his attempts in practice. He was also a "money player"—best when "the chips were down." He was a tireless player and therefore fatigue was not the answer. After hesitating a moment, his reply was: "Well, Coach, I've been having a little trouble lately in shooting them short. I thought I would be sure, so I aimed at the back rim." Needless to say, both shots hit the back rim squarely. It may be a very difficult task, but the more players learn to think *only* of *making* the free throw, the more they will improve their performance.

Free throwing in high school games

National averages are not available to indicate the number of free-throw attempts, or the number of free-throw goals scored in the average high school game. Present rules would indicate, however, that the average high school team might have approximately 30 free throws at the basket in each game. No doubt the same number of close games are won or lost at the free-throw line in high school as is the case in college games; yet the national average until 1953–54 has been around .600. It is encouraging to note, however, that the 1953–54 national average for 1,000 games was .657, actually higher than the college average. Table XX gives free-throw percentages in high school games as reported to the National Federation.

TABLE XX

FREE THROWS—High School
(both teams)

Season	No. of Games	Percentage
1938–39	1000	.453
1942–43	1000	.488
1944–45	1000	.486
1946–47	1000	.501
1947–48	1000	.592
1948–49	1000	.528
1949–50	1000	.544
1950–51	1000	.564
1951–52	1000	.612
1952–53	1000	.609
1953–54	1000	.657
5-year totals 1949–50– 1953–54 inclusive	5000	.597

This table shows the percentage of free-throw attempts scored for both teams, by seasons, as reported to the National Federation.

Good advice on both the college and high school level might be to insist on at least 75 per cent accuracy in practice from each player. No more than two shots in succession should be permitted in the practice sessions. A player who can consistently make 75 per cent under these conditions might be permitted to use any style of shot he chooses. A player who falls very much below this average should be taught the under-hand toss, which is the most accurate for most players.

Free throwing in professional games

Professionals should be better free throwers, and they are. Table XXI gives the National Basketball Association free-throw results for recent years. Please note that the average for the last five years is .722, which shows higher percentages are possible from the free-throw line. This mark might be a good one for college and high school teams to shoot for. Even the professionals could improve their team percentage, however; there are still many professional players who use unorthodox shots, making a fairly low average and thereby

TABLE XXI

FREE THROWS—Professional (N.B.A.)

(both teams)

Season	No. of Games	Average per Game		Percentage
		Attempts	Goals	
1946–47	331	49.6	31.8	.641
1947–48	192	54.0	36.4	.674
1948–49	360	62.4	44.0	.705
1949–50	561	66.0	47.2	.715
1950–51	354	66.6	48.8	.733
1951–52	330	66.4	48.8	.735
1952–53	352	71.6	51.2	.715
1953–54	324	66.0	46.8	.709
5-year totals 1949–50– 1953–54 inclusive	1921	67.3	48.6	.722

This table gives the average number of free-throw attempts and free-throw goals per game, with percentages of attempts scored, for both teams, by seasons, for professional games as reported to the N.B.A.

bringing their team percentage down. It would seem that any professional player should be able to make 80 per cent of his free throws in practice and in games.

Styles of free-throw shooting

New data are not available on the styles of free-throw shooting. However, a study of the styles employed by the Yale squad over the past five years strongly bears out conclusions established in the earlier study. For this reason, the comments and results in Table XXII on page 83 are again given.

Close observation of different styles of shooting used in 52 major games played in New York City during the 1944–45 season indicate that the underhand free throw is the most accurate. Table XXII, Styles of Free-Throw Shooting, page 83, gives the results. In this particular study there were 914 free throws attempted using the underhand style. Of this number 516 were successful, showing a percentage of .565. The two-hand chest shot was used 794 times, 422 with success, giving a percentage of .531. The one-hand shot was used 115 times, 58 with success giving a percentage of .504. In teaching the underhand shot coaches have used the argument that time must be spent in teaching a different type of shot than the player uses from the field. They claim that a player will become proficient from the free-throw line by the use of the same type of shot that he uses from the field and that the additional practice will also aid his field-goal shots. This contention may have had some grounds during the war period when coaches did not have players more than a year and had limited time to spend with their players each day. However, to train players in free throwing is now important enough to be a major part of coaching. It will pay dividends to spend extra time in teaching the underhand free throw to most players.

There are, of course, individual differences and every good

rule has exceptions. If a player is able to make a high percentage of his free-throw attempts using the two-hand chest shot or the one-hand shot he should be permitted to do so,

TABLE XXII

STYLES OF FREE-THROW SHOOTING
(MAJOR GAMES IN MADISON SQUARE GARDEN, 1944–45)

	Underhand (2 hands)			Chest (2 hands)			One Hand			Total		
	FTA*	FTG**	Percentage	FTA	FTG	Percentage	FTA	FTG	Percentage	FTA	FTG	Percentage
1st Half Totals	450	261	.580	395	216	.547	68	38	.559	918	517	.563
2nd Half Totals	464	255	.550	399	206	.516	47	20	.426	910	481	.529
Game Totals	914	516	.565	794	422	.531	115	58	.504	1828	998	.546

* Free-Throw Attempts.
** Free-Throw Goals.

This table shows a comparison of the underhand, chest, and one-hand styles of shooting free throws in fifty-two games. It shows the total number of attempts, total goals scored and percentage of attempts made in the first and second halves and totals. The report is for both teams.

particularly on the college level. Stansbury Peacock, a Yale player, asked if he could shoot his free throws from the chest. Asked if he knew his percentage from the previous year, he said that it was .700. "Pretty high," was the reply. "How about a demonstration?" Stan proceeded to make 39 successive free throws from the chest before he missed.   Needless to say, during that season he shot free throws from the chest and his average was .758.

Tony Lavelli, however, was the greatest free thrower it has been my pleasure to coach.   As a matter of fact, Tony is the best free thrower in the history of college basketball since the days when one man was permitted to shoot all the free throws for his team.   Tony shoots free throws with one hand.   In four years of college basketball, he scored 564 free-throw goals out of 722 attempts—a .781 percentage.   In 1948–49, he scored 215 free-throw goals out of 261 attempts for an .824 percentage, the highest of his entire career.   According to records of the National Basketball Guide no other major college player has broken the records either in a single season or throughout a four-year career in totals or averages per game.   William Anderson of Lafayette holds the all-time college record.   He played in the years from 1915–19 when one man was privileged to shoot all the free throws for his team.   Mr. Anderson's record was 764 free-throw goals out of 930 attempts, an .822 average over the four-year period. He used the underhand shot and taught this style for many years as a coach.   The author agrees with Mr. Anderson but, of course, is always satisfied when a one-hand expert like Tony Lavelli can sink them consistently (see photo, The One-hand Free Throw, in illustrated section).

These examples show that great shooters may use various types of shots.   However, they are the exceptions rather than the rule and the underhand shot is still the most accurate for most players.   Again, the point is made that shooters like Stan Peacock and Tony Lavelli were accurate because their shots, regardless of style, were fundamentally correct and they disciplined themselves to consistent practice periods. Their shots had perfect wrist and finger action, perfect follow-through, and perhaps even more important, these boys *knew* they could make them—they had confidence.

There is no reason why players should not make 80 to 90 per cent of their attempts in practice and why they should not approach this average in games, if the fatigue and mental hazards can be eliminated.

Assists

Definition: An assist should be credited each time a player makes, in the scorer's judgment, the principal pass or tip that leads directly to a field goal. See Chapter 14, page 173, for further details.

We should not finish the chapter on shooting without giving some notice to the importance of assists that help make goals possible. Assists are a matter of judgment and therefore difficulty has been experienced in standardizing the measurement of this important item. However, assists are quite widely recorded and publicized. Many conferences keep a record of assists. The policy certainly furnishes an incentive for players to be play-makers as well as shooters. Those that record assists find that the number of assists per game increases in relation to the number of field goals scored. This is an indication that players, knowing they will receive credit, will make more of an effort to assist. For example, our control group at first showed assists for only about one-third of the field goals scored while in 1953–54 we recorded 60 per cent; that is, if a team scores 25 field goals a game, an average of at least 15 assists would be recorded. Even this percentage seems low.

The professionals (N.B.A.) have the best available records on assists. They started recording assists in 1946–47 and in that year only an average of 6.9 assists were reported out of an average of 25.9 field goals a game—less than 27 per cent. The assists have steadily increased, however, and in the last four years over 70 per cent of the times field goals have been scored, an assist has been credited. In 1953–54 their records show an average of 20.3 assists out of 28.1 field goals a game—nearly 76 per cent.   Perhaps improved observing and recording has had something to do with the increase but players certainly will make more assists when credit is given and this is good for the player, the team and the game.   It seems quite reasonable that an assist should lead to a field goal at least three-fourths of the time if good teamwork is attained. Thus we have the start toward establishing a standard which we may expect from a good team in this department.

6

Basketball Recoveries

Offensive and defensive rebounds

(See photo, The Rebound, in illustrated section)

Definitions: A rebound is credited to a player or team each time the ball is retrieved after a field-goal attempt or free-throw attempt is missed, except when the ball is dead following an attempt. A team rebound is credited to the team that the ball is awarded to when a goal attempt goes out of bounds (1, without being touched by a player, 2, is deflected out of bounds before there is possession, 3, a free-throw attempt misses the rim and is awarded by the official to the opponent out of bounds). An offensive rebound is one that is retrieved by the shooting or offensive team. A defensive rebound is one that is retrieved by the defending or defensive team. If a rebound results in a held ball, the jumper of the team retrieving the jump ball is credited with the rebound.

Rebounding is more important than any other basketball fundamental except shooting. Possession of the ball is worth at least seven-tenths of a point to a team provided it does not lose the ball before getting a shot at the basket, as the shooting average is about .340 (better than one out of three and one-third of two points is approximately seven-tenths). Naturally, the team that gains possession of the ball most frequently, when it is free, will win, provided it can match the other team in shooting accuracy. A study of 132 games during the last five years is given in Table XXIII, Rebounds, on page 89.

In tabulating rebounds observers are urged to credit a rebound to the proper player or team each time a field-goal or free-throw attempt is missed and the ball remains in play. Our N.C.A.A. records, for example, report only an average of 83.9 rebounds per game when the possible number is 102.5. (See Table XXIV.) Our college study, as reported in Table XXIII, shows an average of 114.4 rebounds per game so we can safely assume that there are more than 100 rebounds in the average college game. Of those 100, approximately 58 will become defensive rebounds and 42 will become offensive rebounds, according to our records. The defensive team, naturally, has the advantage as it has the inside positions when the shot is taken. It is therefore misleading merely to record the total rebounds because a team might retrieve half of the rebounds and still not get its half of the offensive rebounds, which are really the ones that count most.

As expected, the winning team usually gains more rebounds than the losing team. Of 100 rebounds, the winners will probably get about 54 as compared to 46 for the losers. The home team usually has an advantage due to the fact that they are more accustomed to the manner in which the ball bounds from the basket or backboard. It is, of course, different on different courts. If the baskets are tight, the rebounds will be long; if the baskets are loose, the rebounds will be short. If the backboard is braced rigidly, the rebounds will be long; if it is braced loosely, the rebounds will be short. Until equipment is standardized, a visiting team should spend part of the practice prior to the game in rebounding to familiarize itself with the conditions. The

TABLE XXIII

Rebounds (control group)

(5-year totals 1949-50–1953-54 inclusive)

	No. of Games	Offensive Rebounds	Average per Game	Defensive Rebounds	Average per Game	Total Rebounds	Average per Game
1st Half (both teams)	132	3130	23.7	4393	33.3	7523	57.0
2nd Half (both teams)	132	3150	23.9	4422	33.5	7572	57.4
Winning Team	132	3252	24.6	4834	36.6	8086	61.3
Losing Team	132	3028	22.9	3981	30.2	7009	53.1
Home Team	132	3243	24.6	4468	33.8	7711	58.4
Visiting Team	132	3037	23.0	4347	32.9	7384	55.9
Both Teams	132	6280	47.6	8815	66.8	15095	114.4

This table shows the offensive, defensive, and total number of rebounds and averages of each per game, for both teams for 132 games, in five seasons. Findings are also given for first half, second half, winning and losing teams, and home and visiting teams.

fundamentals of proper rebounding are important enough to be taught all players so that they get their share of rebounds. Proper balance, timing, jumping, and protection of the ball after it is retrieved are important factors. Individual rebound fundamentals and team rebound organization should demand a major part of the practice periods.

TABLE XXIV

REBOUNDS (N.C.A.A.)

Season	No. of Teams	No. of Games	Average per Game Reported	Average per Game Possible
1950–51	153	3974	84.4	107.2
1951–52	156	4009	84.7	109.1
1952–53	158	3754	84.7	99.8
1953–54	160	3933	81.6	93.9
4-year total	627	15670	83.9	102.5

This table shows the average number of rebounds per game for both teams, by seasons, reported to the N.C.A.A. Bureau. It also gives the average number of rebounds per game that were possible; in other words, the maximum number that might have been reported.

We cannot overemphasize the fact that there will be well over 100 rebounds in every game for the two opposing teams to fight over. Records indicate that if your team can get 60 per cent or better of all rebounds, you can reasonably expect a victory unless your losses of ball and shooting accuracy fall substantially below the standards of your opponents.

Obviously recording and scouting will show the coach the strong rebounding opponents as well as his own strong rebounders. Strategy may be planned accordingly.

Rebounds in high school games

Unfortunately, rebounds are not compiled by the National Federation and from replies received, they are not recorded in very many of the state tournaments. Records available do show that there are well over 100 rebounds in the average high school game so the same emphasis should be placed on high school rebounding as has been suggested for the college game. Players and coaches will be well rewarded for keeping records and emphasizing the fundamentals of this important phase of the game.

Rebounds in professional games

Again, the professionals have been quick to take advantage of tabulating rebounds. They are considered by the National Basketball Association to be an important part of the player and team records. The players are judged and paid according to their shooting percentages and their rebound averages. Naturally some players are delegated to rebound duty more than others; this must be taken into consideration on all levels. The professional averages substantiate the college records very well. Table XXV on page 92 gives the record for the National Basketball Association on rebounds. The reported number is slightly over 100 a game but the average possible number, had all been reported, is 117.4 a game.

Jump-ball recoveries

(See photo, The Center Jump, or Tip-Off, in illustrated section)

Definition: A jump ball recovery is credited to the player retrieving the jump ball. If the ball is tipped out of bounds and awarded to a team, that *TEAM* is credited with the jump ball recovery. There should be a jump ball recovery for every jump ball.

There was a time in basketball when the tip-off was one of

the main plays of the game. Earlier books on basketball show many tip-off plays. With the elimination of the center jump, however, the importance of tip-off and jump ball plays has been minimized.

TABLE XXV

Rebounds—Professional (N.B.A.)
(both teams)

Season	No. of Games	Average per Game Reported	Average per Game Possible
1950–51	354	99.4	122.2
1951–52	330	109.0	119.0
1952–53	352	102.8	114.4
1953–54	324	101.8	113.8
4-year totals 1950–51–1953–54 inclusive	1360	103.3	117.4

This table shows the average number of rebounds per game for both teams, by seasons, for professional games, as reported to the N.B.A. It also gives the average number per game of possible rebounds that might have been reported.

It is true that the jump ball is not as important as some of the other phases of the game, such as the rebound. Our recent study shows an average of only 10.4 jump balls a game, which is a marked decrease from our original study which showed an average of 16 a game. Table XXVI, Miscellaneous Recoveries, on page 93 gives the complete picture.

Since there are more than 100 rebounds a game and only about ten jump balls, only one-tenth the time, in theory, should be spent on jump ball work as compared to rebounding. However, a team does profit by retrieving the ten jump balls. Too many coaches have neglected this part of the game almost entirely and as a result have lost the ma-

jority of the jump balls. The only way to determine a team's
ability in this phase is to record the results. Most teams tip
to certain men; find out who those men are. The jump ball
toward the end of a game when the score is close may be
worth a little time and effort.

TABLE XXVI

MISCELLANEOUS RECOVERIES (control group)
(Jump Balls and Interceptions)
(5-year totals 1949–50–1953–54 inclusive)

	No. of Games	Jump Ball Recoveries	Average per Game	Inter- ceptions	Average per Game
1st Half (both teams)	132	627	4.8	1811	13.7
2nd Half (both teams)	132	744	5.6	1758	13.3
Winning Team	132	730	5.5	1821	13.8
Losing Team	132	641	4.9	1748	13.2
Home Team	132	699	5.3	1837	13.9
Visiting Team	132	672	5.1	1732	13.1
Both Teams	132	1371	10.4	3569	27.0

This table shows the total number of jump ball recoveries and
interceptions and the average number of each per game for 132
games for both teams, first and second halves, winning and losing
teams, and home and visiting teams.

Many players do not understand the technique of tipping
the ball properly. Each player should have instruction in
how to tip the ball ahead, behind, and to either side. It is
equally important that players who expect to receive the tip
know how to properly fake their men out of position and
time their jumps for the ball.

The number of jump balls in high school games are recorded and reported to the National Federation each year. There are 16 jump balls in the average high school game—more than in college games—so time and attention should be allotted accordingly.   Table XXVII, below, gives the records.

TABLE XXVII

Jump Balls—High School
(both teams)

Season	No. of Games	No. of Jump Balls per Game
1938–39	1000	21.7
1942–43	1000	20.4
1944–45	1000	18.0
1946–47	1000	17.5
1947–48	1000	19.2
1948–49	1000	18.5
1949–50	1000	18.6
1950–51	1000	16.8
1951–52	1000	14.1
1952–53	1000	16.2
1953–54	1000	14.5
5-year totals 1949–50–1953–54 inclusive	5000	16.0

This table shows the average number of jump balls per game for both teams, by seasons, as reported to the National Federation.

Unfortunately, neither the N.C.A.A. or N.B.A. (professional) keeps jump ball records.

Interceptions

Definition: An interception occurs each time the ball is lost by the opponents through poor ball handling or bad passing. Credit a player with an interception each time he intercepts a pass or takes the ball away from an opponent. If a player ties up an opponent causing a held ball and his team retrieves the jump ball, credit him with an interception. A *TEAM* interception is credited when an opponent passes the ball out of bounds, for example, and a defensive player does not cause the change of possession. An interception—either player or team—should be credited each time the ball changes team possession due to poor ball handling or bad passing.

"Ball hawks" in basketball are the players coaches are always looking for. Coaches strive to develop men who can press the offense and steal the ball without fouling, players who can intercept a pass or dive for and recover a loose ball on the floor. These players are great contributors to victories. Very often a timely interception gains four points for a team —it saves two points that the opponents may make if they retain the ball and it gains two points that the interceptor's team may make by gaining possession.

In a crucial Madison Square Garden game that will never be forgotten, Oregon led Long Island by a 15-point margin at the start of the second half. Long Island had several great "ball hawks" and their timely interceptions resulted in goals that cut down the Oregon lead. With ten seconds to play, Oregon still held a two-point lead. Out of nowhere came a "ball hawk" who intercepted a pass and fed the ball to a teammate who tied the score. Long Island went on to win in overtime 56–55. Who received the credit?—the player who scored the basket. The interception was soon forgotten.

In spite of its great importance, players are rarely given credit for this skill. Since it can be objectively measured, why not let the player and the public know of his achievement? The interceptor should receive due credit. If players are given this credit it will furnish an incentive for both themselves and other players to improve and excel in this department. As long as scorers get all the praise, many players will want to score above all else—sometimes at the expense of team interest.

The "ball hawks" on the opposing team should be known so that play may be kept away from their areas as much as possible. Great caution should be used so that the ball will not be exposed to them. Certainly more attention should be directed toward this part of the game. Those "four point" interceptions may win many games.

Our recent study of 132 college games over a five-year period is given in Table XXVI on page 93. There are about 27 interceptions in the average college game.

It is most unfortunate that the N.C.A.A., The National Federation (High School), or the Professional (N.B.A.) do not keep records of interceptions.

7

Basketball Errors and Their Implications

BASKETBALL TERMINOLOGY IS NOT WELL ESTABLISHED. Errors are not defined in the rule book as in baseball. For our purposes errors are meant to include losses of the ball (except by shooting for the basket) and personal fouls.

Loss-of-ball

Definition: A loss should be charged to a player each time he is responsible for the ball changing from his own team's possession to the oponents' possession. Such a loss could result from poor ball handling, poor passing, a violation or technical foul (if team possession changes) and these are the types of losses covered in this study. Loss-of-ball may also result from a goal attempt or a goal scored, but these are covered in other parts of the study.

If a player in possession allows himself to be tied up, causing a held ball, and the opponents retrieve the ensuing jump ball, a loss should be charged.

Obviously, a team cannot score without the ball. Therefore, everything that can be done to gain possession of the ball should be stressed by the coach. In addition to *gaining* possession, it is equally important to retain that possession until a scoring opportunity is presented.

Yale University played the University of Illinois in the first round of the N.C.A.A. tournament at Madison Square Garden in 1949. Illinois won the game 71–67. It was a thriller for Illinois to win and a heartbreaker for Yale to lose. Yale had enjoyed a six-point lead with a little more than three minutes to play. *An intercepted pass* gave Illinois a field goal but with two minutes to play, Yale still held a three-point advantage and possession of the ball. A Yale player was open going into the basket for what might have been the clincher. *A bad pass*, however, gave the ball to Illinois and they cashed in with a field goal. Illinois then *intercepted the throw-in* after the goal and scored again. Yale, in possession of the ball, went down the court but was guilty of traveling. This resulted in a fourth Illinois goal *on four straight Yale losses-of-ball*. Now two points behind, Yale again brought the ball to the front court and set up a play. Again, the ball was taken away from a Yale player and turned into a basket. *Five losses* in three minutes gave *five field goals* to the other team. Most coaches can think of many games that have been lost similarly. Loss-of-ball is, then, one of the most serious errors in the game.

Just how much it may cost a team when it loses the ball may be seen in the following illustration: Team A has the ball. Theoretically, this is worth seven-tenths of a point since it will succeed in about one out of three shots if the team does not lose possession (one-third of two points is about seven-tenths). This is based on the assumption that the shooting percentage is .340. When the team loses possession of the ball without gaining a scoring opportunity they obviously give the opponents this seven-tenths point. The minimum average loss, then, would be 1.4 points. The loss might be costly enough to make a difference of four points in the score

—two points that Team A might score if they retained possession and two points that the opponents may score when they gained possession.

It is also conceivable, although a remote possibility, that there could be a maximum cost of eight points to a team that loses the ball. If Team A scored a basket and the shooter was flagrantly fouled in the act of shooting and made both free throws, he would give his team four points. If the ball was lost to the oponents and they executed such a play, the difference in the score would be eight points on one loss-of-ball. At least we may proceed on the supposition that loss-of-ball is costly.

Our recent college study indicates that the average team loses the ball between seventeen and eighteen times a game. The faster game has probably brought about an increase in losses of ball. Table XXVIII on page 100 gives complete results. Many teams lose the ball as many as 30 times during a game. Coaches should keep in mind that if they can cut down the losses by ten in a game, they have given their teams 14 points minimum and it could be many more. It is therefore of great interest to the coach to know how the ball is lost and who loses it, both on his team and on the opposing team. If the coach knows who loses the ball on his own team he may work on fundamentals to improve this situation. If he knows which opponents lose the ball, he may plan strategy that will press those opponents and cause them to lose the ball more frequently.

The ball is lost primarily in three ways: (1) by bad passes, (2) by poor ball-handling, (3) by rule violations such as traveling or broken dribble. The ball may be lost, of course, by taking bad shots at the basket, or by taking any shot that does not score. The ball even changes possession when a goal is scored. However, these latter methods are taken care of through the records of scoring and rebounding.

It should be noted in Table XXVIII that more than three-

TABLE XXVIII

LOSS OF BALL (control group)

(5-year totals 1949–50—1953–54 inclusive)

	No. of Games	Bad Passes	Average per Game	Viola-tions	Average per Game	Poor Ball Handling	Average per Game	Total Losses	Average per Game
1st Half (both teams)	132	905	6.9	555	4.2	853	6.5	2313	17.5
2nd Half (both teams)	132	860	6.5	493	3.7	951	7.2	2304	17.5
Winning Team	132	856	6.5	524	4.0	892	6.8	2272	17.2
Losing Team	132	909	6.9	524	4.0	912	6.9	2345	17.8
Home Team	132	866	6.6	476	3.6	866	6.6	2208	16.7
Visiting Team	132	899	6.8	572	4.3	938	7.1	2409	18.3
Both Teams	132	1765	13.4	1048	7.9	1804	13.7	4617	35.0

This table shows the number of times the ball is lost by bad passes, violations and poor ball handling, and total losses in 132 games in five seasons, with averages per game. It gives this information for both teams, first and second halves, winning and losing teams and for the home and visiting teams.

fourths of the losses are due to bad passes and poor ball-handling. By paying particular attention to the most frequent offenders, instruction may improve the situation markedly. Passing drills that fit into the style of play to be used will help. Violations may also be decreased by covering the rule interpretations thoroughly, and insisting on strict adherence to the rules in all practices and scrimmages.

Our original 13-year study (see Table IX-A in Appendix A) showed a marked decrease in losses during the second half indicating possible early-game nervous tension. The recent study shows about the same number in each half which may mean that players settle down earlier and that coaches have learned that pre-game "pep talks" do not pay off for all players.

As expected, the study shows less losses by the winning team.

Loss-of-ball also occurs more frequently on foreign courts —particularly losses due to violations. This may be due to the fact that the visiting team is usually not familiar with the floor, lighting conditions, and similar factors. Perhaps this would indicate to the coach the advisability of working out on courts away from home prior to the game. If the game is to be played at night, practice should be held at night to get the same lighting conditions. No doubt the mental hazards of playing before unfamiliar and at times unsympathetic crowds are also factors that contribute to this situation.

Eliminate those losses! "A *ball* lost means *points* lost" should be the slogan of every player and coach.

The N.C.A.A. Bureau and the N.B.A. (professional) do not record losses of ball. The National Federation (high school) does record violations. This report is given in Table XXIX on page 102. It will be noted the high school average per game of violations for the last five years is 6.3 compared to 7.9 in the college game. It would be interesting to know how other losses compare but no doubt the totals on all levels are great enough to cause concern and attention.

Personal fouls

(See photo, The Personal Foul, in illustrated section)

The following paragraphs are reprinted from our original study. Progress has been made but some of the comments still apply. We quote from the first edition of this book:

Every coach owes it to the game to minimize as much as possible the committing of personal fouls by his team.

TABLE XXIX

TRAVELING VIOLATIONS—High School
(both teams)

Season	No. of Games	No. of Traveling Violations per game
1938–39	1000	7.3
1942–43	1000	8.2
1944–45	1000	7.5
1946–47	1000	6.8
1947–48	1000	8.1
1948–49	1000	7.0
1949–50	1000	7.3
1950–51	1000	6.0
1951–52	1000	6.0
1952–53	1000	6.6
1953–54	1000	5.8
5–year totals 1949–50–1953–54 inclusive	5000	6.3

This table shows the average number of violations per game for both teams, by seasons, as reported to the National Federation.

Coaches also agree that there is no place in the game at any time for deliberate flagrant personal fouls. It is true, however, that this is one part of the game that needs careful study and attention. It is hoped that this book will help to bring about an improvement in the game by showing that the penalty for the personal foul is not sufficient and therefore needs revision. A study of 75 games indicates that the average team commits an average of 15 personal fouls per game.

The national average is even higher. In 1948, the National Collegiate Athletic Association report showed an average of 18.5 per team and this increased to 19.4 in 1949. Twenty major college teams averaged more than 21 fouls per game in 1949, and Davidson College, the team committing the fewest in the nation, averaged more than 14 per game. In fact, there has been a steady increase in the personal fouls committed since 1944–45 when five fouls were permitted each player instead of four.

The penalty to a team for a defensive personal foul is only one-tenth of a point,* unless it gives the opposing team two free throws. When a foul is committed and the offended team gets one free throw it is worth six-tenths of a point to them since the average team makes 60 per cent of its free throws. When they make the free throw they must give the ball to the other team. Possession of the ball is worth at least five-tenths of a point since the average team scores at least one field goal in four attempts. This leaves one-tenth of a point net gain to the team that is fouled. A team that commits twenty personal fouls in a game might lose only two points (net) in the score. This is not much of a penalty and naturally invites players to foul rather irresponsibly, particularly when behind. As a matter of fact, if one team were to foul the opposing team every time they gained possession of the ball and before they had a chance to score a basket, the fouling team would win by a comfortable margin, since they would match field-goal opportunities against free-

---

* Under old evaluation of ball possession. It is now .7 of a point which could mean an actual loss to the offended team on a one-shot foul.

throw opportunities. There is obviously something wrong with the balance of the game in this instance. The penalty for the personal foul should always be so severe that a player will not consider it advantageous to foul.

One other criticism of the personal foul method is that key players often go out of the game by committing five personal fouls. Increasing the number from four to five, as mentioned, did not remedy the situation nor did it cut down the number of personal fouls committed. On the contrary, it increased the number. In no other game do we lose key players because they make five mistakes in a game. If a player uses rough or unsportsmanlike tactics, he should be dismissed from the game for one infraction, as in football or baseball.

If a football player is guilty of holding several times in a game, he is not asked to leave the game. The penalty, however, is severe enough so that he will not hold if he can possibly avoid it. If the penalty for holding was two yards, for example, there would probably be holding on every play—regardless of efforts of coaches. Officials would also have a tendency to "call" the infraction more frequently; they hesitate before they measure off 15 yards. Holding is not called unless it affects the play.

There are many interference rules in baseball. For example, a base runner may jump in front of a fielder to prevent the fielder from making a play on a ball. The runner is not asked to leave the game, but since he will be called out, the penalty is so severe that he cannot afford to break such a rule. In basketball, regardless of the coach's efforts, players are going to commit fouls when the penalty is not great. We are all familiar with the situation in the last moments of a close game. The trailing team will foul repeatedly in order to gain possession of the ball.

Players should not be deprived of a chance to continue playing because of rule infractions; neither should spectators be deprived of seeing the best players in action late in the game; neither should there be constant, deliberate fouling during the latter part of the game. None of these conditions will be remedied by allowing the players more personal fouls before they are asked to leave the game, or by asking players to refrain from fouling. The only remedy is to make the penalty severe. In other words, if the penalty were severe enough, the player would not commit the foul and there would not need to be a rule that five infractions means the player must leave the game.

It has already been mentioned that knowledge of habitual personal foul offenders is valuable in coaching. Under the present rules plays may be directed at opponents who foul easily or at key men to cause them to commit fouls. The same tactics will, of course, be used against your team if your players cannot play without fouling.

In the Yale-New York University game in Madison Square Garden in December, 1948, an incident occurred that illustrates the point. Many of the sellout crowd came to watch Tony Lavelli. N.Y.U. wisely directed their offense at Tony, and at the half he had committed four fouls. Under these circumstances most coaches take a star player out of the game and hope to be able to use him sparingly before the fifth foul is committed. In this instance, it was decided to change the defensive assignments and Tony played very much "under wraps" defensively during the second half. The choices were: (1) to have him play only offensive ball, (2) let him foul out or (3) have him sit on the bench during the best part of the game. Generally, such a situation is not good for the player, team, or spectator.

In conclusion, the following suggestions are made to help remedy the personal foul situation:

1. More emphasis in coaching individual and team defense. This is particularly important on the junior high and high school level. Since the center jump was eliminated from basketball there has been

a growing tendency to neglect defense. There is a tendency to let the offensive team shoot more freely because the opposing team will get the ball when a basket is scored.

2. Attention by the officials to the rule book so that only actual fouls are called. There is no question of the fact that many of the fouls called in the course of a normal game are not fouls at all according to the rule book. For example, in the latter part of the game, many fouls occur against the team that is trailing and trying to gain possession of the ball. The rules state that a closely guarded player who withholds the ball from play for a period of five seconds shall have a held ball called. The 1949–50 rules say *shall* instead of *may* and it is hoped held balls will be called properly under this rule. The official often waits for bodily contact and then calls a foul. (See photo, The Held Ball, in illustrated section.) Attention to this point alone would cut down the average per game by several fouls.

3. There should be a greater penalty for the defensive foul. The rules committee did not solve the problem in 1949–50 by ruling that, in the last two minutes of the game, the offended team is given a free throw and the ball out-of-bounds following the free throw (made or missed). This rule takes away fast-break opportunities, slows down the game and does nothing about the problem existing during the first thirty-eight minutes of the game.

It is suggested that one free throw be awarded for all defensive fouls and that the free-throw goal count two points. The penalty for the offensive foul should be loss-of-ball to the opposing team— the same as a violation. A player should not be required to leave the game for committing personal fouls. The penalty should be severe enough to take care of the situation. Coaches are urged to try this plan in scrimmages and practice games.

The above paragraphs are all from our first edition.

Now let's take a look at the results of our recent study and some of the problems of the future.

It is gratifying to note recent rule changes that make the penalty more severe for the personal foul. All the changes are moving toward the awarding of a possible two points for the defensive personal foul which we have advocated as the fair penalty since our first study.

Our recent five-year study shows a continuing increase in

personal fouls each year until the 1952–53 season when the "one plus one" rule came in along with the two shot penalty in the last three minutes. Table XXXI (N.C.A.A.) on page 109 is the best table to study on total personal fouls as it includes many more games than our college study. The 1952–53 and 1953–54 records both show decreases for the first time in many years; due no doubt to the more severe penalties.

Still, the number of fouls committed per game is far too many. The present college average is about 42 per game for both teams or 21 for each team. Actually, this means that each of the five players (or his reserve) commits more than four fouls a game. Even more regrettable from the spectator's standpoint is the fact that the new rules have caused many more free throw attempts per game. Please note in Table XIX on page 78 that the N.C.A.A. records show an *increase* for the 1952–53 and 1953–54 seasons of about 15 free throw attempts per game for both teams *even though the number of personal fouls decreased.*

We have known for years that the two most deplorable, unattractive features of basketball are stalling and too many free throws. The 1954–55 penalty—the most severe we have had—gives the additional free throw attempt if the first is successful. Again, this will reduce fouling, which is good; but it will further increase attempts for the simple reason that more free throws are made than missed. We are moving closer to our proposal that the penalty for all defensive fouls be one attempt with the goal counting two points; thus making the penalty even more severe and cutting the number of attempts at least in half.

Please note Table XXX on page 108 for a study of personal fouls under various conditions. Fifty-five per cent of all fouls are committed in the second half, compared to 45 per cent in the first half. Fatigue may be part of the answer here, but the intentional fouling near the end of the game is probably the main reason. We have suggested a time limit the offensive team may have possession before shooting to remedy this situation.

TABLE XXX

Personal Fouls (control group)
(5-year totals 1949–50–1953–54 inclusive)

	No. of Games	Personal Fouls	Average per Game
1st Half (both teams)	132	2616	19.8
2nd Half (both teams)	132	3159	23.9
Winning Team	132	2727	20.7
Losing Team	132	3048	23.1
Home Team	132	2846	21.6
Visiting Team	132	2929	22.2
Both Teams	132	5775	43.8

This table shows the total number of personal fouls and the averages per game for 132 games, in five seasons, for both teams, first and second halves, winning and losing teams, and home and visiting teams.

Contrary to the opinion of some, it still pays high dividends not to foul. The winning team fouls 20.7 times a game compared to 23.1 for the loser.

The home team is called for 21.6 personal fouls per game compared to 22.2 for the visitors. It is interesting to note that the margin here has decreased since our original study (see Table X-A in Appendix A). Perhaps there is less pressure on the officials and conditions are becoming more uniform on home and visiting courts.

Personal fouls in high school games

Table XXXII shows that very complete personal foul data are available from the high schools. The pattern is very much the same as on the college level. First decreases in personal fouls in years were noted in 1952–53 and 1953–54, following the rule changes that made penalties for fouling more severe.

Present high school averages appear to be about 18 fouls a game for each team; still quite high for a 32-minute game.

TABLE XXXI

PERSONAL FOULS—N.C.A.A.

(both teams)

Season	No. of Teams	No. of Games	Average No. Personal Fouls per Game
1947–48	160	3945	36.9
1948–49	149	3737	38.7
1949–50	145	3659	39.0
1950–51	153	3974	42.7
1951–52	156	4009	44.9
1952–53	158	3754	42.5
1953–54	160	3933	42.0
5–year totals 1949–50–1953–54 inclusive	772	19329	42.2

This table shows the average number of personal fouls per game for both teams, by seasons, as reported to the N.C.A.A. Bureau.

Personal fouls in professional games

Table XXXIII shows that the professionals foul more frequently than do high school or college teams. However, professional rules differ from year to year from those of the National Basketball Committee which govern high school, college, A.A.U. and Y.M.C.A. ball.

The professionals have fully utilized the intentional foul in recent years—both by the trailing team to gain possession and by the team ahead to match free throws and run out the time. The peak was reached in 1952–53 when the personal foul total was 57.4 per game for both teams. Although they disqualify on six instead of five fouls, this staggering total meant an average of 5.7 fouls per game for each player on the court (or his reserve). Fouling "specialists" who were dispensable were used frequently toward the end of the game.

TABLE XXXII

PERSONAL FOULS—High School
(both teams)

Season	No. of Games	Average No. Personal Fouls per Game
1938–39	1000	20.8
1942–43	1000	24.2
1944–45	1000	29.1
1946–47	1000	33.3
1947–48	1000	32.3
1948–49	1000	34.9
1949–50	1000	35.3
1950–51	1000	37.6
1951–52	1000	39.6
1952–53	1000	38.2
1953–54	1000	35.7
5–year totals 1949–50–1953–54 inclusive	5000	37.3

This table shows the average number of personal fouls per game, for both teams, by seasons, as reported to the National Federation.

The last minutes of many games, with *both* teams fouling intentionally, consisted of little else but fouling, free throwing, and a slow parade between the two free throw lines.

Many criticized such tactics; but in their way they have rendered the game a service. There are certain aspects unique to the professional game. They are good sportsmen, but if a rule is weak they play the percentages and take full advantage. The intentional foul has not been considered "unethical" in their ranks. They have clearly showed, however, how it can slow down the game and by their tactics they have served warning to high school and college teams, namely: change those rules or this is the game you can soon expect.

TABLE XXXIII

PERSONAL FOULS—Professional (N.B.A.)
(both teams)

Season	No. of Games	Average No. Personal Fouls per Game
1946–47	331	41.6
1947–48	192	44.4
1948–49	360	52.0
1949–50	561	54.0
1950–51	354	51.2
1951–52	330	53.8
1952–53	352	57.4
1953–54	324	50.8
5–year totals 1949–50–1953–54 inclusive	1921	53.4

This table shows the average number of personal fouls per game for both teams, by seasons, as reported to the N.B.A.

Professionals can't tolerate that kind of a game long. They must have spectators and they must put on a show to bring them out. In 1953–54, they tried to clamp down on intentional fouling and succeeded in cutting total personal fouls to 50.8 per game for both teams; still far too many.

In 1954–55, the professionals have put in the time limit rule. The offensive team must shoot within 24 seconds or lose possession. This rule change—long overdue—will greatly reduce intentional fouls, total fouls and stalling.

In conclusion, to meet the important personal foul problem, our recent study would dictate the following considerations which are worthy of further research and experimentation. Some of the suggestions are very similar to those made following our original study.

1. *Penalty for Defensive Personal Foul:* Award one free throw and if successful, the free-throw goal would count two points. If player fouled is in the act of shooting and the goal is made, no free throw is awarded but a personal foul is charged; if the goal is not made the one free throw is awarded, counting two points if made.

This penalty is fair in that it gives what was taken away— the chance to score two points. When the defensive player fouls he does so to prevent the offensive player from shooting or getting into position to shoot. The player fouled should be compensated accordingly. Our study shows ball possession to be worth .7 (35 per cent of 2 points) of a point. A free-throw goal counting two points would be worth 1.3 points (65 per cent of 2 points). The successful free-throwing team would then lose possession, so deducting .7 from 1.3 gives us a net penalty of .6 for the defensive personal foul which is very close to perfect. Therefore, the penalty is proper from both statistical and logical points of view. The two-point goal will greatly reduce the number of free-throw attempts.

2. *Penalty for Offensive Personal Foul:* No free throw. Ball is awarded to fouled oponent out of bounds as in case of a violation but a personal foul is charged. Again, this penalty gives what was taken away. A player who pushes going for a rebound, for example, was trying to get possession illegally so he loses possession. A player charges or screens

illegally to gain scoring position so he loses possession the same as in a violation.

3. *Penalty for Personal Foul When Ball Is Free:* No free throw. Ball is awarded to offended team out of bounds as in a violation but personal foul is charged.

4. *Penalty for Double Foul:* No free throw. Personal fouls are charged and have center-jump between the two offending players. The penalties cancel; why take time to shoot free-throws?

Under the above plans there are no multiple free-throw situations and no decisions between a one-shot or two-shot penalty. It takes a great burden off the officials. Fewer players will be disqualified because of the increase in severity. Free-throw attempts will be less than half the present number during a game. The game is played under the same rules throughout.

To further reduce the number of personal fouls and resultant free-throws and disqualification of players, our study would dictate also a time limit of 30 seconds the offensive team could retain possession without a field-goal attempt. The penalty, however, as dictated by our study, would be a jump ball at the nearer circle rather than loss of ball. The offensive team has not taken an illegal advantage in an attempt to score. The ruling would be the same as a closely guarded player withholding the ball from play. The jump-ball (between player in possession and player guarding him —or if ball is free between two opposing centers) would also give the offensive team a chance to retain possession and the defensive team a chance for possession without fouling. It would not lead to wild shooting or passive defense as might be the case if the penalty were loss of ball.

Again, coaches are urged to try these proposals in scrimmages and practice games.

8

Scouting the Defense

Most of our study, data, and findings thus far have been on the various aspects of offensive basketball. Interceptions and defensive rebounding are defensive items and even control of the ball has defensive implications but in the main our study has been of offensive factors.

Admittedly, we are not giving defense its proper allotment of time and space. The reason is not that the defense is relatively unimportant but rather that performances of defense are hard to measure objectively. Just how much we have neglected defense may be illustrated by a little story.

Egypt was playing Turkey in a Mediterranean Pre-Olympic Basketball Tournament Game at Alexandria in October 1951. Watching the game on our right was an Olympic gentleman from England, on our left one from Denmark. Neither had ever seen a basketball game, so we were a little busy answering questions. Egypt got off to a flying start. They raced down the court and scored five successive field goals to take a 10–0 lead. Turkey called time out. "Egypt has a fast team, and they shoot very well," we commented. "But the other team," said the Danish observer, "Is it not proper to try to stop the opponents from scoring?" Before we could answer, the Britisher, having learned the game quickly, replied, "No, you see, it is a game of passing and shooting skill. One team tries for a goal; then the other team takes the ball and tries its turn at it." It was with a bit of difficulty that we convinced our observers that defense was part of the game of basketball.

We are concerned here, however, with the scouting or analyzing of the defensive performances of players and teams. The entire field is comparatively new and the possibilities are great. If five defensive errors could make a difference of ten points in the score, it would be extremely helpful to know who is making those errors and in what manner. Just as the knowledge of shooting performances has aided greatly in the improvement of shooting accuracy, so would defense improve if we had information about defensive performances. Coaches would know better who and what to teach and players would need to improve glaring weaknesses to maintain a place on the team.

Unfortunately, we do not have defensive data that are adequate to offer as a sampling at this time. We have, however, done considerable experimentation which is sufficient to be of some value. The story of one player is interesting.

One of our guards several years ago was averaging 16 points a game. He was a very accurate shooter. It was obvious, however, that he gave back at least as many points in most games by very poor defensive play. He didn't get back on defense and his individual defense was very poor. Our talks were helpful but the poor defense still was evident; even the bench did not solve the problem. We finally charted the defensive errors in a game without the boys knowing about it. Our "problem guard" made a mere 28 defensive errors and on nine of them, the opponents scored. We lost the game by six points. The results were posted on the bulletin board. We had a better defensive guard—and team—from that time on.

Most defensive scouting or observing is subjective and must be done by one with an adequate knowledge of the game. Some items, however, may be measured objectively. Following is a suggested list of errors that might be checked during the course of a scrimmage or game. Opposite the item, a straight line *1* should be used for each error and the line should be circled ① each time the error results in a free throw goal; or crossed $+$ each time the error results in a field goal for the opponents. A number *2* may be placed above the circle ① if the error results in two free-throw goals. Any forms or symbols, of course, may be used to suit individual preferences or needs.

1. Defensive errors on the ball.
   Number of times a defensive player—
   a. Allows offensive man to drive around him.
   b. Allows himself to be screened.
   c. Allows his man to shoot without deflecting ball or closely guarding him.
   d. Fails to take over a teammate's assignment when necessary.
   e. Fails to recover to take open man when teammate has taken over for him.
   f. Fouls offensive man.
   g. Allows offensive man to get rebound after a shot.
2. Defensive errors away from the ball.
   Number of times defensive player—
   a. Allows offensive opponent to get pass in close scoring position.
   b. Fails to warn teammate of approaching screen.
   c. Fails to take over for teammate.
   d. Fouls offensive man.
   e. Allows offensive man to get rebound after a shot.

In addition to these errors of defense both on and away from the ball, defensive players should be credited with good plays (in addition to rebounds and interceptions), such as:

1. Deflecting a shot.
2. Taking over for a teammate.
3. Successfully preventing a player from driving into scoring territory.

Admittedly, judgment would play a large part in charting the defensive work of a player. However, even a high percentage of accuracy would be very helpful and may have the same effect on defensive improvement as we have noticed in shooting improvement since we started to keep shooting percentages. Don't be surprised if your defensive errors for a single game total 100! And just think—*five less* might change a ten-point loss into a win. Worth a try, isn't it?

9

Scouting Data Pertinent to Psychology of Coaching

UP TO THIS POINT OBJECTIVE DATA HAVE BEEN INTERPRETED mainly for the purpose of coaching to improve various skills. The same objective data will now be interpreted as pertaining to the psychology of coaching.

Physical and mental condition, particularly the latter, have much to do with winning or losing basketball games. Regardless of the skill and all-round ability that a player or team may possess, unless physical condition and mental attitude are adequate, victory cannot be expected. For example, a team often enters a game feeling that there is little chance to win away from home, another may feel that it is unable to win in the second half because of the fatigue element. Still others may feel that they cannot do well because the game is highly competitive and the pressure is too great. Many practice players are not able to come through in games.

It is the purpose of this chapter to point out what the differences are in these various situations. It is hoped that these findings may help coaches to eliminate false impressions and be an aid to them in having their players and teams mentally right for the games. It is not claimed that objective measurements tell the entire story, or even that they are more valuable than subjective observations. It is true, however, that facts are a basis upon which to formulate plans and that knowledge tends to minimize superstitions and false concepts. It might be added that athletes, generally speaking, are among the more superstitious and that more knowledge might improve this situation.

The home team and the visiting team

Many coaches have expressed the opinion that the home court is worth ten points or better to a team. In other words, the team playing at home has a ten-point advantage. In this study, an attempt was made to compare the home games with the games played away from home to determine if a difference does exist, and if so, what the difference is. The reader is referred to Table XXXIV, Home Team Survey, page 120, and Table XXXV, Visiting Team Survey, page 121.

The home team in basketball still has such an advantage, partly imaginary, that it presents a major problem. First, let us consider the actual game results.

Figures can be misleading and particular care and caution is suggested in giving proper interpretations to the findings. Our original study of 448 games showed a winning percentage of .629 for the home team and .371 for the visitors. (See Table XI-A in Appendix A.) Our recent five-year study shows a .598 percentage for the home team compared to .402 for the visitors. Both studies include fairly well-balanced schedules under which it appears that we have something like a 60–40 advantage for the home team.

However, to further supplement these findings, we did additional valuable research.

First, we studied a conference for five years. The Eastern

Intercollegiate Basketball League, where the competition is fairly even, shows the home team winning 138 of 224 games for a .616 percentage, compared to 86 wins, percentage .384, for the visitors. An adequate sampling of other major conferences shows the home team winning from 58 per cent to

TABLE XXXIV

HOME TEAM SURVEY (control group)

(5-year totals 1949–50–1953–54 inclusive)

Shooting Results	No. of Games	Attempts	Goals	Per-centage	Average per Game Attempts	Goals
Total Shots	132	9725	3042	.313	73.7	23.0
Free Throws	132	3932	2552	.649	29.8	19.3

Other Results	No. of Games	Total	Average per Game
Score	132	8636	65.4
Offensive Rebounds	132	3243	24.6
Defensive Rebounds	132	4468	33.8
Total Rebounds	132	7711	58.4
Bad Passes	132	866	6.6
Violations	132	476	3.6
Losses by Ball Handling	132	866	6.6
Total Losses of Ball	132	2208	16.7
Jump Ball Recoveries	132	699	5.3
Interceptions	132	1837	13.9
Personal Fouls	132	2846	21.6

	No. of Games	Games Won by Home Teams	Games Lost by Home Teams	Percentage of Games Won by Home Teams
Home Game Results	132	79	53	.598

This table shows a record of home teams in 132 games. It includes total field-goal and free-throw attempts and goals, total scores, averages per game, and percentages of attempts scored. It also gives totals and averages per game of offensive, defensive and total rebounds; losses by bad passes, violations, poor ball handling, and total losses; jump ball recoveries and interceptions; and personal fouls. It also shows number and percentage of games won and lost on home courts.

62 per cent. We again then may assume the 60–40 advantage for the home team even when competition is fairly even.

But now we must look at another picture. We took the 1953–54 results of 244 college teams, large and small, from

TABLE XXXV

VISITING TEAM SURVEY (control group)

Shooting Results	No. of Games	Attempts	Goals	Percentage	*Average per* Attempts	*Game* Goals
Total Shots	132	9566	2917	.305	72.5	22.1
Free Throws	132	3710	2374	.640	28.1	18.0

Other Results	No. of Games	Total	Average per Game
Score	132	8208	62.2
Offensive Rebounds	132	3037	23.0
Defensive Rebounds	132	4347	32.9
Total Rebounds	132	7384	55.9
Bad Passes	132	899	6.8
Violations	132	572	4.3
Losses by Ball Handling	132	938	7.1
Totals Losses of Ball	132	2409	18.3
Jump Ball Recoveries	132	672	5.1
Interceptions	132	1732	13.1
Personal Fouls	132	2929	22.2

	No. of Games	Games Won by Visiting Teams	Games Lost by Visiting Teams	Percentage of Games Won by Visiting Teams
Visiting Game Results	132	53	79	.402

This table shows records of visiting teams in the same manner that Table XXXIV shows records of home teams.

all over the country, in 2562 games; a very adequate sampling. The home team won an amazing and startling number of these games—1825 for a .712 percentage, compared to only 737 wins or a .288 percentage for the visitors. On the surface, this report could show that the visitors could only expect to win slightly more than one game out of four. A closer examination, however, disputes such a theory. Many teams employ the unfortunate practice of scheduling quite a number of early season "breathers" or easy games *at home.* The results of these games are foregone conclusions and many of them are won by wide margins in the score. The home court advantage, while present, does not have nearly the bearing on the outcome as does the difference in ability of the two teams. In passing, we must point out the lack of wisdom on the part of weak teams who will schedule such games to get on a "big time" schedule, for a monetary gain, or for any other purpose. The practice is most unfair to the players who are asked to face impossible odds.

Comparisons of these studies are most revealing. The nation-wide picture, as just described, has been the basis for the belief that the home team has a ten-point margin and other exaggerated home court advantages.

True, as indicated in Tables XXXIV and XXXV, the home teams lead in all departments; they score more, shoot more and make a higher percentage of their attempts both from the field and free throw line, retrieve more rebounds at both ends, lose the ball less, get more recoveries and commit less personal fouls—compared to the visitors. Yet, the margins are not great. For example, the average home team score is 65.4 compared to 62.2 for the visitors—a difference of 3.2 and not ten or more as some would believe. The field-goal shooting percentage is only .313 at home compared to .305 away and the free throw percentage is also close, .649 to .640.

The margins are so close that attention to a few points could easily erase or reduce the actual 60–40 home court advantage. Assuming that the home team does have an advantage, what are the reasons for and the significance of this fact from a coaching standpoint? All the reasons for the difference cannot be measured objectively, but there are certain facts which may be helpful in the solution of this problem.

The differences may mean that the home team is more accustomed to the court, lighting facilities, and similar factors. It is undoubtedly true also that the matter of fatigue is an important factor in the difference. To remedy this problem, arrive at the scene of games in plenty of time to have adequate rest before playing a game. It is also advisable to take a short work-out on the visiting court to become adjusted to the comparatively strange conditions.

Another factor that contributes to this difference is undoubtedly a purely psychological one. For years we have stressed the fact that the home team does have an advantage. Players often go into games away from home with the feeling that they are playing under a handicap. Coaches may help this situation by pointing out to their players that they actually have more time to rest while traveling than at home, where they are usually busy with studies, and other activities. It should be further pointed out to them that they are playing before spectators who know less about them than do their home fans, and this applies to their weak points as well as their strong points. Many players prefer to play away from home where their closest friends and relatives are not watching them. This is a very important psychological opportunity for the coach.

During the summer of 1953–54, our Yale University team played 30 games in eight countries of South America. Many of the courts were out of doors. They were of every type of surface—tile, dirt, cement and rarely wood. Some were in parks, others in clubs, a few in bull fight rings. Lighting was poor, courts were slippery and other facilities were far below our standards. We played many games with the international ball which is more like a soccer ball than our basketball. Rule interpretations were weird and different to say the least, and there could not possibly be more enthusiastic rooters—100 per cent for the home team. We must hasten to add that our hosts were always friendly and hospitable but the example is used to give home court advantages at their best.

Our boys lost five of the first seven games; some to mediocre teams. Later, adjusting to conditions, the team won 12 of the last 14 games played—against much stronger opponents. The experience was invaluable.

Two of our regulars had been poor home court performers at Yale because they were conscious of friends or relatives watching the games. In South America no one knew them and they started to relax and play ball. They continued to be better competitors during the season that followed.

In contrast, one of our players on our N.C.A.A. championship team at Oregon could play much better if his father, who never saw him lose, was in the stands. You may rest assured the father was escorted to every important game.

Properly meeting the many psychological problems is a great challenge to any coach and on the results hinge wins and losses.

Last, but not least, another very important factor that applies to this problem requires the attention of all coaches and directors of basketball. There is little question but that the home crowd, when encouraged and permitted to become hostile and discourteous toward the visiting team, does give the home team a distinct advantage. Coaches, players, and home fans who attempt to intimidate the officials also give the home team an unfair and unearned advantage. The fact that more personal fouls and violations are called on the home team may have some connection with this; although it is granted that losing teams foul and travel more and visiting teams are the more frequent losers.

Therefore coaches and directors of basketball should eliminate, so far as possible, improper conduct of spectators, players and coaches that in any way intimidate visiting players or officials. This means that booing and other similar tactics must be eliminated. It means also that officials must have, and use, the right to dismiss players and coaches from the game or bench, when the occasion calls for such action.

In conclusion, the following suggestions are offered to bring about a better balance and help equalize the home-visitor situation.

1. Do not schedule games with a home team that is so much stronger that the outcome is obvious. Players have a right to play on their own level of competition where there is a reasonable chance to win.

2. Standardize equipment and facilities so no team will have this home court advantage.

3. Take the pressure off the officials. The home team must not select or appoint them. Appointments should be made through a commissioner and he will be wise to assign officials who do not reside in the area where the game is to be played.

4. Continue to work for standardization of rule interpretations so they will be the same in all areas.

5. Control the home crowds. Insist on proper treatment of visiting players and officials so the game can be played on a neutral basis.

6. Visiting teams should arrive in time to rest and properly prepare for the game. Adequate pre-game practice to familiarize players with all court conditions is advisable.

7. Break down the psychological advantages of the home team which are often greatly exaggerated. Counter them with all possible advantages of the traveling team.

The winning team and the losing team

Table XXXVI, Winning Team Survey, gives the data on the winning team and Table XXXVII, Losing Team Survey, pages 126, 127, gives data on the losing team. Naturally the percentages are higher for the winning team. In many cases, however, there is not a very great difference between the winner and the loser. A particular game will illustrate this point.

TABLE XXXVI

WINNING TEAM SURVEY (control group)
(5-year totals 1949–50–1953–54 inclusive)

Shooting Results	No. of Games	Attempts	Goals	Per-centage	*Average per Game* Attempts	*Average per Game* Goals
Long Shots	132	1261	331	.262	9.6	2.5
Medium Shots	132	3850	1152	.299	29.2	8.7
Short Shots	132	4450	1794	.403	33.7	13.6
Total Shots	132	9561	3277	.343	72.4	24.8
Free Throws	132	4046	2653	.646	30.7	20.1

Other Results	No. of Games	Total	Average per Game
Score	132	9207	69.8
Offensive Rebounds	132	3252	24.6
Defensive Rebounds	132	4834	36.6
Total Rebounds	132	8086	61.3
Bad Passes	132	856	6.5
Violations	132	524	4.0
Losses by Ball Handling	132	892	6.8
Total Losses of Ball	132	2272	17.2
Jump Ball Recoveries	132	730	5.5
Interceptions	132	1821	13.8
Personal Fouls	132	2727	20.7

This table shows records of winning teams in 132 games. It includes field-goal attempts, field goals, percentage of attempts scored, and average number of attempts and goals per game for long, medium, short areas and totals. It also shows free-throw attempts, goals, percentage of free throws scored and averages per game and also the winning team total score and average score per game. It also shows winning team totals and averages per game of offensive, defensive, and total rebounds; losses of ball by bad passes, violations, poor ball handling, and total losses; jump ball recoveries and interceptions; and personal fouls.

Of the five Oregon-Long Island games at Madison Square Garden, the most thrilling was the game in December 1939. Because Oregon had won the National Collegiate Athletic

Association title the year before and Long Island won the National Invitational, there was great rivalry in the game. With 15 minutes to play, Oregon led by 15 points. With one second to play, the score was tied and Dolly King of Long Island missed a free throw, sending the game into over-

TABLE XXXVII

LOSING TEAM SURVEY (control group)

(5-year totals 1949–50–1953–54 inclusive)

Shooting Results	No. of Games	Attempts	Goals	Per- centage	*Average per* Attempts	*Game* Goals
Long Shots	132	1860	424	.227	14.1	3.2
Medium Shots	132	4195	994	.237	31.8	7.5
Short Shots	132	3675	1264	.344	27.8	9.6
Total Shots	132	9730	2682	.276	73.7	20.3
Free Throws	132	3596	2273	.632	27.2	17.2

Other Results	No. of Games	Total	Average per Game
Score	132	7637	57.9
Offensive Rebounds	132	3028	22.9
Defensive Rebounds	132	3981	30.2
Total Rebounds	132	7009	53.1
Bad Passes	132	909	6.9
Violations	132	524	4.0
Losses by Ball Handling	132	912	6.9
Total Losses of Ball	132	2345	17.8
Jump Ball Recoveries	132	641	4.9
Interceptions	132	1748	13.2
Personal Fouls	132	3048	23.1

This table shows records of losing teams in the same manner that Table XXXVI shows records of winning teams.

time. In the overtime period, the teams matched baskets twice, then with 12 seconds to go, Oregon made a free throw and led by one point. In the last three seconds Dolly King again entered the picture. This time he tossed the ball underneath the outstretched arms of the Oregon center—the ball bounced three times on the rim and fell in for the winning basket! Long Island had won the game by overcoming great odds and fighting an uphill battle. Still, a team losing where the margin is this close could hardly be classed as a losing team. In some cases, losing close games of this kind actually gives a team the incentive or counter-irritant to win its succeeding games.

Careful scouting and planning will contribute to the winning habit. Added to this, however, are psychological elements which must supplement statistics, figures, scouting reports, and data of all kinds. Every game should be played with the idea of winning. Unless players and their coach have the confidence that they will win, they should not attempt to play any game. Coaches who pride themselves on being good losers usually lose frequently. They become experts at losing. They should pride themselves on being gracious losers and good sportsmen, and should take every lesson possible from a loss, as well as from a win. But the difference between the winner and the loser is very often the confidence that the coach has in winning a game and the extent to which he can instill that confidence into his players.

Along with these psychological factors, however, data in Tables XXXVI and XXXVII, pages 126 and 127 will indicate the type of performance necessary to be in the winning or the losing class. Teams cannot be expected to win unless they have reasonable ability. It is hoped that information offered here will aid coaches in knowing what to expect from a team and will help to bring the team up to a winning standard.

The greatest differences between winning and losing performances appear to be in shooting accuracy, rebounding and, of course, total score. It is significant to note that the winning team has a shooting percentage of .343 (based on a five year average) compared to .276 for the losers. Note that the losing team takes more long and medium area shots, but that in the short area, the winning team takes many more and hits a much higher percentage. The winning team hits for a percentage of .403 in the short area compared to .344 for the losing team. Even in the medium area, where all shooting is below par, the winning team's percentage is .299 while the losing team's is only .237.

It also should be noted that while the losing team takes a greater total of shots, this is due to the number of shots taken in the two outer areas. In the short area, the winning team takes an average of 33.7 per game compared to an average of 27.8 for the losing team.

The winning team also excels in free throws. They have more attempts (30.7 per game compared to 27.2 for the losing team) and make a .646 percentage while the losing team percentage is .632.

The winning team, then, works the ball in for close shots more often, shoots more accurately in all areas, and has more free-throw attempts and makes a higher free-throw percentage. In factors other than shooting, the difference is not so great, except in rebounding. As expected, the winning team usually has an advantage on the boards. The 132 games studied show that the winning team retrieved an average of 61.3 rebounds a game compared to 53.1 for the losing team.

The difference in score is 12.4 points a game in favor, of course, of the winning team.

These differences correspond surprisingly well to those found in our original 13-year study (see Tables XIII-A and XIV-A in Appendix A). Standards of performance have improved, but the margin between winner and loser is about the same in most departments.

Again, we must study and interpret the findings with caution. The margins between the winning and losing teams in the various departments are not great. This is due to the fact that our sampling, while it does include a normal number of one-sided games, for the most part represents balanced schedules. No doubt if we took national averages, including hundreds of games where the winner ran up huge scores against weak opposition, we would find the difference in score and other departments much greater.   As we have seen in the study of home and visiting teams, such a report would be misleading.   Naturally, the more evenly teams are matched, the less the differences will be.   A team that schedules opponents that are obviously 30 or 40 points stronger could not hope to work from a losing to a winning average when such great differences of ability are apparent.   We have attempted to give a reasonable example that we believe will show the differences for the average situation; which should encourage teams to work toward reasonable winning performances.

In conclusion, greater shooting ability and organization that will get shots from closer areas seem to be the major requisites for the winning team.   Again, keep shooting percentage records *for various areas*.   Also, don't forget the importance of rebounds.

The first half and the second half

The performance of a team in the first half, as compared to that in the second half, is worth the careful attention of the coach.   That is, if the coach likes to win, and it is understood that most of them do.   In scouting one's own team, as well as the opponent's, it should be determined just how effective the team is in each half.   If the opponent is a first-half team and tires in the second half, a coach may plan his strategy and attack accordingly.   If the coach discovers that his own team is a first-half team, he may take measures to correct this situation early in the season.

Of course the major question is how teams become second-half teams.   The answer lies very largely in the fatigue and psychological factors.   Coaches of every championship team agree that to be a champion, a team must be strongest in the second half.   Here, then, is another winning formula.   Know the first- and second-half strength of your own club and of your opponents.   Also, be sure that your team can do two things: improve its performance in the second half over its performance in the first half, and outplay the opponents in the second half. A team that can do this will win most of its games. Remember, you cannot guess at this; you get this information only through careful scouting or analyzing of your own team and of the opponent's.

TABLE XXXVIII

FIRST HALF SURVEY (control group)

(both teams)

(5-year totals 1949–50–1953–54 inclusive)

Shooting Results	No. of Games	Attempts	Goals	Per- centage	Average per Attempts	Game Goals
Total Shots	132	9662	2882	.298	73.2	21.8
Free Throws	132	3381	2216	.655	25.6	16.8

Other Results	No. of Games	Total	Average per Game
Score	132	7980	60.5
Offensive Rebounds	132	3130	23.7
Defensive Rebounds	132	4393	33.3
Total Rebounds	132	7523	57.0
Bad Passes	132	905	6.9
Violations	132	555	4.2
Losses by Ball Handling	132	853	6.5
Total Losses of Ball	132	2313	17.5
Jump Ball Recoveries	132	627	4.8
Interceptions	132	1811	13.7
Personal Fouls	132	2616	19.8

This table shows first-half field-goal and free-throw attempts, goals, percentage of attempts scored, average number of attempts and goals per game for both teams, in 132 games, in five seasons. It also gives totals and averages per game of the score; offensive, defensive and total rebounds; losses by bad passes, violations, poor ball handling and total losses; jump ball recoveries and interceptions; and personal fouls.

Comparative data are available for the average team in both halves. Results are given in Tables XXXVIII, First-Half Survey, above, and Table XXXIX, Second-Half Survey, page 132.

One very significant fact may be derived from these results. For years it has been the belief that team performances become less efficient in the second half. Many have said that the game is too strenuous and that the fatigue element pre-

TABLE XXXIX

SECOND HALF SURVEY (control group)

(both teams)

(5-year totals 1949–50–1953–54 inclusive)

Shooting Results	No. of Games	Attempts	Goals	Per-centage	Average per Game Attempts	Goals
Total Shots	132	9629	3077	.320	72.9	23.3
Free Throws	132	4261	2710	.636	32.3	20.5

Other Results	No. of Games	Total	Average per Game
Score	132	8864	67.2
Offensive Rebounds	132	3150	23.9
Defensive Rebounds	132	4422	33.5
Total Rebounds	132	7572	57.4
Bad Passes	132	860	6.5
Violations	132	493	3.7
Losses by Ball Handling	132	951	7.2
Total Losses of Ball	132	2304	17.5
Jump Ball Recoveries	132	744	5.6
Interceptions	132	1758	13.3
Personal Fouls	132	3159	23.9

This table shows a record of the second half for both teams in the same manner that Table XXXVIII shows the first half record.

vents teams from playing well late in the game. The mental hazard still persists among players that they cannot hold up in the second half. However, results show that even the average team shoots better in the second half and scores an average of 6.7 more points. The shooting percentage jumps from .298 in the first half to .320 in the second half. The average team loses the ball no more the second half. This is another major factor in which fatigue would affect the play.

It is true that in the games studied, free-throw accuracy decreased in the second half. The percentages dropped from .655 in the first half to .636 in the second half. This may indicate that pressure and mental factors are more responsible than fatigue in missed free throws. Certainly, if fatigue alone caused free-throw accuracy to decrease in the second half, it would also cause field-goal shooting accuracy to decrease correspondingly. The fact that there is a pause before the free throw, permitting the player to think over the situation with possible annoyance from the crowd, may be the answer. Also, the pressure is greater in the second half—particularly toward the end of the game.

The increase in personal fouls in the second half may be due partly to fatigue, but there is another cause. We know that fouling increases toward the end of the game because the trailing team must go after the ball.

In any event, coaches can partially disregard the second-half fatigue theory as far as shooting accuracy is concerned. This may be an important psychological aid in coaching. Well-conditioned teams that do not tire in the second half, however, will shoot more accurately than poorly conditioned teams. No doubt the better the condition, the better the accuracy, provided the mental hazards can be eliminated. It is suggested that coaches keep comparisons in first- and second-half scrimmages as well as in games. Every effort should be made to improve individual and team play in each half. An added effort should then be made to make the second half stronger than the first.

First half performances may be improved by proper pre-game policies. The starting team should have adequate shooting, passing and ball handling practice including enough running so they are really ready to go with the opening whistle. Long delays just before the game starts should be avoided. Pre-game "pep talks" should be used carefully if at all—particularly when a team is preparing to meet a strong opponent. The secret here is to relax the players, give confidence; not to increase pressure and nervous tension. Also, remember all boys do not react the same. You may reach one boy and hurt the other four.

Many years ago in our second year of major college coaching, preparing for a championship play-off game, we learned a great lesson. A win would have given Oregon its first championship in 11 years—but it had to wait. We stayed up half the night preparing a pre-game talk which we thought a masterpiece that could not fail. It reached two players very well, but the other three were worthless. They were so nervous they couldn't catch the ball, let alone shoot accurately. They settled down later, but it was far too late. We lost the game in the first ten minutes of play.

The second half performances may best be improved by superior conditioning. Teams should be able to go at top speed for 50 minutes in practice so the 40-minute game will not tire them. The half time intermission should include adequate rest, a good second half plan, something about confidence and the will to win—but all of it must end in time so the team can warm up properly to start the second half. It is most important for a team to have at least five of the 15 minute intermission for this purpose.

Performance on various levels of competition

Coaches are constantly looking for and striving to develop the competitive player—the boy who can come through when a game is close. Many players look great in practice but are unable to reach great heights in strenuous competition.

We receive many inquiries each year from young coaches who ask the question, "How can we teach boys to play as well as they practice?" The reply: "If we knew all the answers to this one, we would win every game." First, just what are the differences of performance on various levels of competition?

Our new study is much more revealing than our original 13-year 460 game survey. The latter compared both teams in major and minor games, scrimmages and practice shooting of the entire squad without defense. The results may be found in Table XVII-A in Appendix A.

Our recent five-year study shows the performances of *the same group* throughout each year, our Yale teams, on each possible level of competition. The study includes shooting only, since it is the most important and most highly specialized skill in the game; also most likely to be affected by varying degrees of competition. We include shooting records of our first squad each year in conference and non-conference games, major and minor games, scrimmages, and in daily practice shooting without defense. A summary of results is given in Table XL, Levels of Competition Shooting, on page 136.

Conference and non-conference games

Most would agree that conference or league games are most important to both player and coach, except for championship play-offs or tournament games. Conference games are championship games—hence competition is at its highest in these games. Our first study, then, is a comparison of shooting in conference and non-conference games (see Tables XLI and XLII on pages 137 and 138).

Major and minor games

Next we studied major and minor games which are only slightly below the conference and non-conference games in competitive comparisons—yet there is a difference. Every conference game is a major game, but every non-conference game is not a minor game. Our list of major games includes the 62 conference games plus 35 non-conference games with major opponents where the competition is at a very high level. Traditional games in particular are included. The minor games include 35 games with non-traditional teams where

TABLE XI

LEVELS OF COMPETITION SHOOTING (control group)
(one team)
(5-year totals 1949–50–1953–54 inclusive)

	No. of Games	FIELD GOALS									FREE THROWS		
		Long Shots per Game		Medium Shots per Game		Short Shots per Game		Total Shots per Game			Attempts per Game	Goals per Game	Pct.
		Attempts	Goals	Attempts	Goals	Attempts	Goals	Attempts	Goals	Total Pct.			
Conference Games	62	10.3	2.0	30.1	7.9	29.4	10.8	68.7	20.7	.302	29.3	19.1	.651
Non-conference Games	70	9.1	2.0	34.2	9.6	32.7	12.6	76.0	24.2	.318	27.6	18.3	.662
Major Games	97	9.2	2.0	31.2	8.5	29.6	10.9	70.0	21.4	.306	28.8	18.7	.650
Minor Games	35	9.2	2.0	35.3	9.7	35.3	14.0	79.8	25.8	.323	27.5	18.6	.675
Scrimmages	100	8.4	2.3	34.9	9.6	40.0	17.2	83.2	29.2	.351	23.8	14.7	.618
Practice Shots (no defense)		Total Attempts	Total Goals	Total Attempts	Total Goals	Total Attempts	Total Goals	Total Attempts	Total Goals	Pct.	Total Attempts	Total Goals	Pct.
		12275 Pct.: .426	5235	15715 Pct.: .537	8445	5955 Pct.: .737	4391	33945	18071	.532	29048	22264	.766

This table shows a comparison in field-goal and free-throw performances of one team in 62 conference games, 70 non-conference games, 97 major games, 35 minor games, 100 game scrimmages, and in practice shooting without defense. The results are totals over a five year period. The table shows the average number of long, medium, short and total field-goal attempts and field goals per game; the percentage of total field-goal attempts scored; the average number of free-throw attempts and free-throw goals per game; and percentage of free-throw attempts scored.

136

competition is not at the highest level. The shooting results of the major and minor games are given in Tables XLIII and XLIV on pages 139 and 140.

TABLE XLI

CONFERENCE GAMES (control group)

(one team)

(5-year totals 1949–50–1953–54 inclusive)

Shooting	No. of Games	Attempts	Goals	Per-centage	Average per Game Attempts	Goals
Long Shots	62	577	127	.220	9.3	2.0
Medium Shots	62	1864	491	.263	30.1	7.9
Short Shots	62	1821	667	.366	29.4	10.8
Total Shots	62	4262	1285	.302	68.7	20.7
Free Throws	62	1818	1183	.651	29.3	19.1

Other Results	No. of Games	Total Points	Average per Game
Score	62	3753	60.5

This table shows the records of one team in 62 conference games over a five-year period. It includes long, medium, short and total field-goal attempts, field goals, percentage of attempts scored and the average number of attempts and goals per game. It gives the same information on free throws and also shows total scores and average score per game.

Please note the general curve from minor games where competitive pressure is lowest, on up through non-conference, major and conference games. Shooting percentages, for example, are .323 in minor games, .318 in non-conference games, .306 in major games and .302 in conference games, which are most competitive. The scores follow the same curve, going from 70.2 points a game in minor games down to 60.5 in conference games. The same pattern is quite apparent in shooting from the various areas. The players took more total shots in conference games, but more were from the medium and long areas. Note that many more short shots were taken in minor games, with a .398 percentage, compared to a .366 percentage in conference games. Free throw accuracy also follows the curve, with a .675 shooting percentage in minor games down to .651 in conference games.

To sum up, then, we may say that the more competitive the game, the poorer the performance in score, short area attempts, field goal and free throw accuracy.

TABLE XLII

NON-CONFERENCE GAMES (control group)

(one team)

(5-year totals 1949–50–1953–54 inclusive)

Shooting	No. of Games	Attempts	Goals	Per- centage	Average per Game Attempts	Goals
Long Shots	70	636	138	.217	9.1	2.0
Medium Shots	70	2397	671	.280	34.2	9.6
Short Shots	70	2286	885	.387	32.7	12.6
Total Shots	70	5319	1694	.318	76.0	24.2
Free Throws	70	1935	1281	.662	27.6	18.3

Other Results	No. of Games	Total Points	Average per Game
Score	70	4669	66.7

This table shows the records of one team in 70 non-conference games over a five-year period in the same manner that Table XLI shows the record of the team in conference games.

Scrimmages

The same group of players each year were checked in shooting performances during scrimmages. We try to approximate game conditions as much as possible. The equivalent of 100 40-minute games is included. The main pressure in scrimmages is to earn or maintain a place on the team. No spectators are present and there is not the real pressure of winning or losing an important game. Also the reserves that form the opposition are not as capable as some opposing teams. The same group of players, now performing under practice rather than game conditions, raise their standards considerably. Only in free throws is the record lower. This may be due to some carelessness and lack of application which seems to be evident in some scrimmages. It could not be due to pressure or fatigue because the other records would be

TABLE XLIII

MAJOR GAMES (control group)

(one team)

(5-year totals 1949–50–1953–54 inclusive)

Shooting	No. of Games	Attempts	Goals	Percentage	Average per Game Attempts	Goals
Long Shots	97	892	194	.217	9.2	2.0
Medium Shots	97	3025	821	.271	31.2	8.5
Short Shots	97	2872	1061	.369	29.6	10.9
Total Shots	97	6789	2076	.306	70.0	21.4
Free Throws	97	2790	1814	.650	28.8	18.7

Other Results	No. of Games	Total Points	Average per Game
Score	97	5966	61.5

This table shows the records of one team in 97 major games over a five-year period. It includes long, medium, short and total field-goal attempts, field goals, percentage of attempts scored and the average number of attempts and goals per game. It gives the same information on free throws and also shows total scores and average score per game.

similarly affected. Table XLV on page 141 gives scrimmage results. Just look at that record! A team that could get an average of 40 short shots a game, have a shooting percentage of .351 in 100 games and score 73.1 points a game, would be close to the top in national standings. If possible in practice why not in games?

Practice shooting

We have always had the policy of shooting a given number of shots from the various areas, depending on individual needs, with results recorded daily. We do the same with free throws, shooting no more than two consecutively.

After techniques are learned, the players take shots as

nearly as possible as they would in games, except no defense is used. The records of our same first squad players in their practice shooting are given in Table XLVI on page 142.

If our scrimmage percentages were high, how do these records look? Imagine a team average of .426 from outside for a season; or an over-all percentage of .532; and the .766 free-throw percentage would be welcome too.

TABLE XLIV

MINOR GAMES (control group)

(one team)

(5-year totals 1949–50–1953–54 inclusive)

Shooting	No. of Games	Attempts	Goals	Per-centage	Average per Game Attempts	Goals
Long Shots	35	321	71	.221	9.2	2.0
Medium Shots	35	1236	341	.276	35.3	9.7
Short Shots	35	1235	491	.398	35.3	14.0
Total Shots	35	2792	903	.323	79.8	25.8
Free Throws	35	963	650	.675	27.5	18.6
Other Results	No. of Games		Total Points		Average per Game	
Score	35		2456		70.2	

This table shows the records of one team in 35 minor games over a five-year period in the same manner that Table XLIII shows the record of the team in major games.

Theoretically, there should be no difference between practice shooting and shooting in games. A player should only take shots he earns—*good shots*. If this type of shot were always taken, it would compare favorably to the practice shot. Therefore, eliminating bad shots may help coaches more closely to approximate the practice shooting average in games.

Defense present, of course, makes a difference, but not 200 percentage points. And what about free throws? No one is guarding the free-thrower in games. Why should the shooting percentage slide from .766 in practice to .651—over 100 percentage points—in conference games?

It is suggested particularly that coaches check carefully the shooting performances of *each individual player* on the various levels of competition. It has been pointed out that team percentages may vary due to lack of ability of some of the

TABLE XLV

SCRIMMAGES (control group)

(one team)

(5—year totals 1949–50–1953–54 inclusive)

Shooting	No. of Games	Attempts	Goals	Per-centage	*Average per Game* Attempts	Goals
Long Shots	100	837	232	.277	8.4	2.3
Medium Shots	100	3485	963	.276	34.9	9.6
Short Shots	100	3997	1722	.431	40.0	17.2
Total Shots	100	8319	2917	.351	83.2	29.2
Free Throws	100	2384	1473	.618	23.8	14.7

Other Results	No. of Games	Total Points	Average per Game
Score	100	7307	73.1

This table shows the records of one team in 100 game scrimmages over a five-year period. It includes long, medium, short and total field-goal attempts, field goals, percentage of attempts scored and the average number of attempts and goals per game. It gives the same information on free throws and also shows total scores and average score per game.

players engaged in a scrimmage or minor game. A player's individual record, however, compared to the record of teammates and opponents, will tell the coach whether or not he is a "money player."

We know the causes for poorer performances in competition must be due to fatigue or a wrong mental attitude. We can remedy the fatigue situation by proper conditioning policies. The proper mental attitude of the player is by far the greater problem. First, find out who your strong and weak competitors are. Records and observations together must be considered. One little aid is to keep a careful running score as suggested in Chapter 14. Knowing the time and score of the game when a player makes a goal will let you know who scores when the score is close; it also lets you know the "hot or cold" players that score in streaks—which may also have to do with fatigue.

TABLE XLVI

PRACTICE SHOOTING (control group)
(one team)
(5-year totals 1949–50–1953–54 inclusive)

Shooting	Attempts	Goals	Percentage
Long Shots	12275	5235	.426
Medium Shots	15715	8445	.537
Short Shots	5955	4391	.737
Total Shots	33945	18071	.532
Free Throws	29048	22264	.766

This table shows a sampling of daily practice shooting by one team over a five-year period. It gives the total attempts, goals and percentage of attempts scored for long, medium, short and total field-goal attempts and for free throws.

When a player's weaknesses are known, each must be treated individually, according to his needs. Some need confidence—nearly all players do. Perhaps techniques need attention; these must be mastered before confidence can be established. Other players are easily distracted—by officials' decisions, comments of fans, newspaper articles, coaches' criticism—or other similar factors. A player must think only of his game and play it to be successful. He must think of making a basket; succeeding—and never of missing or failing.

These lessons are hard to learn and hard to teach. Players and coaches who can combine their efforts to improve mental attitude will have made great progress in solving one of the game's greatest problems.

Subjective observations and the psychology of coaching

Subjective scouting information is equally as valuable as objective data, and this certainly applies in the psychology of coaching.

Personnel observations are particularly important in this regard. Conferences with players about their mental and physical condition are just as important as coaching of skills on the court. Similarly, properly planned strategy and constructive meetings with the squad in which all take part in planning for a game are of paramount importance.

Confidence, competition, cooperation, loyalty and team morale are all products of subjective observations as well as objective data. It is not our intention to infer that teams can be coached entirely as a result of a testing and rating program. The coach must take the entire picture into consideration and develop his team to perform efficiently both mentally and physically.

10

The Tall Man in Basketball

(See *photo*, The Tall Man in Basketball, *in illustrated section*)

THE TALL MAN (FROM SIX FEET FIVE INCHES TO SEVEN feet tall), when properly developed, is the greatest asset a basketball team can have. Regardless of any problem the tall man has presented to the game, coaches should constantly strive to develop and use the "big fellows."

The far West seems to be a territory where many tall men play basketball. Part of this is due to the fact that high school coaches have learned to have patience and work with these men while they are in the growing, awkward, uncoordinated stages. A story of some years ago will illustrate the point:

At the University of Oregon, there was not a single season in twelve years during which we did not have three or four tall men, six feet five inches or over, on the squad. The greatest was Urgel "Slim" Wintermute who stood six feet eight inches. He was center on the national championship team of 1939 and was selected on almost every All-America

144

team that year. Fortunately, he was under a good coach in high school that realized the value of a big man. While many high school coaches would have cut him off the squad, Scott Milligan, coach at Longview, Washington High School, stayed with "Slim" through the awkward stages and as a result, won state honors with him as a senior. When "Slim" Wintermute came to college, he had his full height but weighed only 165 pounds. He was not aggressive and many times during his freshman and sophomore years, it appeared that he might not make the grade as a college player. In the junior year, however, he had developed into a better than average college player. As a senior, he was the difference between just a good college team and a national championship team.

Similar stories can be told about many tall men. It takes patience and work to develop them. But in return, the hard work may pay off in a championship, in addition to the values the boy has received from playing the game. Because of the tremendous value of the tall man, his appearance in the game has created many problems—mostly for the coaches that do not have them.

What shall we do with the tall man in basketball? This has been a leading question in the game for many years. Various rule changes were made to curb the effectiveness of the tall man. The center jump, which used to follow each goal, was eliminated after free throws in 1936 and after all goals in 1938. Now the ball is awarded to the opponent after each goal. It was thought that this would lessen the value of the tall man in the game unless he was a good all-round player, because he could not be used merely for getting the center jump. Result: more tall men and their effectiveness not curbed. The big fellow merely had more stamina from not having to jump, so that he could better play other parts of the game.

The second restriction of the big men was the passing of the three-second rule which prevents the offensive player from standing in the free-throw lane more than three seconds. This change came in 1936 and with certain variations has been continued in the game. Result: still more tall men with no apparent improvement in all-round ability. In other words, the big man is still playing and is just as effective as ever.

Many insist that the tall man should not be legislated against, any more than we should legislate against the fast man, or the expert shot. Many coaches believe that the tall man can be stopped effectively by proper defensive measures. Others believe that the only way to stop a tall man is to have one a little taller and a little better. The entire problem reached a climax in 1944 and 1945 when seven-foot Bob Kurland almost single-handed led Oklahoma A & M to two national championships. During the same era, George Mikan, a six-foot nine inch giant at DePaul University of Chicago, was dominating most of the games in which he played. As a result, additional legislation was considered to curb the tall man. Most of the suggestions had to do with enlarging the three-second area in some way so that the tall man could not take a position so close to his offensive basket. Many still desire a change of this kind although since World War II, this problem has lessened with the improvement in material and coaching.

Many more tall men are in the game now—some of them well over seven feet tall—so the tall man often faces an opponent equally tall. However, we still have a serious problem when a player several inches shorter must guard a tall man near the basket.

Some have advocated putting a height limit on players, thereby eliminating the extremely tall man from the game.

We are reminded of a plea that was made at one of our Olympic meetings in Helsinki in 1952. We had a truly great array of players at Helsinki. Speaking of tall men, led by the veteran Bob Kurland at seven feet one inch and

Marcus Frieberger, a mere seven footer, our group tapered down to Clyde Lovellette, six feet nine inches, Frank McCabe, six feet eight inches, and then to smaller six feet four inch boys. If the squad had a weakness, it was a lack of play making ball hawks like Dean Kelley, who, at five feet eleven inches, was the only member of the 14-player squad under six feet.

The representative from the Philippines, having watched our boys practice, strongly urged the height limit for basketball. He said in part, "I played for the Philippines in the first Olympic basketball games in Berlin in 1936. Our center was six feet tall, but the United States had them six feet five inches. We didn't have a chance. Well, we went home with ideas! It's taken many years but now we have a center six feet five inches tall—*but*—your centers are over seven feet. What do we do now?" The height limit was voted down, however; and, surprisingly, Russia voted with us. They have tall men too.

Most coaches and basketball followers agree that a height limit would not be fair to the tall men. Basketball is one of the few sports that they are able to play; they are seldom outstanding in football or in baseball and no legislation should be put into effect that would deprive them of playing a game that offers them as much all-round value as the game of basketball. We could, of course, have team divisions.

In our original 13-year study, we took the records of 80 tall players over six feet four inches in height. We discovered, among other things, that the tall man of that era scored 94 *per cent* of his total field goals in the short and medium areas. A brief of the original study, giving all essential details, may be found in Table XX-A in Appendix A.

We have now completed a similar new study of tall men over six feet four inches who have played in college games during the seasons 1949–50 through 1953–54. Table XLVII on page 148 gives complete findings.

The study includes 99 players appearing in 555 games. However, many players appeared in only parts of games so no averages per game were computed.

TABLE XLVII

SHOOTING BY TALL MEN (control group)

	No. of Players	No. of Games*	Attempts	Goals	Shooting Percentage	Percentage of All Attempts Taken in Area	Percentage of All Goals Made in Area
Long Shots	99	555	217	49	.226	5.2	3.6
Med. Shots	99	555	1506	393	.261	36.1	28.9
Short Shots	99	555	2450	919	.375	58.7	67.5
Total Shots	99	555	4173	1361	.326	100.0	100.0

* Number of games in which players appeared. Many players played only parts of games, therefore use of number of games to determine average attempts and goals per game would be misleading and inaccurate.

This table shows the field-goal shooting performances of 99 college players from six feet four inches and taller in height, appearing in 555 games in seasons 1949–50 to 1953–54 inclusive. It shows the total number of attempts and goals scored by these men and also the totals in the long, medium and short areas. It also gives shooting percentages and per cent of all attempts taken and goals scored in each area.

For a similar study of tall men prior to 1949–50, see Table XX-A in Appendix A.

Field-goal attempts and goals scored were charted in the three areas—long, medium and short—for these men. The results follow the same trends as those found in our original study and are very significant. Standards of performance have, of course, improved.

The shooting averages compare favorably to the average for all players in each area, but this does not tell the complete story. These men took 59 per cent of their shots and made 68 per cent of their goals in the short area. The average player takes 42 per cent of his shots and makes 51 per cent of his goals in this area. This represents a great difference. In the medium area, the tall man takes 36 per cent of his total shots and makes 29 per cent of his goals. The average player takes 42 per cent of his shots and makes 36 per cent of his goals in this area. Therefore, there is not such great difference in the medium area. In the long area, however, the tall man takes only 5 per cent of his shots and makes less than 4 per cent of his goals, while the average player takes 16 per cent of his shots in this area and makes 13 per cent of his goals.

In other words, the tall man now makes over 96 per cent of his total field goals in the short and medium areas. These figures would indicate that he is a threat mainly in the areas close to the basket.

Several suggestions seem to be in order that will improve the game and still enable the tall man, if he is a good all-round player, to participate. Some of these follow:

1. Widen the free-throw lane from 6 to 12 feet and make this entire lane a restricted three-second area. This would not only keep the tall man, or any player, out of that area, but it would open up the middle lane so that zone defense would be of less value and teams would work the ball into the basket with less difficulty. The change would relieve congestion under the basket. It also prevents the cheap field goal resulting from the tip-up goal following a missed free throw. Smaller men, with superior quickness would have a good chance for rebounds. In an experimental game using the widened lane, between Yale and Springfield in 1952, a player 5 feet 9 inches tall led the rebounders with 14; this would be hardly possible under present rules.

It is indeed strange that the rules permit an offensive player to stand within three feet of the basket on either side of the lane but do not permit a player to stand any place in the lane out to the foul line—a distance of fifteen feet from the basket. It would seem that the somewhat antiquated markings of the court rather than the needs of the game have dictated the rules.

We made the widened lane proposal following our original study and have strongly advocated it since 1944 when it was presented to New York sportswriters and coaches.

The Fordham-Columbia experimental game played in 1945 and described in Chapter 11 was played with the suggested widened lane (see illustrated section).

A vote of the spectators attending the game was taken. Seventy per cent voted for the change. The officials that worked the game and many of the coaches present favored the change also.

It is gratifying to know that two major groups have adopted the widened lane as a result of our early study and proposal.

Following our introduction of the plan in Army service basketball games in Italy in 1945, the rule was adopted by the International Federation. Naturally, our neighbor countries with fewer tall men were quick to see the advantages. The widened 12-foot lane was used in the Olympic games in London in 1948 and again in Helsinki in 1952. It is part of the international rules and they wouldn't change back for anything.

The second major group to adopt the widened lane was the N.B.A. (professional). No other league in the world has so many tall men. They had to legislate further against the big fellow. After several seasons, the professionals like the change. Even George Mikan, for many years a great star with the Minneapolis Lakers following his college All America days at DePaul, is quoted as saying, "The widened lane may cost me the scoring title, but it's the best thing that has happened to basketball since the elimination of the center jump." Incidentally, here is probably the greatest of all tall players commending the two changes made to legislate against the tall man. The answer: George Mikan would be a star no matter what they do to the rules because he can play basketball.

If the widened lane is good for international and professional basketball, why not for high school, college, A.A.U. and Y.M.C.A. teams. Some have argued that the widened lane would aid and increase the use of the zone defense. Such is not the case at all; if any difference developed it would favor man to man defense. We have watched many Olympic games and our Yale team played with the twelve-foot lane on our thirty-game South America tour. More teams used man to man than zone; the type of defense made no difference.

Some high school people feel the widened lane would take away too much scoring area on small courts. Actually, it would relieve congestion near the basket and put the limited scoring area available to better advantage. Even if their argument had merit, it is too bad to have rules detrimental to the game to accommodate antiquated court conditions.

We sincerely hope, for the good of the game, the 12-foot lane will soon be adopted.

2. Our second proposal is more radical. We recommend allowing two points for field goals scored in the short and medium areas—out to a radius of 24 feet from the basket. We recommend counting three points for field goals scored beyond the 24-foot radius. This change would further decrease the comparative value of the tall man who is only effective in scoring in the closer areas. Merit of this plan is completely discussed under Area Basketball in Chapter 11. While the widened lane merit is proven and ready for adoption, area scoring needs further research and experimentation.

Coaches should try these proposals in scrimmages and practice games. They may be part of the answer to the ever-increasing tall man problem.

3. Coaches should teach big men a shot that may be used in the long area so that defensive players will not be safe in running back

to the keyhole and waiting for the opponent. If big men could shoot long shots accurately, it would (a) tend to relieve congestion under the basket on both offense and defense, (b) open up the game, (c) cut down the effectiveness of the zone defense and (d) make the big man a greater asset to his team.

4. In playing against an opposing player who is tall and can only score close to the basket, defensive measures should be taken accordingly. First, a defensive player may play in front of him or to the side so that it is difficult to get the ball to him. Second, defensive players away from the ball may drop into the keyhole to help tie up the tall man, and third, measures may be used to effectively screen him from the backboards.

5. Have patience and work hard to develop the big man. Try to have big men on your squad because, no matter what changes are made in the rules, a good big man will always be valuable in basketball.

11

A Proposed Area-Method of Scoring

THE HOME RUN IS THE MOST SPECTACULAR PLAY IN BASE-
ball. Parks have been built for particular hitters so that the
fans will see an occasional home run. The baseball has been
made more lively so that the home run will be more possible.
Correspondingly, the long field goal is the most spectacular
play in basketball. In spite of this fact, it is used sparingly
in many sections of the country. The home run in baseball,
of course, is worth more than the single. In basketball, however, the long field goal from, let us say, 40 feet out, counts
the same as the field goal under the basket. Since the data
indicate clearly that it is much more difficult to score from
the longer areas, why should not goals from the longer areas
be worth more than goals under the basket?

In addition to the percentage differences in shooting from
different areas, there are two other major reasons for consider-
ing an area-method of scoring—the reasons are the zone defense and the tall man.*

---

* The area-method of scoring in basketball is suggested for use by instructors
and intramural coaches as an interesting variation of the regular game. "Area
basketball" has proved popular to those who have tried it.

The zone defense

It has been observed that many teams are using this type of defense which does not project out much more than 24 feet from the basket. In many sections of the country teams that are using the one-hand shot almost exclusively are not effective in shooting beyond this distance. Therefore when those two situations exist—the team that cannot shoot long and the zone defense—there is not much of a basketball game after the defense is set. If more credit is given for the long field goal, it might draw out the zone defense and also encourage all players to learn a shot that can be made from a long distance.

The fact has been pointed out in Chapter 10 that the tall man does most of his scoring in the areas close to the basket. If a score in this short area counted less, it would minimize the importance of the tall man and he would not be used unless he could play all of the game well.

Further, to restrict the tall man it was suggested in Chapter 10 that the restricted three-second area be enlarged. The suggestion was made that the free-throw lane be increased from a width of six feet to 12 feet. The same rules that are now in use would then apply. However, on a jump ball in the lane, the ball is tossed up at the free-throw line and no one is allowed inside the lane until the ball is tapped. This widened lane is suggested to permit the smaller man to have a better chance to get rebounds, to relieve congestion under the backboards, and to restrict the tall man in scoring under the basket.

Other advantages to the area-method of scoring are that: (1) it gives the team behind a better chance in the latter part of the game; (2) it is more attractive to spectators since they see the "home run" of basketball more often; (3) it encourages a more wide-open style of play which appeals to players and spectators.

The Fordham-Columbia experimental game

The suggestions that have been mentioned were made to the New York basketball coaches and sportswriters in 1944. As a result, an experimental game was played between Columbia University and Fordham University in the Columbia gymnasium, February 7, 1945 (see illustrated section). Because three scoring areas were thought too complicated for the officials, it was decided to divide the court into two areas. The short area extended from the basket to a radius of 21 feet and the long area was that area beyond a radius of 21 feet. The rules were as follows: for each field goal made inside the 21-foot area the usual two points were scored; for each field goal made outside the 21-foot area, three points were scored. If the shooter touched the area line on the take-off, only two points were allowed. However, if the shooter's impetus carried him inside the short area after the shot, the goal counted three points.

The foul lane was widened from 6 to 12 feet and the regular three-second rule applied throughout the entire new area; that is, no offensive player was permitted to remain in this area for more than three seconds with or without the ball.

Excerpts from Irving T. Marsh's account of the game in the New York *Herald Tribune*, February 8, 1945, are as follows:

From the spectators' point of view, the new rules provided more excitement, more wide-open basketball and a decided accent on set shooting.

The crowd voted 60–40 in favor of the 3-point basket for a long shot scored outside a twenty-one foot arc and 70–30 in favor of widening the foul lane.

Most of the coaches present, however, were not too pleased with the new regulations, but nearly all agreed that widening the foul lane had distinct merit since it opened up the game and prevented mad scrambles under the basket as well as dropping the emphasis on big men.

To this observer the new rules definitely provided a game with more action and much more excitement, but if it really gets wild and wooly there is no telling what may happen. The scorers and officials particularly found it extremely difficult to keep up with the play, but both men who worked the game, Chuck Solodare and John Norton, liked the innovations in spite of the added burden.

The game might have been even more successful and proved the points better if one of the teams had used a zone defense. Unfortunately both teams played man-to-man. Also, neither team had any exceptionally tall players.

Following this game other games were played in various sections of the country and the author conducted numerous games of this type among service teams. In practically all cases the reaction was favorable to both changes.

In one Army game a team was 12 points behind with two minutes to go. Four long field goals were scored and because each counted three points, the score was tied and the game went into overtime. The original leader finally won by two points. This indicates how the area-scoring plan gives the team behind a better chance.

Games with area scoring

Two suggestions are offered for experimentation with area scoring to further cope with the problems of the tall man and the zone defense. First, our original proposal was to count one point for a field-goal in the short area, two points for a goal in the medium area, and three points for a goal in the long area. This plan has merit in that it gives due credit for shots from various distances from the basket in keeping with our findings.

It will be recalled, in our original survey, we made a special study using this scoring method. Here is a brief review of that study.

Sixty major games in which there was a difference in the score of five points or less were selected from the various season records included in the survey. These games were then scored by the area method of counting one point for a goal in the short area, two points for a goal in the medium area, and three points for a goal in the long area. The area scores were then compared to the original scores. In twenty-eight of the sixty games, the original losing team either tied the score or won under the area method. It is significant to note that in practically all of these games where the winner was changed there was a tall man on the original winning team. It is also evident from the data of the entire survey that lessening the value of the goal in the short area would minimize the advantages of the tall man.

Admittedly, the plan is complicated as it involves marking the court into three areas, although tape is now available that makes temporary markings quite simple. The plan is also rather difficult to officiate and may never be practical for inter-school competition. It does, however, properly award shooting ability and is highly recommended for intra-class and intramural competition.

Secondly, we have a recommendation based on more recent study. The plan is very similar to the one used in the Columbia-Fordham experimental game in 1945; it has only two scoring areas. We have seen in our recent five year study how shooting in the long area by tall men continues to decline. They make less than four per cent of their goals outside the twenty-four foot radius; in fact all players make only about one-eighth of their total goals in the outer area. Naturally, the trend continues to favor the zone defense and use of tall men near the basket.

Our simple plan is to mark an arc on the court with a 24-foot radius from the plane of the backboard. All field goals scored outside this arc count three points; those scored inside the arc count two points. A player's last contact with the floor in the take-off for the shot must be outside of the arc to receive three points; he may land inside the arc after the shot is taken. In the same way, a player would receive only two points for a goal if, in the attempt, he took off inside the arc and jumped backward landing outside the arc; in other words the take-off position determines the point value of the goal. This plan is a little better than the twenty-one foot area used previously as it is really not quite right to award three points for a goal twenty-one feet out. The 24 to 36 or more foot area represents a really long shot. It is worth three points.

A new study was made of 29 games to test this plan. The games were those ending with five or less points representing the winning margin; all were major games from seasons 1949–50 through 1953–54. We counted three points for all field goals scored by each team outside the 24-foot radius and on this basis adjusted the original score to the "area" score. In more than half—15 to be exact—of the games, the original losing team either became the winning team or substantially narrowed the margin. The reasons are obvious. The original winner usually had the height advantage and the losing team resorted to—and made—more shots from outside. The game scored by the area method gives a much more equal balance to both teams.

In summary, the two-area scoring proposal might have the following beneficial effects on the game.

1. Zone defense will decrease as outside shooters must be guarded closely.

2. Tall men will have to play all the game better. Their scoring value will be decreased. They cannot be solely key-hole players—either on offense or defense.

3. Players will increase practice and mastery of the long two-hand set shot—almost a lost art in the game now; and more of the offensive area of the floor will be utilized.

4. The trailing team will have a better chance—with good outside shooting they could catch up in a hurry.

5. Fans would see the "home run of basketball" frequently; they would like the change immensely.

6. Players will like it too. Coaches will be inclined to take the

wraps off on long shooting restrictions. What player doesn't like to shoot from outside?—one of the big thrills for the player.

7. Last but not least: Since the zone defense will no longer be practical, the outside defense will be tight which will open up the alleys for many more drive-in plays; another popular player thrill and one of the greatest crowd pleasers.

Major changes should never be made without sufficient evidence of their worth and this must come through research and experimentation. Many coaches and followers of basketball fought against the elimination of the center jump, and it took years to bring about this change. The Pacific Coast Conference finally tried the plan for one entire season and this resulted in the change. Now it is agreed that it is an improvement in the game.

If the tall man and the zone defense are problems in basketball, the plan suggested here may be the answer. It should certainly never be made illegal to use the tall man or the zone defense, but rules of the game may be altered to make it of less advantage to use them.

Again, none of the proposals in this Chapter are made with the idea of changing the rules immediately. Yet, the suggestion is made that coaches try out the proposals, experiment with area scoring and see if the results seem to be helpful to the game.

12

The Player Analyzes His Own Game

MOST PLAYERS MUST MAKE THEMSELVES GREAT BY CONSTANT practice. It is alleged that the great pianist Paderewski was once approached after a concert by an admirer who said: "That was wonderful. I wish I could play like that." The artist replied, "No, I'm afraid you wouldn't want to. It was necessary for me to practice 12 hours a day for 13 years in order to play as I do."

A player who expects to be an outstanding performer in highly competitive basketball will find it necessary to make certain sacrifices. He must, of course, be willing to keep himself in good physical condition. This means that he must refrain from smoking and drinking alcoholic beverages. He must not have habits that are detrimental to the very best possible physical condition and endurance. In addition to having the physical requirements and a correct mental attitude, the player must be willing to put basketball first among all his activities, except for his studies, during the season.

Major sports are now so highly specialized that it is necessary for boys to do some practicing in their chosen sport out of season. It is the trend now for coaches to specialize. Many schools engage a different coach for each major sport and they frequently hold practice sessions during other than the regular playing season. To keep up with the highest competition, therefore, it is also necessary for players to specialize. The best basketball players play the game whenever possible all year 'round. Most players at least practice shooting in the off-season.

Boys come into the coach's office throughout the year and ask if they may turn out for basketball. They want to be varsity players. After a 30-minute talk, a coach can tell whether or not they have a chance. If a player has reasonable ability, it depends largely on how much he wants to sacrifice and specialize to be a good competitive player.

Coaches may guide, counsel, and aid them but to get to the top, the players themselves must assume the major responsibility.

One way to practice constructively after techniques are learned is to scout or analyze one's own game. For example, in practice shooting keep a daily or weekly chart as illustrated in Form J, page 162. Please note that our practice shot form allows for both one-hand and two-hand shots in the medium area and divides the 12-foot short area into two divisions. These break-downs of course are optional. By recording the number of attempts and goals from various areas and for the various types of shots, a player soon learns his proficiency and how best to spend his time to improve.

If reports are kept in scrimmages and games, a player should be given access to the findings so that he may know his ability and achievement. He can then work accordingly to improve. Our charts are scrutinized carefully by players after scrimmages and games and great interest is shown by each player regarding his achievement. This means there will be an effort toward improvement in most cases.

At first, some players do not like to know about their

shooting percentages and other records. Just as baseball players are conscious of their batting averages, so some basketball players feel that knowing their records makes them too conscious of the percentage factor and causes them to "tense

PLAYER'S NAME *Johnson, Frank*

SHOT CHART

DATE		LONG 24'-36'		MEDIUM SET 12'-24'		MEDIUM IN MOTION 12'-24'		SEMI SHORT 8'-12'		SHORT TO 8'		FREE THROW		OTHER FUNDAMENTALS
MONTH	DAY	A	G	A	G	A	G	A	G	A	G	A	G	
Feb. 5	Fri.	50	17	50	28	50	24	50	36	50	42	100	87	*Indiv. defense; Rebounding.*
TOTAL														
PCT.														

A – ATTEMPTS
G – GOALS

FORM J

PRACTICE SHOT FORM

Note: The player should keep a daily record of practice shooting from various areas. He should total the attempts and goals and divide the number of goals by the number of attempts to determine the percentage or "shooting average."

up" in scrimmages or games. However, after becoming accustomed to the idea, all players seem to like it. Players must adjust themselves to it eventually because the basketball shooting averages are now public knowledge just as batting averages are in baseball.

It has been the author's custom to make up a season report on each player at the end of the year. An example of this is found in Form G, pages 38–39. In light of these findings, suggestions are made to each player that he may use to improve his game during the off-season and a prescribed program is outlined for him. After a season under this plan, players eagerly come into the office to receive their report each Spring. Of course, keeping proper records is basic to this plan.

Individual rating scales may be of great value to the player. An example is offered on Form K, page 164. Self-analysis and rating by the player is also strongly recommended. This brings his rating to the player in the most meaningful way and he may work accordingly. Coaches, of course, may also use these scales as an aid in the selection of squad and team and for instructional purposes. Often the player's rating and the coach's rating may be combined, with a conference resulting. A constructive plan for player improvement may follow.

It must constantly be kept in mind by the coach that each player is different. Practice sessions in which all players receive exactly the same type of instruction should be minimized. On the basis of the player's rating, a program should be prescribed that will fit his particular needs.

The rating scale offered in Form K is not claimed to be technically valid. The 25 factors are not weighed as to importance and everyone may not agree that these are the proper or total factors which make up the successful player. It does include, however, the generally accepted factors. By receiving a mark of four in each factor, a player could score one hundred on the rating. If a player's score falls below three in any factor, real effort should be made to improve this skill. It will be noted that it is impossible for the player to improve some of the factors listed. For example, a small player cannot help his size. This means he will need to work harder on the other points to make up for this handicap. A

Individual Player Rating Scale — Form K

SCALE
1. VERY POOR
2. FAIR
3. ABOVE AVERAGE
4. EXCELLENT

NAME	OFFENSIVE FOOTWORK	DEFENSIVE FOOTWORK	DRIBBLING	PASSING	WRIST ACTION	BALL HANDLING	BALL HAWKING	SHORT SHOTS	FOUL AREA SHOTS	LONG SHOTS	FREE THROWS	INDIVIDUAL OFFENSE	INDIVIDUAL DEFENSE	OFFENSIVE BACKBOARD WORK	DEFENSIVE BACKBOARD WORK	APPLICATION OF FUNDAMENTALS	SPEED ON COURT DRIVE	AGGRESSIVENESS	COMPETITIVE ABILITY UNDER FIRE	TRAINING CONDITION	MENTAL ATTITUDE	INTELLIGENCE	ALERTNESS	PROPER CUTTING & FLOOR PLAY	SIZE & BUILD	NATURAL ABILITY	TOTAL SCORE	INDIVIDUAL RATING ON SQUAD
Jones	3	2	3	3	4	3	3	2	1	4	3	1	3	3	3	4	3	2	3	3	3	3	8	3	4	3	74	5

FORM K

Individual Player Rating Scale. (From *Basketball Illustrated* by Howard A. Hobson. Copyright, 1947, by A. S. Barnes and Company.)

164

player can, however, improve on most factors, both objective and subjective. The individual player will be aided in improving the objective factors from the survey data that establish standards indicating good or bad performances.

Subjective factors may also be improved if the player will analyze himself carefully. For example, many players have developed skills to a high degree but because of a poor mental attitude, are unable to excel in competition. Worry about being "off one's game," consciousness of spectators, lack of confidence, the wrong attitude toward the coach or other players, fear of being taken out of the game for mistakes, and what people or the newspapers say, are only a few of the examples that keep players from performing to the best of their ability.

Players may get help in analyzing their game by asking teammates for their opinions about both the objective and subjective factors. The intelligent player is one who is willing to help his teammates and, in turn, to be helped by them.

Still another aid is the use of moving pictures. If a movie camera is available, pictures of players in action executing the various skills will be invaluable. Coaches will also find it valuable to take moving pictures of games when possible. There is no better aid in individual instruction than a picture that will show the player exactly how he performs.

Generally speaking, then, the successful player must (1) be willing to make any sacrifice that is necessary to be in fine physical condition, (2) have the proper mental attitude toward the game, (3) have determination and confidence that he can succeed, (4) constantly analyze his game by keeping careful records, (5) try to improve on the basis of these findings after consultation with the coach. He should also make it a habit to go into the coach's office often to talk things over. This is helpful to both player and coach.

13

Scouting the Officials

COACHES AND OTHER BASKETBALL AUTHORITIES AGREE that, because so much is left to the judgment of the official, basketball is the most difficult of all games to officiate. The records show that the average team commits more than 20 personal fouls during a game. At least, the officials call that many. For both teams that makes a total of at least 40 decisions on personal fouls alone. If we add to this violations, out-of-bounds decisions, held balls, and technical fouls it is reasonable to assume that basketball officials have at least seventy-five decisions to make during the progress of a forty-minute game. Each of these decisions may vitally affect the game and a team's chances to win. Basketball officials are usually part-time workers; officiating is a side-line for them. For this reason, comparatively few of them make a thorough study of the game. It therefore falls upon the coach, the only person spending the major portion of his time working at the game, to help in problems of officiating. Again, this book does not deal with playing or officiating techniques, but rather with facts derived from studying and analyzing the game, which may lead to improvement in all its phases.

There are certain significant results which should concern

the official. It has been pointed out that the home team wins more than 60 per cent of its games. This in itself is, of course, not the fault or concern of the official, except for certain contributing factors. For example, personal fouls are called much more frequently on the visiting team than they are on the home team. Even more serious is the fact that violations are called more frequently on the visiting team than on the home team. Many times, of course, this is proper and it is admitted that no two games, or even parts of games, are the same. However, the results in regard to these two factors are too consistent to be overlooked. Other data are available that show numerous instances where the same officials, working several games in which the same teams participated, called more fouls and violations on the visiting team than on the home team. Also, more players on visiting teams are put out of games on fouls than are members of home teams.

Indications are that there is a tendency for the official unconsciously to favor the home team. This is not because the official is dishonest or unethical; it is because he is under the same pressure that confronts a judge or jury trying a case in a community where local feelings and prejudices run high. This situation may partially be eliminated by engaging officials from an outside area who have no interests of any kind in the community where the game is played. It has also been suggested that officials be trained, recommended, and assigned by a neutral, central bureau representing the Conference or Association under whose auspices the teams play.

Scouting the official is another way to help the officiating problem. If it is fair to measure the achievement of a basketball player during a game by analyzing his performance, why is it not equally fair to do the same to the official? Data gathered in this manner will soon point out which officials are inclined to work games without being influenced by local pressure, which ones yield to this pressure, and which ones do or do not have the general ability to officiate.

The suggested procedure is as follows: Assign an observer to each official through one entire game and chart the official on the number of personal fouls, violations and other factors that he calls on each team during the game. The results are then totaled for the entire game. If records of this kind are kept on every game that an official works throughout the season, some indication of his ability will be insured. The measurements for a large number of games, or a comparison of data on the same official working with the same teams playing at home and away, will be of some value.

In addition to objective data there should be subjective observations, and they must be made by an expert. The commissioner of officials usually does this in college conferences. If there is no commissioner, the officials' associations should send out men to scout officials. Subjective observations should include the appearance, physical condition, and professional poise of the official, his judgment and responsibility in calling plays, and his attitude toward players, spectators and coaches.

A composite report of all of the data should be recorded and sent in to the official's association or the commissioner's office, whichever may be the central bureau. This report may be sent in on a form similar to Form L, page 169. This particular form, with some modifications, has been used in the Pacific Coast Conference.

A suggestion is offered that may be an improvement over that exemplified in Form L and in quite general use nationally. Coaches, in our opinion, should not be requested to rate officials on a game in which that coach's team participates. First, the coach has sufficient other duties during the game; most would consider that an understatement. A coach cannot properly analyze the play of his team and that of the opponents, do even a reasonably good coaching job,

DATE_____

TEAM "A" (Visitors)_____ Score_____

TEAM "B" (Home)_____ Score_____

OFFICIALS "C"_____ "D"_____ PLACE_____

* * * * * * * *

I. ANALYSIS OF OFFICIAL'S WORK: (In checking "Yes" or "No" column use either "C" or "D," or both.)

Satisfactory

A. Subjective

   1. Prompt Appearance for Game   Yes___ No___

   2. Physical Condition   Yes___ No___

   3. Professional Poise   Yes___ No___

   4. Speed in Action   Yes___ No___

   5. Prompt and Decisive Judgment Calling Plays   Yes___ No___

   6. Judgment in General   Yes___ No___

   7. Assumed Equal Responsibility Calling Plays   Yes___ No___

   8. A Spirit of Comradeship rather than Hostility   Yes___ No___

   9. Assumed Complete Command of Game   Yes___ No___

  10. Official Combination and Team Work   Yes___ No___

  11. 1953–4 Rule Interpretation Calls   Yes___ No___

B. Objective

   1. Personal Fouls Called on Home Team _____

   2. Personal Fouls Called on Visiting Team_____

   3. Violations Called on Home Team   _____

   4. Violations Called on Visiting Team   _____

   5. Held Balls called on Both Teams   _____

REMARKS: (State briefly conditions which prompt you to check column "NO.")

II. CONDITIONS AND INTERPRETATIONS WHICH AROSE IN THIS GAME THAT CALL FOR SPECIAL ATTENTION FOR OUR NEXT MEETING:

Signature of Coach_____

Signature of Athletic Director_____

FORM L

REPORT ON OFFICIALS

and at the same time watch and judge the officiating. Secondly, a coach in such a situation is naturally prejudiced. He is quite likely to notice mistakes that go against his own team rather than those that hurt the opponents. An official's work should be judged, if possible, by a qualified person not connected in any way with either team or the institution which the team represents.

One important item, not listed in Form L, is worthy of mention. The person assigned to analyze the work of an official would do well to check the number of calls made that do not affect the play; that is, whistle tooting on situations that do not give a player or team an advantage. These calls should be eliminated. One of the great criticisms of our present game is "too much whistle tooting." Hypertechnical officials that referee according to the literal letter of the rule do the game a great disservice. Judgment must be exercised in officiating any game. In baseball, for example, if a batter steps out of the batter's box and hits the ball, the rules say he is out. Batters step out of their box in hitting the ball quite often but it is rarely called because the batter has gained no advantage. To interpret the rule literally would ruin the game. Off-side could be called on nearly every play in a football game. Someone almost always has a finger or hand over the neutral zone. What a farce the game would be if all these were called when no advantage is gained. Why, then, do so many basketball officials go so literally by the book? Quite often at the national tournaments, we have asked a group of nonpartisan coaches to check the number of calls made by the officials that could have been ignored without affecting the play. We have never failed to eliminate *at least one-third* of all calls made. Examples: A player lifts the pivot foot a fraction early starting a dribble in the back court with no opponent near him. Ignore the infraction. A player causes negligible contact going after a rebound.

The opponent gets the ball and play is not affected. Why call it?

Some argue that players will learn bad habits under this proposal. Such is not the case. If they violate the rules and are called *when* it affects the play, they will learn to form proper habits accordingly. Some officials say they must call every infraction to protect themselves. They should not be officiating. Proper judgment is the greatest asset an official can have.

It is hoped that these suggestions on the scouting of officials will be of some help to the officials themselves and a means of improving the entire officiating problem.

Officials may also be aided through their commissioners. These men are appointed for conferences or leagues and should be qualified to observe, train, appoint and assign officials. Standard interpretations of rules will also be a great aid to the officials, particularly in intersectional play. Moving pictures of officials in action, as well as of rule interpretations will also be helpful. Clinics and demonstrations are still other possibilities which should be utilized. Last, bringing records kept during games to the official's attention, as we do in the case of players, will help him and will tend to eliminate the weaker officials. At best, basketball will always be a difficult game to officiate. Improvement depends on cooperation between officials, coaches, players, and spectators.

Officials have an opportunity to aid the game by their conduct on the court. Decisions should be made promptly and clearly, but the official who is an exhibitionist has no place in basketball. The game is for the players, and officials should stay in the background as much as possible. Also, their manner should not have a tendency to antagonize players or spectators. The official who knows the rules and their interpretations thoroughly, who is in the physical condition his duties require, and who has the professional dignity and poise to carry out his assignment efficiently but without showmanship, will do much to improve basketball. Coaches should make an effort to train young officials by using them during scrimmages. Officiating should also be included in physical education courses that include basketball.

14

Box Score
for Sportswriters—
Improved
Game Reporting Plan

IT HAS ALREADY BEEN STATED THAT BASKETBALL IS PLAYED by some 20 million and watched by more than 100 million people each year. This interest indicates that there must be a correspondingly large number of people who read about the games in the newspapers. Sportswriters, radio commentators, telecasters, and others who report games to the public, therefore, should seek to report as many interesting facts of the game as possible. In baseball, for example, the score of the game and the number of runs each player scores is not all that is reported to the public. A rather elaborate box score is included and it is followed by a summary giving most of the available facts about the game. Similar information is available in basketball, so why not follow the same procedure?

Admittedly, it would be too complicated for a reporter to record all of the details that are included in a scout report.

| HOME TEAM | | FINAL SCORE [ ] | | VS VISITING TEAM | | | FINAL SCORE [ ] |
| DATE | PLACE | REFEREE | UMPIRE | TIMERS | | SCORERS | |

FOULS	PLAYER	POS.	NO.	FIELD GOALS	FREE THROWS	RECOVERIES	LOSSES	TOTAL POINTS
$P^1 P^2 P^3$	Nelson	F	8	IXIIXI/IIXI	IXI/XIIXI	III/IIII	III/II	9
TIMES OUT	GAME TOTALS			60-20	15-10	84	23	46
	PCT.			.333	.667			

RUNNING SCORE

1 2 3 4 5 6 7 8 9 10 11 12 13 14 15 16 17 18 19 20 21 22 23 24 25 26 27 28 29 30 31
32 33 34 35 36 37 38 39 40 41 42 43 44 45 46 47 48 49 50 51 52 53 54 55 56 57 58 59 60 61 62 63 64
65 66 67 68 69 70 71 72 73 74 75 76 77 78 79 80 81 82 83 84 85 86 87 88 89 90

1 2 3 4 5 6 7 8 9 10 11 12 13 14 15 16 17 18 19 20 21 22 23 24 25 26 27 28 29 30 31
32 33 34 35 36 37 38 39 40 41 42 43 44 45 46 47 48 49 50 51 52 53 54 55 56 57 58 59 60 61 62 63 64
65 66 67 68 69 70 71 72 73 74 75 76 77 78 79 80 81 82 83 84 85 86 87 88 89 90

FORM M

REPORTER'S SCORE SHEET

EXPLANATION OF FORM M

This is a suggested reporter's score sheet for one team, but such a score sheet should not be kept by the official scorer. He should be assigned to record only the "minimum essentials" as listed in a regular score book. A reporter, however, could easily keep the additional data as suggested in Form M and he may always check with the official book on the items included in the official records before making up his permanent summary columns. The heading at the top, the running score and times out entries at the bottom are self-explanatory. Explanation of the columns is as follows:

Column 1—*Fouls:* P1—first personal foul
                         P2—second personal foul, etc.

"   2—*Player:* This indicates the player's name.

"   3—*Pos.:* Position

"   4—*No.:* Player's jersey number

"   5—*Field Goals:* This column includes field-goal attempts and field goals scored. A vertical line indicates a field-goal attempt and an X indicates a field goal scored.

"   6—*Free Throws:* This column includes free-throw attempts and free throws made. Again a free-throw attempt is a vertical line and an X is a free throw made.

"   7—*Recoveries:* Includes offensive and defensive rebounds, interceptions and retrieved jump balls. A vertical line indicates a recovery.

"   8—*Losses:* This column includes losses-of-ball by bad passes, violations, or poor ball handling. A vertical line indicates a loss.

"   9—*Total Points:* Total points are equal to the number of field goals made (2 points each) plus the number of successful free throws (1 point each).

Game totals are merely the addition of each column.

In the totals under "field goals" and "free throws" the first number indicates the attempts and the second number indicates the baskets made or scored; percentages are arrived at by dividing the number of baskets made or scored by the number of attempts.

Note: Diagonal line divides game into two halves. Everything on left of diagonal line is first half; everything on right of diagonal line is second half.

Name	Fouls	FG	FT	Rec.	LB	TP
Nelson	3	10-3	8-3	7	5	9
TOTAL	15	65-22	18-10	64	21	54
Pct.		.338	.555			

FORM N

BASKETBALL SUMMARY—BOX SCORE

However, a simplified record with the most important statistics could easily be kept on a form similar to the one described in Form M on page 174.

It will be noticed that this model form includes all avail-

EXPLANATION OF FORM N

This summary, or box score, is, of course, taken from the score sheet. It gives a total for each player and for the team. The explanation of the columns is as follows:

Column 1—*Name of player*

"   2—*Fouls:* This includes the total number of personal fouls called on the player during the entire game. It also includes technical fouls which would be indicated by T^1, T^2, etc. in Form M.

"   3—*F.G.:* Field-goal attempts and field goals. For example, 10–3 means 10 field-goal attempts and 3 field goals.

"   4—*F.T.:* Free-throw attempts and goals. For example, 8–3 means 8 free-throw attempts and 3 free-throw goals.

"   5—*Rec.:* Total recoveries

"   6—*L.B.:* Total loss-of-ball

"   7—*T.P.:* Total points

The totals at the bottom are, of course, the team totals and again the percentages are arrived at by dividing the number of goals by the number of attempts.

able information now kept in the ordinary score book. It adds to this field-goal attempts, recoveries, and losses-of-ball. From this information, individual player and team percentages and averages may easily be computed and recorded. In this manner, season records for players and teams may easily be kept the same as in baseball.

From the data accumulated in this type of score sheet, a box-score summary suitable for use in the newspapers could easily be made. An example is given in Form N on page 176. This summary gives the reader at a glance the important statistics on each player during the progress of the game as well as team totals and percentages. If this type of box score requires too many columns, a summary may be used at the bottom, as is done in baseball. This summary might include the personal fouls, and if necessary, the recoveries and losses, eliminating those columns from the box score proper.

This simplified plan is suggested as a start toward reporting the most essential game information. In some cases there may be a demand for more detailed information, as has been the case in baseball. It is possible that reporters who care to keep detailed statistics might include a summary of such things as offensive rebounds, defensive rebounds, violations, bad passes, ball-handling losses, interceptions, jump-ball recoveries, baskets responsible for, and assists. All but the latter two may be objectively recorded. A complete summary using abbreviations no more complicated or detailed than is commonly used in baseball would be possible. Again, it should be stressed that this latter, more complicated plan is only necessary for those who desire complete information. As the public becomes more familiar with this type of reporting the demand for additional details will follow.

The running score

It will be noted in Form A on pages 16–22 that the complete scout report includes an elaborate running score. This type of running score was not included in the reporter's score sheet Form M on page 174, because it would be impossible for one person to keep this type along with all the other scoring records. However, the values of the complete running score are so great that it would be well to have one person devote his time to keeping it on a separate form. A very complete running score plan is given below to show the possibilities.

RUNNING SCORE

SCORE	1	2	3	4	5	6	7	8	9	10	11	12	13	14	15	16	17	18	19	20
PLAYER SCORING	11			11	9	11	7		9		7	11		6		7	11		11	
TIME OF SCORE	19½			18	17	16½	16		15¾		15	14½		14		12	11½		10	
TYPE OF SHOT LOCATION	1-L		2-L						3-C	3-C				1-R	1-R				1-L	

FORM O

COMPLETE RUNNING SCORE

SCORE Box: Draw a diagonal line through proper number each time score is made. This shows the exact score of both teams at all times during the game.

PLAYER SCORING Box: Place the jersey number of the player scoring the goal directly beneath the score number. This furnishes very valuable information since it shows which players are consistent and which ones have "cold" streaks. It also gives information for reporting the game so that players will be given proper credit for making important goals.

TIME OF SCORE Box: Starting with twenty minutes and going to zero, each time a goal is scored, place the *remaining time* to the nearest quarter minute directly under the score number. This provides extremely valuable information as to when a team or player has long periods without scoring. This may involve a fatigue element for example. It also makes it possible to compare the exact score of both teams at any time during the game. This is important information for sportswriters.

LOCATION—TYPE OF SHOT Box:

For location of shot:

    1—short shot (cripple); out to twelve feet from basket.

    2—medium shot; from twelve to twenty-four feet from basket.

    3—long shot; beyond twenty-four feet.

For type of shot:

    L—left-hand shot

    R—right-hand shot

    C—chest shot

    U—underhand shot

    H—hook shot

    O—overhead shot

    J—jump shot

Example—1-R would indicate short area, right-hand shot.

The information in this box will aid coaches and sportswriters. It will give the type of shot and the location on the court from which each goal is made. This makes it possible to describe a game much more vividly and, of course, will aid coaches in instructional work.

Scoring rules for basketball

Scoring rules for basketball should be as complete as they are in baseball. The following rules were drawn up by the author at the request of the National Collegiate Athletic Association with the assistance of Mr. Homer Cooke of the N.C.A.A. Bureau. The rules now have the approval of that bureau, although not all of the items are recorded and reported by the Bureau so far. The rules submitted have been used in both our original and recent surveys. Some of the rules were given in Chapter 3 in describing scouting methods. The complete list is given here with approved rulings and recorders are urged to use them so that consistency and standardization may be achieved. Approved rulings are cases in point that are a part of all official rules.

SECTION 1—FIELD-GOAL ATTEMPTS:

Article 1: An attempt shall be charged to a player any time he shoots, throws or taps the ball at the basket, when, in the opinion of the scorer, he is attempting to score a goal, except when he is fouled in the act of shooting and the goal is *not* made.

Article 2: Tip ups shall count as field-goal attempts, because the player tips the ball with the intention of scoring a goal.

Article 3: Blocked shots shall count as field-goal attempts. The player whose shot is blocked is attempting to score a field goal.

> *Question:* Team A Player, while shooting, is fouled by Team B Player and goal is made. Is this a field-goal attempt?
>
> *Answer:* Yes. Since a goal was made, an attempt must be charged. If the goal was not made, no attempt would be charged.
>
> *Question:* Team A Player shoots but fouls Team B Player by charging after the ball leaves his hands. Is this a field-goal attempt?
>
> *Answer:* Yes, as goal, if scored, would count in this case. If foul were called before ball left shooter's hands, ball would be dead before shot and no field-goal attempt would be charged.

SECTION 2—REBOUNDS:

Article 1: A rebound is credited to a player or team each time the ball is retrieved after a field-goal attempt or free-throw attempt is missed. A rebound must be credited following each unsuccessful goal attempt, except when ball is dead following free-throw attempts.

Article 2: A *team* rebound is credited to the *team* that the ball is awarded to when a goal attempt goes out-of-bounds (a) without being touched by a player (b) is deflected out-of-bounds before there is possession (c) a free-throw attempt misses the rim and is awarded by official to opponent out-of-bounds.

> *Question:* Team A Player and Team B Player retrieve rebound simultaneously and held ball is called. Who is credited with rebound?

> *Answer:* If neither player had clear possession prior to the held ball, credit player whose team retrieves the jump ball. For example, if Team A Player tips jump ball and it is retrieved by his team, credit Team A Player with the rebound.

> *Question:* Team A Player does not catch rebound but tips it out to a teammate. Is he credited with a rebound?

> *Answer:* Yes, if the ball goes to a member of Team A. However, if it goes to Team B Player, the latter is credited with the rebound.

SECTION 3—RECOVERIES (Other Than Goals or Rebounds):

Article 1: The ball changes from one team's possession to the opponent's in one of the following ways:

1. Following opponent's successful goals.
2. Defensive rebounds.
3. Interceptions.
4. Jump balls (when ball is retrieved by team not originally in possession).
5. Violations.
6. Offensive personal fouls (when opponent retrieves rebound resulting from an ensuing missed free-throw).
7. Technical fouls on offensive team.
8. Double foul where original possessor loses following tip-off.

Goals and rebounds are covered elsewhere.   Credit other recoveries as indicated by the following articles.

Article 2: Interceptions:

An interception occurs each time a player or team takes the ball away from the opponent.   Examples are intercepted pass; taking the ball from an opponent's hands; stealing the ball on a dribble.

Question: Team A Player has ball and Team B Player ties it up causing a held ball.   Is this an interception?

Answer: Credit Team B Player with recovery *if* his team retrieves the jump ball.   If not, there is no change of possession and no recovery is credited.

Question: Team A Player makes a bad pass that goes out-of-bounds and ball is awarded to Team B.   Is this an interception?

Answer: Yes.   Credit B with a *Team* recovery as the ball changed possession.

Article 3: Jump Balls:

A jump-ball recovery is credited each time the ball is tossed between two players and a player's team gains possession.   This includes tip-offs.   Credit the recovery to the player retrieving the ball.

Question: On a jump ball Player A taps the ball out of bounds and it is awarded to Team B.   Is a recovery credited?

Answer: Yes.   Credit a *Team* jump-ball recovery to Team B as that team gained possession.

Article 4: Fouls:

When ball changes possession due to an offensive foul, credit a recovery to the player who was fouled.   In case of a technical foul by offense where no individual player is fouled, credit a recovery to the *team* that is fouled.   If double foul is called and jump-ball that follows causes a change in team possession, credit a recovery to *team* retrieving ball.

SECTION 4—LOSSES:

Article 1: A player or team loses the ball in one of the following ways:

1. Scoring a goal.
2. Losing a rebound to defensive team.
3. Bad pass or poor ball-handling resulting in interception by opponents.

4. Violations.
5. Allowing ball to be tied up and losing resulting jump ball.
6. Committing a technical foul when one's team is in possession of the ball.
7. Committting an offensive personal foul when the resulting free throw is missed and the opponents retrieve the rebound.

Goals and rebounds are covered elsewhere. Charge other losses each time a player or team is responsible for the opponent gaining possession of the ball. Such cases are:

Article 2: When a player in possession loses ball to opponents due to bad pass, poor ball-handling or dribbling, or due to a violation, charge the player or team with a loss.

> *Question:* Team A Player has ball and withholds it from play or allows Team B Player to tie it up causing held ball. Is a loss charged?

> *Answer:* If held ball results in possession by Team B, charge Team A Player with a loss. Otherwise no loss is charged as ball did not change possession.

> *Question:* Team A Player is dribbling and Team B Player slaps ball out-of-bounds. Is Team B Player charged with a loss?

> *Answer:* No. Team B Player did not have possession and ball did not change team possession. Had Team B Player caught the ball and then fumbled or slapped it out-of-bounds, he would be charged with a loss.

SECTION 5—ASSISTS:

Assists are a matter of judgment on the part of the scorer. We have considered many factors that might be classed as assists in aiding a teammate score a field goal. For example, a screen properly set for a teammate may enable the latter to drive in for a goal. However, at the start, we perhaps should only include passes or tips to players that result in field goals as assists. The N.C.A.A. bureau has already stopped reporting assists because of so much lack of uniformity but it is hoped the move is temporary. The N.B.A. (professional) records assists as do numerous conferences and the public certainly should have such information.

Article 1: Credit a player with an assist each time he makes, in the scorer's judgment, the principal pass or tip contributing directly to a field goal. Further, only one assist is to be credited for each field goal and only when it is primarily responsible for that goal.

Question: Team A Player retrieves defensive rebound, dribbles to side and passes to teammate in mid-court. Latter could have scored but passes to another teammate who scores the goal. Who gets the assist?

Answer: Major contribution was probably made by first passer in this case. The last pass before goal is scored is usually but *not always* the assisting pass.

Question: When player scoring has dribbled in for the goal may an assist be credited to a teammate?

Answer: Yes. If there was an important pass that led to the dribble and goal, credit an assist to the passer.

Question: Team A Player retrieves offensive rebound and passes ball (or tips ball) to teammate, who scores field goal directly on the play. Is an assist credited?

Answer: Yes. Credit Team A rebounder with an assist since his tip or pass led directly to a field goal. He is also, of course, credited with a rebound.

Question: Team A Player tips ball on a jump-ball play to a teammate who scores directly on the play. Is an assist credited?

Answer: Yes. The successful tip led directly to a field goal.

Section 6—Points-Responsible-for:

FORWARD

Careful judgment must be exercised by the reporter to be sure a defensive player is not unjustly charged with points an opponent scores. Even in assigned man-to-man defense it is necessary to change men due to screens or for other reasons. While it is desirable to place defensive responsibility for all points scored, individual players must not be penalized where there is serious doubt.

Article 1: Each time a point or points are scored, charge the opposing player or team with those points. If responsibility cannot be charged to an individual player, charge the points to the team.

In placing responsibility for field-goal scores, place the responsibility on the player who has or should have the responsibility at that particular time.

Free-throw scores are always charged to the player committing the foul.

Question: Player A goes in for offensive rebound and his opponent beats him back and scores field goal.   Is Player A charged with the points?

Answer: No. If teammate took over his assignment as he should, the teammate would be responsible. If no one took over and if Player A had no reasonable chance to recover, charge responsibility to *Team*.

Question: Defensive Player A jumps at opponent and allows opponent to drive around him and score field goal. Teammate tries to take over but is too late. Who is responsible?

Answer: Charge Player A who made the major mistake in this case. Had Player A been unavoidably screened and teammate did not properly take over, the latter would have been responsible.

Question: Team A uses a zone defense. Can responsibility be charged to individual defensive players in this case?

Answer: Yes. Just as definitely as in man-to-man. Charge responsibility to player who is guarding or should be guarding shooter in that area. Also penalize zone defensive players who commit fundamental man to man defensive errors that lead to scores.

Errors

Errors are not included in the rules submitted. A suggested definition is: An error shall be charged to a player each time he commits:

1. A personal foul
2. A technical foul
3. A violation
4. Causes his team to lose the ball in any other manner than in a try for a goal.

Further development of scoring plan

Sportswriters are in agreement that a reasonable amount of this type of data will be helpful in writing interesting but impartial stories on the games.

As a case in point, there was a game in Madison Square Garden in which a certain highly publicized player scored twelve points, although the defense against him was very strong.   Because of the twelve points most of the press reports were very flattering to the player.   He accounted for the twelve points by scoring four free-throw goals and four field goals.   The game chart showed that the player took 32 shots in order to get the four field goals, giving him an average of .125.   Actually, his shooting performance was the poorest of any player on the court that night.   Therefore the press report of this particular game was misleading—it did not tell the whole story.   Many times the star rebounder, for example, receives little recognition because there is no evidence of his work.

Great progress has been made in recent years in reporting more of the technical data of games to the public and this is most gratifying.   Many papers now carry more elaborate box scores and some use summaries beneath the box scores. However, we have only scratched the surface in this department.   Field-goal attempts, rebounds and assists are the items most have added to the older traditional items such as personal fouls, field goals, free-throw attempts and goals, and total points.   Other equally important items might easily be made available.   Some of these are described in the paragraphs that follow.

At the start, we should urge a greater effort toward uniform terminology—particularly in abbreviations used in reporting games to the public.   For example does FG mean field goal or foul goal; does FTM mean free throws missed or free throws made.   Many variations appear in box scores often with no explanatory list.   The public naturally can only guess.   The following abbreviations and terms are suggested and, again, have the approval of the N.C.A.A. Bureau.

FG   — Field Goals
FGA   — Field-Goal Attempts
FT   — Free Throws

FTG — Free-Throw Goals
RB — Rebounds
ORB — Offensive Rebounds
DRB — Defensive Rebounds
PF — Personal Fouls
Tec — Technical Fouls
TP — Total Points
TO — Times Out
A — Assists

Following are other abbreviations for items not as commonly used but that may be added in the future.

TL — Total Losses of Ball
TR — Total Recoveries
PRF — Points Responsible For
LV — Losses of Ball from Violations
LBP — Losses of Ball from Bad Passes
LBH — Losses of Ball from Poor Ball Handling
RTU — Recoveries from Tie-Ups
RJB — Recoveries from Jump Balls
RI — Recoveries from Interceptions

Writers and commentators will always use variations in terminology to describe a game. In baseball, for example, a home run will always also be called a four-bagger, a circuit clout, a homer and other similar names. A field goal is called a basket, a bucket, a goal, etc. The proper term, however, is field goal and perhaps our younger game should have reasonable uniformity until the public is better acquainted with the various terms. Our glossary attempts to make some progress in defining terms in a hope for better uniformity.

The suggestions made in this chapter should help to eliminate guess work and give reporters and sportswriters more concrete information on which to base their stories.

15

The Spectator—
Watching the Game

HIGH SPEED AND FREQUENT SCORING PRODUCE THRILLS IN basketball that are not found in many other games. However, partly because basketball is a comparatively new game, and partly because complete statistical reports have not always been available to the public, the average spectator has a limited knowledge of the sport. As a result, many who watch basketball games are unaware of many of the things that they should look for to make the game more interesting and meaningful to them.

Spectators watch a game for different reasons and therefore react differently during the game. Some watch because their school team is playing and they feel a responsibility to support the team; others watch a game because a friend or relative is playing on one of the teams; still others attend because they are interested in basketball as a sport. The last group probably includes many who have played the game. A fourth group includes those who are professionally interested, such as players, coaches and scouts.

Regardless of a spectator's purpose, the information and

188

suggestions furnished in this chapter may in some measure give a more intelligent understanding of the game.

Some coaches watch between 100 and 150 basketball games each season. In watching these games they look particularly for certain things, depending on their interest. If the coach's own team is playing, he of course attempts to analyze both individual and team play. He knows the individual assignments and the plan that has been outlined for the team and his main interests are whether these are being carried out, and whether they are successful against the opponent. Many coaches follow an individual player constantly through several minutes of the game to see how he is performing. In other words, coaches analyze all phases of the game when their team is playing.

In watching a game where future opponents are playing, a scout's analysis, as described in the earlier chapters, should be the observer's intention.

Many times, coaches of college or professional teams watch games for the purpose of scouting new material. In these games there is a different interest. Here the coach looks for potential ability such as speed, aggressiveness, competitive ability, coordination, skill, size, and similar attributes. These observers are not greatly interested in analyzing team play and individual assignments.

It has been observed that when watching the game for one of these professional purposes there is seldom reason for, or evidence of, the observer screaming, screeching, and shouting as the game progresses. When a person allows himself to be "taken away" by the game and becomes a rooter, he ceases to be an analytical coach or scout.

Players often watch games in order to learn and to improve their own techniques. In such cases they are seldom strong rooters. Players analyze the game with a concentration and interest similar to those of a coach or scout.

The average spectator is not expected to watch a basketball

game with the sole purpose of making a complete analysis of it. For this reason, he cannot be expected to react quite like an experienced scout, coach, or player. The point should be made, however, that the greater the spectator's knowledge of the game, the more intelligently he will be able to watch it and control his reactions. It is not our intention to discourage or take away the spectators' joy in rooting for their favorite team. It is desirable, however, that spectators be able to control themselves properly at the games and a greater understanding of the game will aid in this.

The observations made at a high school tournament will illustrate this point. Two very prejudiced rooting sections, one on each side of the court, comprised most of the attendance. It was obvious that the majority of the rooters had very little knowledge and understanding of the game. Their interest, of course, was to see their favorite team win. Constant bedlam and uproar started with the first whistle and lasted throughout the game. As a result, the players received undue and unjust criticism. Coaches were also criticized and in the spectators' opinion the officials were seldom right because each decision had to go against one team or the other. At times, spectators of this type reach a stage of hysteria which is undesirable for all concerned. Of course, there were a few spectators who apparently went merely to see the "spectacle" and sat passively, waiting for the end. They are comparable to the lady who courteously accompanied her baseball-minded husband to a game. She sat quietly through seven innings. Then the pitcher beaned the batter, at which point, rejoicingly, the lady jumped to her feet, exclaiming, "Good, now let's go home; he's hit him at last."

Greater knowledge will lessen the nervous strain, anxiety, and superstitions often apparent in the rooters' sections during ball games. Spectators should know what to expect from players, teams, and officials so that they will not hope for the impossible.

In baseball many spectators keep the score during the progress of the game. Since basketball programs are now used extensively, they should include an arrangement for keeping

NAME	NO.	POS.	AGE	HT.	WT.	FIELD GOALS	FREE THROWS	PER. FOULS	TOTAL POINTS
*Hauptfuhrer,B.F.	17	F	21	6'4"	190				
*Rockwell, J.R.	16	F	19	6'3"	185				
*Prior, W	18	C	20	6'5"	195				
*Gannon, J.	11	G	25	5'11"	185				
*Brady, W	12	G	25	5'10"	175				
Crosby, C	7	F	19	6'	155				
Henry, W	14	F	22	6'1"	183				
McCurdy, W.	9	F	21	6'	170				
Guthrie, J	5	C		6'5"	210				
Mobraaten,N.F.	3	F	18	6'1"	178				

FIRST HALF SCORE _____   FINAL SCORE _____

NAME	NO.	POS.	AGE	HT	WT	FIELD GOALS	FREE THROWS	PER. FOULS	TOTAL POINTS
*Lavelli, T	8	F	19	6'3"	185				
*Anderson,J.F.	11	F	19	6'2"	170				
*Joyce, R	9	C	20	6'5"	194				
*Redden, J.	6	G	20	5'9"	163				
*Peacock, S	7	G	20	5'10"	170				
Osbourn, J	5	G	19	6'2"	185				
Nadherny, F	14	F	20	6'	193				
Jackson, L	15	G	21	5'10"	190				
Johnson, C.	4	C	21	6'4"	180				
Upjohn, H	10	F	18	5'11"	160				

FIRST HALF SCORE _____   FINAL SCORE _____

* INDICATES PROBABLE STARTING PLAYER
USE VERTICAL LINE FOR FIELD-GOAL ATTEMPT
USE X FOR FIELD GOAL SCORED

USE O FOR FREE-THROW ATTEMPT
USE ⊗ FOR FREE THROW SCORED
USE P1, P2 ETC. FOR PERSONAL FOUL

FORM P

BASKETBALL PROGRAM FOR SPECTATORS

the score as illustrated in Form P on page 191. This might well include an individual chart, see Form E, page 32. This would make it possible to chart the performances of your favorite player during the game. The same form could be used to chart an entire team, if so desired. Plans of this kind will develop a more meaningful spectator interest.

Teachers of basketball could greatly aid spectators by giving clinics, talks, and demonstrations of various kinds for the general public. These sessions might include such things as interpretations of the rules, demonstrations of fundamentals, simple plays, and moving pictures.

Demonstrations conducted in connection with early season games are possible. Talks and showing of basketball films to student bodies, service clubs, alumni groups, and other similar gatherings, may be very valuable.

Teachers of physical education courses that include basketball might well devote part of the course to spectator interest.

Spectators, of course, can also improve their knowledge of the game by reading the rules book and some of the many books on the sport (see Appendix for list of suggested readings).

16

Conclusions
and Interpretations
on Scouting

THE FOLLOWING LIST OF CONCLUSIONS AND INTERPRETA-
tions should be of help to coaches, players, officials, sportswriters, and spectators, in accordance with their respective
interests and needs.

Our data indicate similar findings and trends in high
school, college, and professional basketball. Therefore, the
following interpretations and conclusions may reasonably be
applied to all three levels. Findings given, however, are based
on college games unless otherwise indicated.

* 1. Scoring in basketball has practically doubled since 1937 but
there was an actual decline in 1953–54; the first in modern history.
This may indicate the game has reached its scoring peak. At present, the average college team scores about 69 points a game; a high
school team averages nearly 58 points a game; the professionals
average close to 80 points.

---

* Sections indicated by asterisks are based on most recent available averages.
The reader is urged to consult carefully all tables from which figures may be
taken for any period and for an average five-year period.

2. Shooting may be measured objectively and averages computed.

* 3. Shooting averages have increased greatly in recent years but the peak has probably not been reached. Most agree the keeping and publicizing of shooting averages have aided this increase in accuracy. The present college shooting average is about .340; an increase of about 50 percentage points in the last five years. High school data are not sufficient to draw conclusions but the trend and averages seem to approximate the college standards. The professional shooting percentage was .373, highest in history, in 1953–54.

4. Shooting accuracy lessens as the distance of the shot becomes greater. Shooting averages may be misleading unless we know the areas from which shots were taken.

* 5. Over one half of the field-goal scoring and more than 40 per cent of all shots are from the short area (within a radius of 12 feet from the basket). The shooting average in this area is .397. This has defensive implications for the coach.

* 6. Results of shooting in the medium area (between a radius of 12 and 24 feet from the basket) indicate that poor shots are taken in this area. The average is only .266. Over one-third of field-goal scoring and more than 40 per cent of all shots are from this area.

* 7. In the long area (beyond a radius of 24 feet from the basket) shooting has been neglected and should receive particular attention. Only about *one-ninth* of the field-goal scoring and a little more than *one-sixth* of all shots are from this area.
The shooting average, as in all areas, is improving. It is now about .264.

* 8. The average college team takes about 70 shots a game and makes 24; we estimate high school teams average from 60 to 65 attempts and score an average of 20 goals; the professionals average about 75 attempts and 28 goals a game.

9. One-hand and two-hand shots are equally effective in the medium area but the two-hand shot is preferable in the long area.

* 10. Free-throw accuracy is improving rapidly but has not reached its peak, except possibly by professionals. College free-throw shooting averages drop from .766 in practice to .648 in

games. This might easily be improved by minimizing the mental and fatigue hazards. Latest high school averages are .657 while the professionals consistently make over 70 per cent of their attempts.

11. The underhand style of free throw is the most accurate for most players. However, some of the top free throwers use other styles.

* 12. The college team has an average of over 32 free-throw attempts a game and scores 21. The professionals attempt an average 33 and are successful in over 23 a game. Figures are not available for high school averages per game.

* 13. There are conservatively more than 100 rebounds in the average college, high school or professional basketball game. Next to shooting, rebound recoveries are the most important fundamental. The number of rebounds may be accurately measured during a game and it is valuable to the coach to know where the rebound strength lies.

It is not sufficient to record total rebounds; offensive and defensive rebounds should be designated. About 58 per cent of all rebounds will become defensive rebounds as the defensive team has the inside position.

* 14. Jump balls are relatively few in a game. There are only about 10 in the average college game and 16 in a high school game. Less time should be spent on this phase of the game than on more important ones such as rebounding, shooting, etc.

* 15. The college team makes an average of more than 13 interceptions a game; a warning to be more careful in passing and ball handling.

* 16. Possession of the ball is worth an average of at least .7 of a point.

* 17. Loss of ball costs a team an average of 1.4 points and could cost as much as eight points.

* 18. Personal fouls are still a major problem in the game. College teams commit an average of 21 a game, high school teams nearly 18, and professional teams average over 25. However, there have been decreases recently since rules have made the penalty more severe. We still recommend a penalty of one free-throw counting two points for all defensive personal fouls.

* 19. The home team has a distinct advantage.   Home teams win about 60 per cent of their games when the teams are fairly evenly matched.   However, the present national average of all college games played shows the home team winning over 70 per cent. The home team excels in all departments studied but the margins are small when teams are evenly matched.   Psychological factors must be studied.   Other factors are scheduling, officiating, rule interpretations and home-audience behavior.

* 20. The winning team has a slight advantage over the losing team in most phases of the game.

The greatest difference is in shooting accuracy with a fairly substantial difference in rebounds next.   The winning team has a shooting percentage of .343 compared to .276 for the losers.   The winning team also shoots more frequently and better in the short area and is more accurate from the free-throw line.

21. The average team is actually stronger in the second half in field-goal shooting and in retaining possession of the ball.   This indicates that the game is not too strenuous physically.   Tension of players in the first half may lessen the advisability of pre-game "pep talks."   Poor shooting in the first half may be improved by longer warm-up periods.   The fact that free-throw accuracy lessens in the second half would seem to be due largely to psychological factors.

22. Shooting accuracy lessens as the competition becomes more intense.   Therefore, all that can be done to relieve tension should be attempted.   Many psychological factors are indicated.

* 23. The tall man (over six feet four inches) does most of his scoring close to the basket.   Ninety-six per cent of his scoring is within a radius of 24 feet of the basket.   Enlarging the three-second area as now used in professional and international games would tend to lessen the value of the tall man unless he can play all of the game well.

24. Players may analyze and improve their game through the use of fundamental rating charts.

Players must specialize, discipline themselves to practice, be in proper physical and mental condition and make certain sacrifices in order to become top performers.

25. As an aid to officiating, careful scouting of officials is suggested.   Observations and reports should be made by neutral, quali-

fied persons, preferably from the commissioner's or officials' bureau. All possible local pressures on the officials should be removed.

26. A reporter's score sheet and box score are suggested for the use of sportswriters and others so that they may better report the games to the public. Standardization of terminology is also a great need.

27. It is possible for spectators to keep score or scout their favorite players during a game. Greater knowledge may lessen nervous strain and anxiety for the spectator.

28. Objective scouting may be done by a trained observer but subjective scouting must be done by a basketball expert. Many factors in basketball cannot be objectively measured. Subjective findings are equally important and should be considered as such by the coach.

29. Complete scout records on players, teams, and opponents should be kept each season for future reference. These may be obtained from game scout reports.

30. Basketball defense is still obviously neglected. We need to observe, measure and record defensive performances so more information will be available and standards may be established.

31. There is a need for further research in the field of basketball, particularly on the secondary school level.

Our greatest basketball problems, at least from a spectator's point of view are:

A. Stalling—particularly near the end of the game.

Suggested Remedies: 1. Time limit offensive team may have possession of the ball before shooting. (Already adopted by the N.B.A. (professional).) Penalty, however, should be jump ball.

2. Close adherence to rule where jump ball is indicated when closely guarded player withholds ball from play five seconds.

B. Intentional and Frequent Personal Fouls.

Suggested Remedies: 1. Time limit rule as stated above.

2. Continue to make the penalty more severe. We recommend one free-throw counting two points for defensive fouls; loss of ball to opponents on offensive fouls or when ball is not in possession of either team.

3. Officials should call only fouls that give player or team advantage or affect the play.

C. Disqualifying of key men due to personal fouls.

Suggested Remedies: 1. More severe penalties and time limit rule will probably aid this situation.

2. Coaches must teach better defense and, to meet all these problems, must be willing to "play the game" and not "beat the rules."

D. Too many Free Throws:

Suggested Remedy: Very simple. Merely award one free throw counting two points as suggested above. Above plans will also reduce number of fouls which will reduce number of free-throw situations. The number of free throws under these plans will be less than half the present number.

E. The Tall Man.

Suggested Remedies: 1. Widen the free-throw lane to 12 feet (already adopted by international and professional rules).

2. Experiment with proposal to decrease the value of the field goal within the 24-foot radius of the basket compared to the long-area field goal.

Appendix A—Tables

THE FOLLOWING LIST OF TABLES INCLUDES TABLES FROM OUR original study of 460 college games over a 13-year period, from 1936–37 through 1948–49. The tables are included here for comparative and historical reference.

List of tables

XIX-A.   Minor Games
XX-A.   Shooting by Tall Men

TABLE I-A

ALL GAMES SCORING

Season	Number of Games	Score	Average Score per Game
1936-37	31	2185	70.5
1937-38	36	2985	82.9
1938-39	41	3326	81.1
1939-40	32	2748	85.9
1940-41	43	3537	82.3
1941-42	32	2588	80.9
1942-43	35	2985	85.3
1943-44	32	2763	86.3
1944-45	52	5306	102.
1945-46	37	3855	104.2
1946-47	32	3537	110.5
1947-48	27	3174	117.6
1948-49	30	3787	126.2
Game Totals (both teams)	460	42776	93.0
Major Games (both teams)	382	35715	93.5
Minor Games (both teams)	78	7061	90.5
Winning Team	460	24253	52.7
Losing Team	460	18523	40.3
Home Team	448	21614	48.2
Visiting Team	472	21162	44.9

This table shows total scores and average scores per game for both teams, by seasons, for 460 games. Similar information is given for major and minor games, winning and losing teams, and home and visiting teams.

TABLE II-A

TOTAL SHOTS

Season	Number of Games	Field-Goal Attempts	Field Goals	Percentage	Average Field-Goal Attempts per Game	Average Field Goals per Game
1936-37	31	3082	790	.256	99	25
1937-38	36	4198	1090	.260	117	30
1938-39	41	4956	1249	.252	121	30
1939-40	32	4101	1115	.272	128	35
1940-41	43	5188	1411	.272	121	33
1941-42	32	3790	996	.263	118	31
1942-43	35	4294	1168	.272	123	33
1943-44	32	4004	1112	.278	125	35
1944-45	52	8319	2154	.259	160	41
1945-46	37	5238	1491	.285	142	40
1946-47	32	4715	1361	.289	147	43
1947-48	27	4201	1204	.287	156	46
1948-49	30	5081	1460	.287	170	49

(Table II-A continued on next page)

TABLE II-A

(cont.)

Season	Number of Games	Field-Goal Attempts	Field Goals	Percentage	Average Field-Goal Attempts per Game	Average Field Goals per Game
Game Totals (both teams)	460	61167	16601	.271	133	36.1
Major Games (both teams)	382	50995	13762	.270	133.5	36.0
Minor Games (both teams)	78	10172	2839	.280	130.4	36.4
1st Half	460	30129	7977	.265	65.5	17.3
2nd Half	460	31038	8624	.278	67.5	18.8
Winning Team	460	31209	9554	.306	67.8	20.8
Losing Team	460	29958	7047	.235	65.1	15.3
Home Team	448	30002	8398	.280	67.0	18.7
Visiting Team	472	31165	8203	.263	66.0	17.4
Intra-Squad Scrimmages (both teams)	75	10520	3457	.329	140.3	46.1
Practice Shots		14925	8474	.568		

This table shows field-goal attempts and field goals by both teams, by seasons, for the 460 games; percentages of attempts scored and average number of attempts and goals per game. It gives similar information for major and minor games, first and second halves, winning and losing teams, and home and visiting teams; also, a sampling from intra-squad scrimmages, and practice shots without defense.

TABLE III-A
SHORT-AREA SHOOTING *

Season	Number of Games	Field-Goal Attempts	Field Goals	Percentage	Average Field-Goal Attempts per Game	Average Field Goals per Game
1936-37	31	1021	367	.359	33	12.
1937-38	36	1394	511	.367	39	14.
1938-39	41	1381	517	.374	34	13.
1939-40	32	1112	436	.392	35	14.
1940-41	43	1468	611	.416	34	14.
1941-42	32	1065	413	.388	33	13.
1942-43	35	1449	572	.395	41	16.
1943-44	32	1377	560	.407	43	18.
1944-45	52	3765	1275	.339	72	25.
1945-46	37	1968	735	.373	53	20.
1946-47	32	2138	796	.372	67	25.
1947-48	27	1906	675	.354	71	25.
1948-49	30	2096	770	.367	70	26.
Game Totals (both teams)	460	22140	8238	.372	48.1	17.9
Major Game Total (both teams)	382	18435	6768	.367	48.3	17.7
Minor Game Total (both teams)	78	3705	1470	.397	47.5	18.8
Winning Team Total	460	12494	5043	.404	27.2	11.0
Losing Team Total	460	9646	3195	.331	21.0	6.9
Intra-Squad Scrimmages (both teams)	75	4501	1964	.436	60.0	26.2
Practice Shots		3810	3304	.867		

* Short shots are those taken within a radius of twelve feet from the basket.

This table shows total shots with percentages and averages as in Table II-A but for short shots only.

TABLE IV-A
MEDIUM-AREA SHOOTING *

Seasons	Number of Games	Field-Goal Attempts	Field Goals	Percentage	Average Field-Goal Attempts per Game	Average Field Goals per Game
1936-37	31	1349	288	.213	44	9.
1937-38	36	1859	396	.213	52	11.
1938-39	41	2347	513	.219	57	13.
1939-40	32	1830	449	.245	57	14.
1940-41	43	2358	548	.232	55	13.
1941-42	32	1555	363	.233	49	11.
1942-43	35	1916	402	.210	55	11.
1943-44	32	2013	423	.210	63	13.
1944-45	52	2906	598	.206	56	12.
1945-46	37	2276	525	.231	62	14.
1946-47	32	1875	428	.228	59	13.
1947-48	27	1356	308	.227	50	11.
1948-49	30	2032	461	.227	68	15.
Game Totals (both teams)	460	25672	5702	.222	55.8	12.4
Major Games (both teams)	382	21247	4730	.223	55.6	12.3
Minor Games (both teams)	78	4425	972	.220	56.7	12.4
Winning Team (total)	460	12644	3169	.251	27.5	6.9
Losing Team (total)	460	13028	2533	.194	28.3	5.5
Intra-Squad Scrimmages (both teams)	75	4848	1261	.260	64.6	16.8
Practice Shots		3085	1632	.529		

* Medium shots are those taken between a radius of twelve feet and a radius of twenty-four feet from the basket.

This table shows total shots with percentages and averages as in Tables II-A and III-A but for medium shots only.

TABLE V-A
Long-Area Shooting *

Season	Number of Games	Field-Goal At-tempts	Field Goals	Per-centage	Average Field-Goal At-tempts per Game	Average Field Goals per Game
1936-37	31	712	135	.190	23	4
1937-38	36	945	183	.194	26	5
1938-39	41	1228	219	.178	30	5
1939-40	32	1159	230	.198	36	7
1940-41	43	1362	252	.185	32	6
1941-42	32	1170	220	.188	37	7
1942-43	35	929	194	.209	27	6
1943-44	32	614	129	.210	19	4
1944-45	52	1648	281	.171	32	5
1945-46	37	994	231	.232	27	6
1946-47	32	702	137	.195	22	4
1947-48	27	939	221	.235	35	8
1948-49	30	953	229	.240	32	8
Game Totals (both teams)	460	13355	2661	.199	29.0	5.8
Major Game Total (both teams)	382	11313	2264	.200	29.6	5.9
Minor Game Total (both teams)	78	2042	397	.194	26.2	5.1
Winning Team	460	6071	1342	.221	13.2	2.9
Losing Team	460	7284	1319	.181	15.8	2.9
Intra-Squad Scrimmages (both teams)	75	1171	232	.198	15.6	3.1
Practice Shots		2905	1046	.360		

* Long shots are those taken beyond a radius of twenty-four feet from the basket.

This table shows total shots with percentages and averages as in Tables II-A, III-A and IV-A but for long shots only.

TABLE VI-A

Free Throws

Season	No. of Games	Free-Throw At-tempts	Free-Throw Goals	Per-centage	Average Free-Throw At-tempts per Game	Average Free-Throw Goals per Game
1936-37	31	1043	605	.580	34	20
1937-38	36	1356	805	.594	38	22
1938-39	41	1406	828	.589	34	20
1939-40	32	857	518	.604	27	16
1940-41	43	1154	715	.620	27	17
1941-42	32	1013	596	.588	32	19
1942-43	35	1100	649	.590	31	19
1943-44	32	1006	539	.536	31	17
1944-45	52	1828	998	.546	35	19
1945-46	37	1478	873	.591	40	24
1946-47	32	1339	815	.609	42	25
1947-48	27	1224	766	.626	45	28
1948-49	30	1377	867	.630	46	29

This table shows total free-throw attempts and free-throw goals made by both teams for the 460 games. It also shows percentage of attempts scored and average number of attempts and goals per game.

The table also shows free-throw attempts and free-throw goals

TABLE VI-A

(cont.)

Season	No. of Games	Free-Throw At-tempts	Free-Throw Goals	Per-centage	Average Free-Throw At-tempts per Game	Average Free-Throw Goals per Game
Game Totals (both teams)	460	16181	9574	.592	35.2	20.8
Major Games (both teams)	382	13703	8191	.598	35.9	21.4
Minor Games (both teams)	78	2478	1383	.558	31.8	17.7
1st Half (both teams)	200	3235	1932	.597	16.2	9.7
2nd Half (both teams)	200	3579	2091	.584	17.9	10.5
Winning Team	460	8449	5145	.609	18.4	11.2
Losing Team	460	7732	4429	.573	16.9	9.6
Home Team	448	8164	4818	.590	18.2	10.8
Visiting Team	472	8017	4756	.593	17.0	10.1
Intra-Squad Scrimmages (both teams)	75	2134	1204	.564	28.5	16.1
Practice Shots		5275	4112	.780		

made, percentages of goals scored, and average number of attempts and goals per game for major and minor games, first and second halves, winning and losing teams, home and visiting teams, and in intra-squad scrimmages and in practice shots without defense.

TABLE VII-A

REBOUNDS

	No. of Major Games	Offen- sive Re- bounds	Aver- age per Game	Defen- sive Re- bounds	Aver- age per Game	Total Re- bounds	Aver- age per Game
1st Half (both teams)	75	1564	21	2327	31	3891	51.9
2nd Half (both teams)	75	1601	21	2375	32	3976	53.0
Winning Team	75	1653	22	2536	34	4189	55.9
Losing Team	75	1512	20	2166	29	3678	49.0
Home Team	75	1643	22	2430	32	4073	54.3
Visiting Team	75	1522	20	2272	30	3794	50.6
Both Teams	75	3165	42.2	4702	62.7	7867	104.9

TABLE VIII-A

MISCELLANEOUS RECOVERIES
(JUMP BALLS, AND INTERCEPTIONS)

	No. of Games	Jump Balls	Average per Game	Inter- ceptions	Average per Game
1st Half (both teams)	75	552	7.4	578	7.7
2nd Half (both teams)	75	608	8.1	518	6.9
Winning Team	75	634	8.5	546	7.3
Losing Team	75	526	7.0	550	7.3
Home Team	75	560	7.5	528	7.0
Visiting Team	75	600	8.0	568	7.6
Both Teams	75	1160	15.5	1096	14.6

TABLE IX-A

LOSS-OF-BALL

	No. of Games	Bad Passes	Average per Game	Violations	Average per Game	Poor Ball-Handling	Average per Game	Total Losses	Average per Game
1st Half (both teams)	75	467	6.2	329	4.4	471	6.3	1267	16.9
2nd Half (both teams)	75	362	4.8	257	3.4	450	6.0	1069	14.3
Winning Team	75	429	5.7	300	4.0	475	6.3	1204	16.1
Losing Team	75	400	5.3	286	3.8	446	5.9	1132	15.1
Home Team	75	449	6.0	260	3.5	423	5.6	1132	15.1
Visiting Team	75	380	5.1	326	4.3	498	6.6	1204	16.1
Both Teams	75	829	11.1	586	7.8	921	12.3	2336	31.1

This table shows the total number of times the ball is lost by bad passes, violations and poor ball-handling, and total in seventy-five games with the averages per game (both teams). It also shows the totals and averages for the first and second halves, for the winning and losing teams, and for the home and visiting teams.

Table VII-A (*left, top*) shows the offensive, defensive and total rebounds retrieved by both teams for 75 games. It also shows the average number of rebounds by both teams per game. Findings are also given for first half, second half, winning and losing teams, and home and visiting teams.

Table VIII-A (*left, bottom*) shows the total number of jump balls and interceptions made in 75 games with the averages per game (both teams). It also shows the totals and averages for first and second halves, for the winning and losing teams, and for the home and visiting teams.

TABLE X-A

PERSONAL FOULS

	No. of Major Games	Personal Fouls	Average per Game
Winning Team	75	1069	14.3
Losing Team	75	1183	15.8
Home Team	75	1073	14.3
Visiting Team	75	1179	15.7
Both Teams	75	2252	30.0

This table shows the number of personal fouls committed by both teams in 75 games with the average per game for the winning and losing team, home and visiting team and totals for both teams.

Table XI-A *(right)* shows a record of the home team in 448 games. It includes field-goal and free-throw attempts and goals, total scores, and average score per game. Percentages of attempts scored and averages of attempts and goals per game are also given. For 75 home games, it includes total number and average per game of rebounds; losses of ball by bad passes, violations, and poor ball handling; jump-ball recoveries; interceptions; personal fouls. It also shows number and percentage of games won and lost in 434 home games.

TABLE XI-A

HOME TEAM SURVEY

Shooting Results	No. of Games*	At-tempts	Goals	Per-centage	Average per Game	
					At-tempts	Goals
Total Shots	448	30002	8398	.280	67.0	18.7
Free Throws	448	8164	4818	.590	18.2	10.8

Other Results	No. of Games	Total	Average per Game
Score	448	21614	48.2
Rebounds	75	4073	54.3
Bad Passes	75	449	6.0
Violations	75	260	3.5
Losses by Ball-Handling	75	423	5.6
Total Losses-of-Ball	75	1132	15.1
Jump Balls	75	560	7.5
Interceptions	75	528	7.0
Personal Fouls	75	1073	14.3

	No. of Games**	Games Won by Home Teams	Games Lost by Home Teams	Percentage of Games Won by Home Teams
Home Games Results	434	273	161	.629

* Only home team court games counted.
** Games not included played on neutral courts.

TABLE XII-A

VISITING TEAM SURVEY

| Shooting Results | No. of Games | At-tempts | Goals | Per-centage | Average per Game | |
					At-tempts	Goals
Total Shots	472	31165	8203	.263	66.0	17.4
Free Throws	472	8017	4756	.593	17.0	10.1

Other Results	No. of Games	Total	Average per Game
Score	472	21162	44.9
Rebounds	75	3794	50.6
Bad Passes	75	380	5.1
Violations	75	326	4.3
Losses by Ball-Handling	75	498	6.6
Total Losses-of-Ball	75	1204	16.1
Jump Balls	75	600	8.0
Interceptions	75	568	7.6
Personal Fouls	75	1179	15.7

	No. of Games*	Games Won by Visiting Teams	Games Lost by Visiting Teams	Percentage of Games Won by Visiting Teams
Visiting Game Results	434	161	273	.371

* When both teams travel both are counted as visiting teams. Games not included played on neutral courts.

Table XII-A shows a record of the visiting team in the same manner that Table XI-A shows a record of the home team.

TABLE XIII-A

WINNING TEAM SURVEY

Shooting Results	No. of Games	At-tempts	Goals	Per-centage	Average per Game	
					At-tempts	Goals
Long Shots	460	6071	1342	.221	13.2	2.9
Medium Shots	460	12644	3169	.251	27.5	6.9
Short Shots	460	12494	5043	.404	27.2	11.0
Total Shots	460	31209	9554	.306	67.8	20.8
Free Throws	460	8449	5145	.609	18.4	11.2

Other Results	No. of Games	Total	Average per Game
Score	460	24253	52.7
Rebounds	75	4189	55.9
Losses-of-Ball	75	1204	16.1
Jump Balls	75	634	8.5
Interceptions	75	546	7.3
Personal Fouls	75	1069	14.3

This is a table that shows the record of the winning team in 460 games. It includes total field-goal attempts and field goals, percentage of attempts scored, average of attempts and goals per game for long, medium, short areas, and total. It also shows winning team free-throw attempts, goals, percentage of free throws scored, and averages per game. It shows the winning team total score and average score per game. It also shows the winning team record in 75 games of rebounds, losses-of-ball, jump balls, interceptions, and personal fouls; totals and averages per game.

TABLE XIV-A

LOSING TEAM SURVEY

Shooting Results	No. of Games	At-tempts	Goals	Per-centage	Average per Game	
					At-tempts	Goals
Long Shots	460	7284	1319	.181	15.8	2.9
Medium Shots	460	13028	2533	.194	28.3	5.5
Short Shots	460	9646	3195	.331	21.0	6.9
Total Shots	460	29958	7047	.235	65.1	15.3
Free Throws	460	7732	4429	.573	16.9	9.6

Other Results	No. of Games	Total	Average per Game
Score	460	18523	40.3
Rebounds	75	3678	49.0
Losses-of-Ball	75	1132	15.1
Jump Balls	75	526	7.0
Interceptions	75	550	7.3
Personal Fouls	75	1183	15.8

This is a table that shows a record of the losing team in the same manner that Table XV shows a record of the winning team.

Table XV-A *(right, top)* shows first-half field-goal attempts, field goals, percentages of attempts scored, average number of attempts and goals per game, in 460 games (both teams). It also shows first-half free-throw attempts, goals, percentage of free-throw attempts scored, and averages per game. For 75 games it shows first-half rebounds, losses-of-ball, jump balls and interceptions; totals and averages per game.

Table XVI-A *(right, bottom)* shows a record of the second half (both teams) in the same manner that Table XV-A shows the first-half record.

214

TABLE XV-A
FIRST-HALF SURVEY
(both teams)

Shooting Results	No. of Games	At-tempts	Goals	Per-centage	Average per Game	
					At-tempts	Goals
Total Shots	460	30129	7977	.265	65.5	17.3
Free Throws	200	3235	1932	.597	16.2	9.7

Other Results	No. of Games	Total	Average per Game
Rebounds	75	3891	51.9
Losses-of-Ball	75	1267	16.9
Jump Balls	75	552	7.4
Interceptions	75	578	7.7

TABLE XVI-A
SECOND-HALF SURVEY

Shooting Results	No. of Games	At-tempts	Goals	Per-centage	Average per Game	
					At-tempts	Goals
Total Shots	460	31038	8624	.278	67.5	18.8
Free Throws	200	3579	2091	.584	17.9	10.5

Other Results	No. of Games	Total	Average per Game
Rebounds	75	3976	53.0
Losses-of-Ball	75	1069	14.3
Jump Balls	75	608	8.1
Interceptions	75	518	6.9

TABLE XVII-A

LEVELS OF COMPETITION SHOOTING

	No. of Games	Field Goals						Total Shots			Free Throws		
		Long Shots		Medium Shots		Short Shots							
		At-tempts	Goals	At-tempts	Goals	At-tempts	Goals	At-tempts	Goals	Per-centage	At-tempts	Goals	Per-centage
Major Games (both teams)	382	11313	2264	21247	4730	18435	6768	50995	13762	.270	13703	8191	.598
Minor Games (both teams)	78	2042	397	4425	972	3705	1470	10172	2839	.280	2478	1383	.558
Scrimmages (both teams)	75	1171	232	4848	1261	4501	1964	10520	3457	.329	2134	1204	.564
Practice Shots	*	2905	1046	3085	1632	3810	3304	14925	8474	.568	5275	4112	.780

* Non-competitive shooting—no defense.

This is a table that shows a comparison in field-goal and free-throw performance of teams playing in 382 major games, 78 minor games, 75 scrimmages, and in practice sessions without defense. It shows long, medium, short, and total field-goal attempts, field goals, and percentage of total field-goal attempts made. It also shows total free-throw attempts, free-throw goals, and the percentage of free-throw attempts scored.

TABLE XVIII-A

Major Games *

Shooting	No. of Games	At-tempts	Goals	Per-centage	Average per Game	
					At-tempts	Goals
Long Shots	382	11313	2264	.200	29.6	5.9
Medium Shots	382	21247	4730	.223	55.6	12.3
Short Shots	382	18435	6768	.367	48.3	17.7
Total Shots	382	50995	13762	.270	133.5	36.0
Free Throws	382	13703	8191	.598	35.9	21.4

Score	No. of Games	Total Points	Average per Game
	382	35,715	93.5

* A major game is a conference game or its equivalent in which competition is at its highest level.

This is a table that shows the record of both teams in 382 major games. It includes long, medium, short, and total field-goal attempts and field goals, percentage of attempts scored, and the average number of attempts and goals per game in each category. It gives the same information on free throws and also shows total scores and average score per game.

TABLE XIX-A

Minor Games *

| Shooting | No. of Games | At-tempts | Goals | Per-centage | Average per Game | |
					At-tempts	Goals
Long Shots	78	2042	397	.194	26.2	5.1
Medium Shots	78	4425	972	.220	56.7	12.4
Short Shots	78	3705	1470	.397	47.5	18.8
Total Shots	78	10172	2839	.280	130.4	36.4
Free Throws	78	2478	1383	.558	31.8	17.7

Score	No. of Games	Total Points	Average per Game
	78	7061	90.5

* A minor game is a non-conference or practice game in which the competition is not at its highest level.

This is a table that shows the record of both teams in 78 minor games in the same manner that Table XVIII-A shows the record of both teams in major games.

TABLE XX-A

SHOOTING BY TALL MEN

	No. of Players	No. of Games*	At- tempts	Goals	Shoot- ing Per- cent- age	Per Cent of All At- tempts Taken in Area	Per Cent of All Goals Made in Area
Long Area Shots	80	676	824	145	.176	9.4	5.6
Med. Area Shots	80	676	3322	750	.226	38.1	29.0
Short Area Shots	80	676	4576	1692	.370	52.5	65.4
Total Shots	80	676	8722	2587	.297	100.0	100.0

* Number of games in which players appeared. Many players played only parts of games, therefore use of number of games to determine average attempts and goals per game would be misleading and inaccurate.

This table shows the field-goal shooting performances of 80 college players from six feet four inches and taller in height, appearing in 676 games in seasons 1936–37 to 1948–49, inclusive. It shows the total number of attempts and goals scored by these men and also the totals in the long, medium, and short areas. It also gives shooting percentages and per cent of all attempts taken and goals scored in each area.

Glossary

A.A.U.—Amateur Athletic Union.

ABUSED AREA—The medium area where players seem to take more bad shots.

ALLEYS, OPENING UP—To open up a scoring lane or path to the basket.

ALL-ROUND PLAYER—A player who is expert in all phases of the game.

ANGLE, PROPER—Defensive term meaning the act of taking a position between the offensive player and the basket at a certain angle.

AREA, LONG—The area beyond a 24-foot radius from the basket.

AREA, MEDIUM—The area between a radius of 12 and 24 feet from the basket.

AREA, SHORT—The area within a radius of 12 feet from the basket.

AREAS—Certain designated parts of the playing court.

AREA-SCORING METHOD—A suggested method of awarding different points for field goals scored from different areas.

ASSIST—A pass made by a player that directly contributes to a field goal.

ATTEMPT—An attempt to score a goal; a shot.

BACK COURT—That part of the court between the center line and the end line behind a team's opponent's basket.

BALL-CONTROL GAME—A conservative offensive plan used to protect a lead; a percentage game.

BALL-HANDLING—Ability of the player to control the ball well in all situations.

BALL HAWK—A player who is expert in retrieving the ball; a ball recovery expert.

BASKET—The ring eighteen inches in diameter with white net, through which the ball is thrown to score a goal; also used interchangeably with field goal.

BASKET SHOOTING—Shooting the ball at the basket.

BASKET SHOOTING CHARTS—Charts or forms used to record attempts and goals.

BATTER'S BOX—Baseball term; the area designated by the batsman's lines in which the batter must stand while swinging at the ball.

BENCH—Section reserved for team officials and for players while not participating in the game.

BENCH A PLAYER—To remove a player from the game; to demote a player who has been a regular player by having him sit on the bench while another replaces him.

BENCH WARMER—A player who sits on the bench.

BOARDS—Basketball backboards.

BOTTLE UP—A defensive term which means to stop the offense from functioning effectively.

BOX SCORE—Summary of the game records.

BREAK, THE—The fast break.

BUCKET—Keyhole area; around the basket; bucket means basket.

CALL, CALLS—Referee's decisions.

CATCALLS—A term attributed to spectators' cheers that are unsportsmanlike. Remarks that are uncomplimentary.

CATCHING—The act of catching or receiving the ball.

CEILING—Top achievement; the ceiling has not been reached means the maximum has not been attained.

CENTER—Name of one of the positions on a basketball team.

CENTER JUMP—The two centers jump for the ball which is tossed up between them at the start of the game, at the start of the second half and at certain other times; a tip-off; a jump ball.

CHALK TALK—A meeting on basketball.

CHANGE OF PACE—The act of moving at different and alternating speeds over the court.

CHANGING MEN—A defensive term meaning that defensive players change assignments.

CHARGING—A personal foul caused by a player making personal contact by a charge into an opponent—more frequently committed by the offensive player.

CHART—A form on which objective or subjective data are recorded.

CHARTING—Recording of objective data during the course of a game or scrimmage.

CIRCUIT CLOUT—Basball term; a home run.

CLINCHER—A goal that seems to assure victory.

CLUTCH—A period when the game is close.

CLUTCH PLAYER—A player who plays well in the clutch or when the game is close.

COACH—One who teaches a team or squad the game of basketball.

CONFERENCE GAME—A game scheduled with a team in the same conference or league.

CONTROL GROUP—Players, teams, and games used in our recent five-year college study. The group consists of Yale University teams and its opponents.

CONVERTED FREE THROW OR SHOT—A free throw or shot that is successful; a goal.

COURT—The playing floor.

CRACKER BOX GYMNASIUM—A small gymnasium—under regulation size.

CRASHING THROUGH—A defensive term meaning that the defensive player stays directly with his assignment on screen plays by staying between his man and the screener.

CRIPPLE—A type of shot—an easy short shot.

CROSS SCREENING—Players cross to screen out opponents from basket on rebounds.

CROSS UP—The act of doing what the opponents do not expect.

CROWD PLEASER—A style of play or performance that is pleasing to the audience.

CUTAWAY—Offensive term meaning that player cuts for the basket after setting a screen. Used when defense changes assignments too fast.

CUTTER—A player who runs or cuts on the court, usually for the basket.

CUTTING PLAYS—Plays that use players who cut or run from one position to another.

DEAD BALL—A ball becomes dead after goals, when time expires ending a period, following referee's whistle when ball is in play, etc. (see rules book for complete list).

DEFENSE, ALL COURT—A style of defense in which players are guarded tightly in all parts of the court.

DEFENSE, COMBINATION—A combination of man-to-man and zone defense.

DEFENSE, FORCING—A pressing defense; a tight defense; an effort to force the offensive team into action.

DEFENSE, INDIVIDUAL—A player's individual defensive techniques such as defensive footwork, ball hawking, and guarding.

DEFENSE, KEYHOLE—A team defense that plays in the keyhole area and does not force play in the outer areas; a loose defense.

DEFENSE, LOOSE—A sagging defense; a defense that converges to the center; a defense that does not press.

DEFENSE, LOOSE, AWAY FROM THE BALL—A defense in which the defensive players guarding men not near the ball play well away from their men; used to congest the keyhole area.

DEFENSE, MAN-TO-MAN—A defense that gives each player a definite opponent to guard.

DEFENSIVE, SLIDING—A defense that enables players to stay with regular assignments.

DEFENSE, SWITCHING—A defense that permits players to change defensive assignments repeatedly.

DEFENSE, ZONE—A defense that gives each player an area of the court to cover.

DEFENSIVE BACKBOARD WORK—Defensive rebound techniques.

DEFENSIVE FOOTWORK—Various techniques of footwork employed by a player while on defense.

DEFENSIVE PERSONAL FOUL—A personal foul committed by a player while on defense.

DEFENSIVE PLAYER—A player on the team not in possession of the ball; a player attempting to prevent an opponent from scoring.

DISQUALIFY ON FOULS—The exclusion of a player from the game; mandatory after committing his fifth personal foul (or sixth in professional basketball).

DOGGED—A defensive term meaning the act whereby an opponent is guarded closely at all times.

DOUBLE FOUL—A situation in which two opponents foul each other simultaneously.

DOUBLE UP—Defensive term meaning to put two players against one.

DRAW THE DEFENSE OUT—An offensive plan to make the defensive players come to the outer areas of the court in order to relieve congestion near the basket.

DRIBBLE—Throwing, batting, bouncing, or rolling the ball and touching it again before it touches another player.

DRIBBLE, BROKEN—A discontinued dribble in which the ball comes to rest in one or both hands of the dribbler; a violation.

DRILLS—Exercises given to train players in basketball skills.

DRIVE IN—A player's effort to dribble hard toward the basket in an effort to score.

DROP OFF—Defensive term meaning to play loose or away from an opponent.

DUNKING—A word used to describe the action of a tall man who jumps high and reaches above the rim of the basket to drop the ball through the basket.

ERRORS, BASKETBALL—Loss of ball, and personal fouls.

FAKE—An offensive fundamental action that draws a defensive player out of position.

FAN—A spectator.

FAST BREAK—A system of team offense that attempts to advance the ball to the front court for scoring opportunities before the defense is organized.

FEED—A pass; to feed the ball to a player is to pass it to him.

FIELD—The playing floor.

FIGURE 8—An offensive plan in which all five players move in a manner that forms the figure 8.

FIRST STRING—The first squad or the first team.

FIVE-YEAR STUDY—Our recent study of 132 college games from 1949–50 through the 1953–54 season.

FLOOR PLAY—General ability in playing the game offensively aside from shooting, such as ball handling, passing, and dribbling.

FOOTWORK—Various movements of the basketball player in which the feet are used.

FORWARD—Name of one of the positions on a basketball team. Originally thought of as an offensive player who played in the front court.   Forwards and guards now perform similar duties.

FORCE PLAY—To press the team with the ball in an effort to make them play faster.

FOUL AREA—Keyhole area.

FOUL, DELIBERATE—An intentional foul.

FOUL OUT—Being forced to leave the game after committing five personal fouls.

FOUL, PERSONAL—A player foul which involves contact with an opponent while the ball is in play or after the ball is in the possession of a player for a throw-in from out-of-bounds.

FOUL, TECHNICAL—A foul that does not involve contact; not a personal foul.

FOULING SPECIALISTS—Players who are in the game to commit intentional personal fouls—which is a deplorable practice.

FOUR BAGGER—A baseball term; a home run.

FREE BALL—A ball not in possession of either team that is in play.

FREE SHOOTING GAME—A game in which many field goal attempts are tried.

FREE THROW—Privilege given a player to score one point by an unhindered throw for goal from a position directly behind the free-throw line.

FREE-THROW ATTEMPT—A try or attempt or shot at the basket made in an effort to score a free throw.

FREE THROWER—A player in the act of shooting a free throw.

FREE-THROW LANE—Areas at each end of the court; an area between the foul line and the end line.

FREE-THROW LINE—A line fifteen feet out from the basket from which free throws are attempted.

FREE-THROW PERCENTAGE—Percentage of free throws made; number of free-throw attempts divided into number of free throws scored; free-throw shooting average.

FREEZE THE BALL—To hold the ball and make no effort to score.

FRONT COURT—That part of the court between the end line behind a team's own basket and the center line.

FUNDAMENTALS—Elementary skills of the game such as dribbling, shooting, passing, and similar skills.

FUNDAMENTALS, GROUP—Fundamentals executed by two, three, or four on a side.

FUNDAMENTALS, INDIVIDUAL—Fundamentals executed by one player or one player on a side.

GALLOP—A term used to describe a player running at full speed.

GAMES ABROAD—Games played away from home.

GIVE-AND-GO—An offensive plan in which players pass the ball to a teammate and run for the basket or to another position— usually for a return pass.

GLASS BOARDS—Backboards made of glass.

GOAL—Made when the ball enters the basket from above and remains in or passes through.

GOAL, FIELD—Goal scored from the field or playing floor other than a free throw; a field goal counts two points.

GOAL, FREE-THROW—A goal scored from the free-throw line as a result of a penalty. A free-throw goal counts one point.

GOING THROUGH—A defensive term meaning that a player stays with his assignment on screen plays by going through a gap between his defensive teammate and the screener.

GUARD—Name of one of the positions on a basketball team. Originally thought of as a defensive player who played in the back court. Guards and forwards now perform similar duties.

HAND OFF—Act of handing the ball to another player.

HEART, THE—Will to win. Competitive ability.

HEAVE—A goal attempt—a shot.

HEIGHT LIMIT—A proposed plan that would bar players more than a specified number of feet and inches tall from the game.

HELD BALL—When two players have one or both hands on the ball so firmly that neither can gain possession without undue roughness. Ball is tossed between the two players who jump for it. Also used interchangeably with "jump ball."

HELD-BALL RECOVERY—A retrieve of the ball on a jump for the ball following a held ball.

HOLD THE COURT—Term applied to basketball shoes. Shoes that will not slip on the basketball floor.

HOME COURT—The playing floor of the home team.

HOME RUN OF BASKETBALL—A long shot that, it is suggested, might count three points instead of two points as at present.

HOMER—A home run in baseball; a person who is partial to the home team.

"HOT" OR "COLD" PLAYER OR TEAM—An inconsistent player or team; one who does well for a time and then performs poorly for a time.

INTENTIONAL FOULING—The act of committing a personal foul deliberately.

INTERCEPTION—Taking the ball away from an opposing player or team while the ball is in play; for example, an intercepted pass.

INTRA-SQUAD—Between squad members. Groups that are members of the same squad.

INTRAMURAL—Between two groups that are members of the same institution.

JUMP BALL—A jump ball takes place when the official tosses the ball up between two opposing players.

JUMP, GETTING THE JUMP ON A TEAM—The act of getting ahead of the other team at the start.

KEYHOLE—The areas from the end lines inside of the free-throw lanes including the free-throw circles.

KEY MAN—A valuable player.

LEACHING—A defensive term meaning to guard an opponent closely at all times.

LEFTY—Left-hand shot at the basket.

LET FLY—To shoot at the basket in a careless manner.

LIVE BALL—A ball is live after it is put in play such as when it leaves official's hands on the toss for a jump ball, when a throw-in touches a player inbounds or when ball is placed at disposal of a free thrower.

LOOSE BALL—A ball not in possession of either team.

LOSS OF BALL—Possession of the ball changing from one team to the other.

MAJOR GAMES—A conference or league game or the equivalent.

MAJOR SPORTS—Generally regarded as those sports that have the most participants and spectator appeal, such as football, basketball, baseball, track, swimming, and hockey.

MAKE DEFENSE SHOW—An offensive plan to cause the defense to make the first move or to commit itself.

MATERIAL—Players available to a coach to work with or teach.

MENTAL HAZARD—A disconcerting factor that a player has to contend with that may affect his mental attitude during the game.

MID-COURT—Center area of playing floor.

MINOR GAME—A non-conference or practice game.

MONEY PLAYER—A player who is a good competitor when the game is close.

MULTIPLE FREE THROWS—A succession of free throws attempted by the same team.

NATIONAL FEDERATION—The National Federation of State High School Athletic Associations.

NATIONAL INVITATIONAL—A basketball tournament sponsored by the Metropolitan Sports Writers of New York City.

N.B.A.—National Basketball Association—a professional league.

N.C.A.A.—National Collegiate Athletic Association.

NEUTRAL COURT—A playing floor that is the home court of neither team.

NON-CONFERENCE GAME—A game scheduled with a team outside one's own conference.

OBSERVATIONS, OBJECTIVE—Observations that can be made by two or more persons with the same results.

OBSERVATIONS, SUBJECTIVE—General observations not included under objective observations; in this study, subjective observations are made by a basketball expert.

OBSERVER—One who watches the game as an analyst; a recorder of objective or subjective data; a scout.

OFFENSE, INDIVIDUAL—A player's individual offensive techniques such as faking, dribbling, passing, and shooting.

OFFENSIVE BACKBOARD WORK—Offensive rebound techniques.

OFFENSIVE FOOTWORK—Various pivots, stops, and turns executed by a player while on offense.

OFFENSIVE PERSONAL FOUL—A personal foul committed by a player while on offense.

OFFENSIVE PLAYER—A player on the team that has possession of the ball; a player attempting to score.

OFFICIALS—The referee and umpire of the game. They are assisted by two timekeepers and two scorekeepers.

ONE-ONE (OR ONE PLUS ONE) RULE—A rule which from 1952–53 through 1953–54 awarded, under certain conditions, an extra free throw if the first was unsuccessful.

OPPONENTS—Players or teams to be played against.

ORIGINAL STUDY—Our study of 460 college games from 1936–37 through 1948–49 upon which Part I of the first edition was based.

OUTFIT—A team.

OUT-OF-BOUNDS—The territory beyond the sides and ends of the court.

OUT-OF-BOUNDS PLAYS—Offensive plays employed when the team has possession of the ball for a throw in from out-of-bounds.

OUTSIDE TEAM OR PLAYER—A team or player that shoots well from the long area—outside a 24-foot radius from the basket. A team that shoots well "from outside" shoots well from the long area.

OVERTIME—An extra playing period in effect after the regular period of the game, when a game is tied.

PASS—PASSING—Tossing or throwing the ball from one player to the other.

PASS, BASEBALL—A one-hand pass, similar to a baseball throw, usually a long pass.

PASS, BOUNCE—A pass in which the ball is bounced once before it reaches its destination.

PASS, CHEST—A pass with one or two hands that starts with the ball held near the chest.

PASS, HOOK—A wrist action, one-hand pass made over the head.

PASS, ONE-HAND—A pass in which the ball is passed or tossed with one hand.

PASS, ROLL—A pass in which the ball is rolled on the floor.

PASSIVE DEFENSE—A non-aggressive, loose defense.

PEP-TALK—Coach's remarks to a team prior to, during, or between halves of a game to stimulate or cause greater effort.

PERCENTAGE BASKETBALL—A style of play that stresses ball control and taking only close shots where the shooting percentage should be high.

PERCENTAGE, SHOOTING—Number of shots or attempts divided into number of goals or baskets scored.

PIVOT—A step or steps taken by a player in different directions with one foot while the other foot is held in place.

PIVOT AREA—Keyhole area.

PIVOT, DOUBLE—An offensive plan that uses two pivot or post men.

PIVOT, FRONT—A pivot in which the player turns or pivots forward.

PIVOT MAN—An offensive player who plays in pivot area; keyhole area.

PIVOT, REAR—A pivot in which the player turns or pivots to the rear.

PIVOT, SINGLE—An offensive plan that has only one man playing offensively in the keyhole area.

PIVOT, TRIPLE—An offensive plan that uses three pivot or post men.

PLAYER NUMBER—Number on jersey of the player.

PLAYING TECHNIQUE—Skill employed by the players.

PLAY-MAKER—A player who excels in creating situations that will enable his teammates to score.

PLAY-OFFS—Games played at the end of the regular schedule— usually to determine a championship.

PLAYS—Offensive plans of a team to score goals.

PLAY THE BALL—To press or force defensively; to go after free balls.

PLAY THE PERCENTAGE—The policy of playing by certain established standards; a conservative plan.

POINTS—Credit for goals; free-throw goals count one point each and field goals count two points each.

POINTS-RESPONSIBLE-FOR—Points that a defensive player permits his opponent to score.

POST—Keyhole area. Player assuming the position of a post.

POST, DOUBLE—An offensive plan that uses two post men.

POST MAN—A player who takes a position similar to that of a post so that teammates will cut past him and cause their defensive players to come in contact with him.

POST, TRIPLE—An offensive plan that uses three post men.

PRESS—PRESSING—To play a tight defense; to play close to the player with the ball in an attempt to take the ball from him.

PRESSURE ON PLAYERS, OFFICIALS—Various factors such as public opinion, competition, publicity, game outcome and numerous other influencing factors that one is subjected to in carrying out his assignment.

PROBLEM GUARD (OR PLAYER)—One who presents particular and difficult problems.

QUICK CHANGE—Defensive term in which players change defensive assignments quickly on screen plays.

RATING SCALE—A rating plan by which a player is rated in relation to others on the squad.

REBOUND—A retrieve of the ball from the backboard after an unsuccessful shot at the basket.

REBOUND, DEFENSIVE—Retrieve of the ball from the opponent's backboard.

REBOUNDER—A player who retrieves the ball from the backboard; a retriever of rebounds.

REBOUND, OFFENSIVE—A retrieve of the ball from a team's own backboard.

REBOUND, TEAM—A rebound that is awarded the team; one not recovered by an individual player.

RECENT STUDY—Our study of 132 college games from 1949–50 through the 1953–54 season; our five-year study.

RECOVERY—A retrieve of a ball not in possession of either team or a retrieve of a ball in possession of an opponent.

REGULAR—A player on the first team; one who plays regularly.

RESERVE—A substitute player.

RETRIEVING—Gaining possession of a free or loose ball.

REVERSE—Offensive act of player who makes a quick stop and reverses his direction.

ROAD TRIP—A trip made to play basketball games away from home.

ROLL—Offensive term meaning that player turns for basket after setting screen.   Used in similar manner as the cutaway.

ROLL, DOUBLE—A roll by two players consecutively.

ROOTERS—Enthusiastic spectators.

RUN OUT THE TIME—Practice of stalling or using delaying tactics until time expires ending a period.

SCANDALS—The discovery in 1950 of gambling and games purposely won or lost in college basketball.

SCORE—Point or points resulting from a goal or goals.

SCORE, RUNNING—The progressive score of each team during the game, point by point.

SCORING PEAK—The highest possible scoring achievement.

SCOUT—One who watches the game as an analyst; a recorder of objective or subjective data; an observer.

SCOUTING—Analyzing individual and team performances, objectively and subjectively.

SCOUT REPORT—Recorded objective and subjective observations of either or both teams during the game.

SCREEN—To set up a post on which a teammate may screen his defensive player; to screen a player from an area.

SCREEN, MOVING—A situation in which the player doing the screening is on the move and not stationary.

SCREEN, STATIONARY—A situation in which the player doing the screening is in a stationary position while screening.

SCRIMMAGE—An intra-squad game.

SEAT—To accommodate with a seat. A pavilion that will seat a certain number of people will accommodate that number.

SECOND GUESSING—The custom of offering the correct way of doing something after it is done; having the right answer after something fails.

SECOND-HALF TEAM—A team that plays better in the second half.

SET PLAYS—Offensive team plays used to attack a team defense that is set or organized.

SETTLE DOWN—The state of a team or player when nervous tension is overcome and the performance is normal.

SHOOT—To try for a goal by tossing, throwing, or tapping the ball toward the basket.

SHOOTING AVERAGE—Percentage of shots made; similar to batting average in baseball.

SHOT—A try for a goal by tossing, throwing, or tapping the ball toward the basket.

SHOT, BACKBOARD—A shot in which the ball hits the backboard before going through the basket.

SHOT, BAD—A shot that is not fundamentally correct.

SHOT, BLOCKED—A shot deflected by a defensive player.

SHOT, CHEST—A two-hand shot that starts from a chest position; usually a set shot.

SHOT, EARNED—A good shot; a shot that the defense cannot block.

SHOT, FIELD—A shot from the field or playing floor other than a free throw; a field-goal attempt.

SHOT, GOOD—A shot that is fundamentally correct; a shot that cannot be guarded; a shot that is accurate.

SHOT, HOOK—A wrist-action, one-hand shot made over the head.

SHOT, INSIDE—A player who shoots short area shots. Also, shots taken in short areas.

SHOT, LAY-IN—A short shot off the backboard or laid just over the rim of the basket.

SHOT, LAY-UP—A short shot in which the ball is banked off the backboard.

SHOT, LONG—A shot taken in the long area, outside of a twenty-four foot radius from the basket. This area is considered the two-hand shot area.

SHOT, MEDIUM—A shot taken in the medium area between a radius of twelve feet and twenty-four feet from the basket.

SHOT, ONE-HAND—A shot in which the ball is pushed or thrown toward the basket by one hand.

SHOT, OUTSIDE—A player who shoots long-area shots. Also, a shot taken in the outer area.

SHOT, OVERHEAD—A type of shot in which the starting position of the ball is over the head.

SHOT, PIVOT—A shot taken following a pivot or turn by the shooter; usually taken in the keyhole area.

SHOT, PRACTICE—A shot taken in practice sessions where no defense is encountered; not a scrimmage or game shot.

SHOT, REBOUND—A shot that is the direct result of a rebound.

SHOT, SET—A shot taken from a stationary position.

SHOT, SHORT—A shot taken in the short area within a radius of twelve feet from the basket.

SHOT, SOUND—A good shot; fundamentally correct.

SHOT, UNDERHAND—A shot in which the ball starts from a position below the waist.

SHOW, MAKE A TEAM—A plan to make the opposing team lead with its attack or make the initial move or show its intent.

SHOW, PUT ON A—To play a spectacular type of game to please the audience.

SLAM BANGERS—Offensive term meaning players that are careless in their play. Erratic play.

SLEEPER—A player who ignores defense and waits only for opportunity to score. Player sent down court quickly to catch defense asleep.

SLOW BREAK—Offensive term meaning a system where team plays slowly and attacks defense after it is organized. A ball-control game.

SPARK PLUG—A fiery player who instills team with courage and desire to win.

SPECTATOR—One who watches the game as a non-participant.

SPLIT THE POST—Two offensive players cutting on either side of a post man.

SPORTSWRITERS—Gentlemen of the press who report the games to the public and who write about the game.

STALL—To keep possession of the ball and make no effort to score.

STANCE—Position of the arms, legs, and body.

STARTS—A type of footwork. Method of starting to run on the court.

STEAL THE BALL—To take the ball away from an opponent.

STOPS—A type of footwork. Method of stopping on the court.

STRATEGY—Plans, either offensive or defensive, to be used in playing a game.

STREAKS IN SCORING—Inconsistent scoring. A team that has periods of heavy and then light scoring scores in streaks.

STYLE OF PLAY—General pattern or plan that a team employs on offense or defense.

STYLE OF SHOOTING—The form or style a player employs in shooting, such as the one-hand shot, the underhand shot, and the hook shot.

SUBSTITUTE—A player who enters the game to replace a regular player.

SYSTEM—General offensive or defensive plan a team employs.

TAKE-OFF—The last position of the feet while in contact with the floor, when a player is in the act of shooting.

TAKE OVER—A defensive term meaning that a player takes a teammate's defensive assignment when necessary.

TEAMWORK—Ability of players on a team to play well together.

TENSE UP—Condition of a player, meaning to stiffen. Not relaxed. When a player is not able to act in a well coordinated manner.

TEN-SECOND RULE—Rule whereby it is necessary to advance the ball from the back court to the front court within ten seconds. Penalty for infraction is loss of ball to opponents.

THIRTEEN-YEAR STUDY—Our study of 460 college games from 1936–37 through 1948–49; our original study.

THREE AGAINST TWO—A situation in which three offensive players are against two defensive players.

THREE-SECOND RULE—Rule that makes it illegal for an offensive player to stand in the keyhole area from the foul line to the end line for more than three seconds.   Penalty is loss of ball to opponents.

TIE-UP—When a player causes a held ball to be called while it is in control of an opponent.

TIME LIMIT—The rule proposal whereby the offensive team is limited in the length of time it may retain possession of the ball without attempting a field goal.

TIMING—Method of jumping at the proper time to retrieve the ball.

TIP-OFF—A center jump.

TIP OR TIPPING—The act of tipping the ball with the fingertips; a tap.

TIP-UP—A goal attempt made by the player tipping the ball toward the basket.

TOSS—A shot at the basket; also, a pass.

TRAILER MAN—A player who follows behind the ball as a safety man.

TRAILING TEAM—The team that is behind in the score.

TRAVELING—Running with the ball; a violation.

TRAVELING SQUAD—Group of players who are included on basketball trips.

TROUBLE MAKER—A player who has a poor attitude.   One who causes dissension on the squad.

TURN, REVERSE—A type of footwork where the player turns to go in the opposite direction.

TURN, SIDE—A type of footwork where the player turns to go to the right or left side.

TWO AGAINST ONE—A situation in which two offensive players are against one defensive player.

TWO-SHOT PENALTY—The penalty for certain personal fouls that awards two free-throw attempts.

UNDER FIRE—In major competition.

UNDERHAND TOSS—A free-throw attempt in which the ball is released through an underhand motion. An underhand shot.

UNDERSTUDY—A substitute.

UNORTHODOX SHOTS—Field-goal attempts that are of an uncommon or unusual style.

VIOLATION—Certain infractions of the rules not classed as fouls, such as running with the ball, illegal dribble, kicking the ball, and similar offenses. Penalty for most violations is loss of ball to opponents.

VISITING COURT—The playing floor of the visiting or traveling team.

WEAVE—A method of players moving from one position to another so that they exchange positions in a manner resembling a weave.

WHEN CHIPS ARE DOWN—A period when game is close.

WHISTLE-TOOTING—A rather critical term applied to officials who blow the whistle too much.

WILD SHOOTING—Hurried or careless shooting.

WORK IN—The plan of attempting to create situations which will make possible field-goal attempts close to the basket.

WORK OUT—A practice.

WORK THE BALL IN—An offensive plan to get shots in the short area near the basket.

WRIST ACTION—The ability of a player to use his wrists in a coordinated manner in passing, catching, shooting and similar techniques.

Y.M.C.A.—Young Men's Christian Association.

ZONE—Refers to zone defense.

ZONE 2–1–2—A zone defense that stations two men near the basket (one on each side), one man in the center, and two men in the outer area.

ZONE 2–3—A zone defense that stations three men near the basket and two men in the outer area.

ZONE 3–2—A zone defense that stations two men near the basket (one on each side) and three men in the outer area.

ZONE 1–3–1—A zone defense that stations one man under the basket, 3 men across the court about even with the free-throw line, and one man in the outer area.

Annotated Bibliography
of Basketball Books

EVERY BASKETBALL COACH SHOULD BE FAMILIAR WITH THE literature in the field. This is important not only for a knowledge of the history and progress of the game, but for all coaching purposes. It is also important for basketball scouting. Only through a thorough knowledge of the game as expressed by those actively engaged in the field will coaches be able to analyze the game. Players, sports writers, spectators, officials, and others interested in the game should also do some reading in the field.

Our first edition carried an annotated bibliography of all books written on basketball, to the best of our knowledge, from the game's origin through 1948. We now include all books through September, 1954, if they have been listed in the *Cumulative Book Index* or have been brought to our attention if privately published.

The literature in the field of basketball has become so great that several categories with suggestions now seem appropriate.

Basketball is growing fast and changing every year. A book more than ten years old, while it may contain much material still usable, cannot possibly be adequate for the reader who wants up-to-date technical information. Our first category, therefore, includes books published from 1945 through 1954.

The ten years prior to the 1945–1954 period saw some radical changes in the game, such as the elimination of the center jump following goals. A change in literature naturally followed and some good books were written in this era. Our second category includes books published from 1935 to 1944, inclusive, and these books are recommended as supplementary material.

Books published prior to 1935 are recommended mainly as historical references and comprise the third group in our bibliography.

A fourth category includes books on basketball of a nontechnical nature that are not text books. Included are the known story books for juveniles that have flooded the market recently. Some of these books, unfortunately, are of questionable character value and should be carefully reviewed before purchasing.

Our final recommendation would be to acquire as first preference recent books produced by well known and established publishers. Their insistence on up-to-date material and high quality of work makes the difference. Some good books are privately published but they should be reviewed before adding them to one's library.

Group I—1945–1954 inclusive

This list includes recent text books and other books essential to coaches, players, or others interested in technical basketball information.

American Association for Health, Physical Education, and Recreation, National Section on Women's Athletics, *Official Basketball and Official Rating Guide for Women and Girls.* Annual publication.

Allen, Forrest C., and Harold E. Foster and Edward S. Hickey, *How to Improve Your Basketball.* Chicago: The Athletic Institute, 1950. 80 pp.

A booklet by three outstanding coaches representing the National Association of Basketball Coaches. Covers fundamentals with small but numerous illustrations and includes brief comment on the history of basketball, rules, common terms, and suggested bibliography. Very good for the young player.

Anderson, Forrest, *Basketball Techniques Illustrated*. New York: A. S. Barnes and Company, 1952. 95 pp.

A book covering the fundamentals, with drawings rather than photographs. Mr. Anderson formerly coached at Bradley University and now coaches at Michigan State College.

Balch, J. W., *California Offense for Basketball*, rev. ed. Santa Barbara, California: The Author, 1949. (Book not reviewed.)

Balch, J. W., *Theory for Basketball Offense*. Santa Barbara, California: The Author, 1949. (Book not reviewed.)

Bancroft, Jesse H., *Games*, rev. ed. New York: The Macmillan Company, 1950, pp. 412–414, 450–465, Basketball.

List of lead-up games for basketball; games of basketball skills for all age levels through elementary grades; regular basketball as it applies to elementary school children.

Bee, Clair F., *Winning Basketball Plays*. New York: A. S. Barnes and Company, 1950. 176 pp.

Mr. Bee edits basketball plays, well diagrammed, by leading basketball coaches of the United States.

Browning, Omar, *How to Get the Most Out of Basketball; for the Spectator, for the Player, for the Coach*. Bartlesville, Oklahoma: Phillips Petroleum Co., 1949. 70 pp.

A pamphlet on the game prepared by Mr. Browning while coach of the Phillips Oilers, National A.A.U. champions. Mr. Browning was also Head Coach of the U.S. Olympic basketball team in 1948.

Browning, William, *Basketball: Fundamentals, Defense, Offense, Officiating, Coaching, Rules*, 2nd ed. New York: Pitman, 1952. 156 pp. Illustrated.

A booklet in Pitman's games and recreation series.

Bruce, Robert M., *Annotated Bibliography of Basketball Literature*. The National Association of Basketball Coaches, 1947. 151 pp.

An indexed, annotated bibliography of books and periodical publications on basketball through April, 1947. An excellent reference and source of information. Robert Bruce did this work as a master's thesis at Springfield College.

Buchanan, Lamont, *The Story of Basketball in Text and Pictures*. New York: Stephen Paul, 1948. 188 pp.

A very interesting book with many large illustrations of basketball from its infancy through the 1948 season. Highlights of various periods described. Chapter on statistics lists championship teams, All America selections, and other similar information.

Bunn, John W., and others, *The Art of Officiating Sports*. New York: Prentice-Hall, Inc., 1950. 388 pp.

Includes basketball officiating. The most recent and up-to-date source of information on officiating. Highly recommended.

Bunn, John W., *The Art of Basketball Officiating*. Springfield, Massachusetts: M. F. Stibbs, 1948.

A modern and much needed book covering all phases of basketball officiating.

Bunn, John W., *Scientific Principles of Coaching*. New York: Prentice-Hall, Inc., 1955. 306 pp.

Includes a chapter on principles of physics and mechanics as related to fundamental basketball skills.

Chamber's Encyclopedia. New York: Oxford University Press, 1952. Vol. 2, p. 150.

One very short paragraph on the origin, history, and rules of basketball. Not a good source for information about the game.

Colliers Encyclopedia. New York: P. F. Colliers and Son Corporation, 1950. Vol. 3, pp. 223–227.

Most complete encyclopedia coverage of basketball. Five pages devoted to the origin, rules, officiating, rule changes, methods of play, offensive and defensive skills, team offense and defense, outstanding teams, and women's basketball. Includes a court diagram and illustrations of officials' signals.

Converse Rubber Company, *Basketball Yearbook*. Malden, Massachusetts: Converse Rubber Company. Annual publication.

Records and pictures of leading college and high school teams; articles on basketball by leading coaches; Chuck Taylor's All America selections; national tournament summaries. A valuable basketball booklet for all coaches even though advertising is the motive. Back copies should be kept for reference.

Dean, Everett S., *Progressive Basketball*. New York: Prentice-Hall, Inc., 1950. 271 pp. Illustrated.

First published at Stanford University in 1942. The new and revised edition is one of the best texts on the game. All departments of the game are covered together with coaching methods and philosophy. Mr. Dean coached at Indiana and Stanford before retiring in 1951.

Durbin, Brice, *All American Basketball Drills, Practices and Mental Qualities*. Columbus, Kansas: Portrait Publications, 1945. Revised 1947, 1953.   61 pp.

This pamphlet deals more with the values and ideals of the game than playing techniques.   Part One—All American Ideals; Part Two—Mental Qualities; Part Three—Drills and Practices; Part Four—An Understanding Mind.   Contents are partly based on results of questionnaire from 88 college players who received All America recognition in 1953.   Mental qualities of a great competitor are from recommendations of six coaches or athletic directors.   No illustrations or index.

Durbin, Brice, *Portrait of a Basketball Player*. Burns, Kansas: News Printing Company, 1947.   32 pp.

A pamphlet on the philosophy of basketball; values to participants; ideals; not a text on techniques.

Encyclopedia Americana.   New York, Chicago: Americana Corporation, 1952.   Vol. 3, pp. 312–313.

A very much improved section on basketball over earlier editions.   This one is by Irving Marsh of the New York *Herald Tribune* and briefly but adequately covers the origin, history, rules, rule changes, and general development of the game over the years.

Encyclopaedia Britannica.   Chicago, Toronto, London: Encyclopaedia Britannica Inc., 1951.   Vol. 3, pp. 181–182.

A more complete treatment of the game than in earlier editions. Paragraphs are devoted to origin, history, rules, philosophy, strategy, equipment, popularity, and major developments of the game.

Gullion, Blair, *One Hundred Drills for Teaching Basketball Fundamentals*.   Washington University, St. Louis: The Author, 1933. Revised 1953.   52 pp.

A monograph featuring practice drills as a method of teaching fundamentals and improving skills.   Includes 94 diagrams.

Gullion, Blair, *Techniques and Tactics of Basketball Defense*. Washington University, St. Louis: The Author, 1951.   200 pp.

One of the author's basketball monographs dealing exclusively with defense.   Includes 63 diagrams and 23 pictures.

Healey, William A., *Coaching and Managing High School Basketball*, 3rd ed.   Danville, Illinois: Interstate Printing Company, 1952.   194 pp.

Designed for the high school coach. History and growth of basketball; fundamentals, team offense and defense; suggestions to coaches; basketball tests; purchase and care of equipment; recent developments in basketball, are all well covered. Practical and easy to understand. Diagrams, illustrations, bibliography. Distributed by the National Federation of State High School Athletic Associations, Chicago, and by A. S. Barnes and Company, New York.

Hobson, Howard A., *Basketball Illustrated*. New York: A. S. Barnes and Company, 1948. 86 pp.

A well illustrated elementary book for boys and young coaches. Recommended for the beginner. Covers all fundamentals thoroughly. Gives examples of offensive plays and defensive formations. Features training, conditioning, and self-testing activities for the player. 102 illustrations; 14 diagrams.

Hobson, Howard A., *Scientific Basketball*, 2nd ed. New York: Prentice-Hall, Inc., 1955. 268 pp. Illustrated.

The only basketball book devoted exclusively to objective measurements and subjective observations with their various implications. Shooting percentages are a special feature. Includes special study of 592 college games with supplementary material from N.C.A.A., high school, and professional games. Chapters for the coach, player, spectator, official, and sports reporter.

Hobson, Howard A., *The All America Basketball Player Record and Scout Book*. New Haven, Conn.: Walker-Rackliff Co., 1948.

Hobson, Howard A., *The Official Basketball Scout and Record Book*. New Haven, Conn.: Walker-Rackliff Co., 1948.

The above two books are not texts but are for recording player and team achievements for game and season reports. Each covers 35 games. They are included in this bibliography because they supplement the material in the author's text, *Scientific Basketball*.

Hobson, Howard A., *Thirteen Basic Basketball Shots*. New Haven, Conn.: The Seamless Rubber Company, 1952. 26 pp.

An illustrated booklet covering the various types of shooting in basketball with instructions and suggestions.

Holman, Nathan, *Holman on Basketball*. New York: Crown Publishers, Inc., 1950. 323 pp. Illustrated.

A good book for any basketball coach. History and progress of the game from its origin; fundamentals covered thoroughly; team offense and defense with examples from other coaches' systems; illustrated; indexed.

International Amateur Basketball Federation, *Official Basketball Rules for Men as Adopted by International Basketball Federation for the Olympiad*. New York: Amateur Athletic Union of United States. Published every four years.

    Gives official international rules.

Lawrence, H. B., and G. I. Fox, *Basketball for Girls and Women*. New York: McGraw-Hill Book Company, Inc., 1954. 254 pp. Illustrated.

    The latest book on girls' basketball.

McCracken, Branch, *Indiana Basketball*. New York: Prentice-Hall, Inc., 1955. 210 pp. Illustrated.

    A new book by the head coach at Indiana University, Big Ten champions in 1953 and 1954. Includes chapters on conditioning and training, scouting, and practice sessions, as well as good coverage of individual and team skills.

Meissner, Wilhelmine E., ed., *Official Basketball and Officials Rating Guide for Women and Girls, Containing Rules*. New York: A. S. Barnes and Company. 112 pp. Annual publication.

    Published for National Section on Women's Athletics of the American Association for Health, Physical Education and Recreation.

    Standards for women's basketball; progressive basketball programs for grades one to twelve; basketball in service programs; officials rated for each state; official basketball rules and interpretations; selected bibliography. The first requisite for coach or teacher of basketball; also valuable for players and spectators.

    This is an annual publication. Back copies should be kept for reference.

Meissner, Wilhelmine E., and Elizabeth Y. Myers, *Basketball for Girls*, rev. ed. New York: A. S. Barnes and Company, 1950. 87 pp.

    Fundamentals thoroughly covered; offense and defense for each player; equipment, fundamentals of teaching; officiating; diagrams and illustrations. Modern and practical. One of the best books on girls' basketball.

Morley, Leroy, and others, *Fundamentals and Techniques for Winning Basketball*. Danville, Illinois: School Aid Company, 1951. 117 pp. Illustrated. (Book not available for review.)

National Collegiate Athletic Bureau, *The Official Basketball Guide*. New York: The Author. Annual publication. Approximately 270 pp.

The official rules of the National Basketball Committee are given in a separate attached part of the *Guide;* comprising about 40 pages, this section may be purchased separately. The rest of the *Guide* includes college game results of the previous year, schedules of the next season, records, news items of conferences, and other similar information. A must for all coaches and of great value to players, sports writers, and others interested in the game. Mr. Oswald Tower, Andover, Massachusetts, edits the official rules book and also acts as the official interpreter of the rules.

National Federation of State High School Athletic Associations, *Official Basketball Rules.* Chicago: The Author. Annual publication. Approximately 65 pp.

A publication of the official basketball rules of the National Basketball Committee. Intended for high school use. Includes records and statistics of high school basketball with state tournament results of the previous year. Back copies should be kept for reference.

National Federation of State High School Athletic Associations, *Basketball Case Book.* Chicago: The Author. Annual publication. Approximately 106 pp.

Edited by Mr. H. V. Porter and Mr. Oswald Tower. Official rule interpretations are given through the use of more than 500 play situations. Very helpful for coach and player.

National Federation of State High School Athletic Associations, *Basketball Player Handbook.* Chicago: The Author. Annual publication. Approximately 50 pp.

A booklet edited by Mr. H. V. Porter and others. Divided into five parts: the rules, problems and administration; basketball play situations; duties of players; pre-game training; and game administration.

Newsom, H. A., *Basketball for the High School Coach and the Physical Education Teacher.* Dubuque, Iowa: W. C. Brown, 1952. 164 pp. Illustrated. (Book not available for review.)

Quaker Oats National Basketball Board, *How to Play Basketball.* Chicago: The Quaker Oats Co. Annual publication. 30 pp.

A booklet published each year covering the fundamentals and plays from notes of outstanding coaches serving on the Quaker Oats Basketball Board.

Rupp, Adolph F., *Championship Basketball.* New York: Prentice-Hall, Inc., 1948. 239 pp.

Adolph Rupp's philosophy and system of basketball as used at the University of Kentucky. A very complete basketball book covering all phases of the game. Coaching stories are a feature. 107 diagrams. Index.

Adolph Rupp has coached National Championship teams at the University of Kentucky. He was the United States College Olympic Coach in 1948.

Teauge, Bertha, *Basketball for Girls*. Ada, Oklahoma: The Author, 1953.

A booklet by the coach at Bying High School in Ada, Oklahoma.

V-Five Association of America, *Basketball*, rev. ed. Annapolis: United States Naval Institute, 1950.

This book is one of a series of books on sports first written during World War II primarily for service programs. The revised edition includes ideas of several basketball coaches and has value as a text for the coach. Distributed by A. S. Barnes, New York.

Welsh, Ray, *Winning Basketball*. Minneapolis: Burgess Publishing Company, 1947. 144 pp.

The author edits offenses and defenses by 80 high school and college coaches of the United States.

Group II—1935-1944 inclusive

This list includes text books and similar publications that may be useful as supplementary material to books listed in Group I.

Allen, Forrest C., *Better Basketball*. New York: Whittlesey House, McGraw-Hill Book Company, 1937. 490 pp.

Probably the most complete book on basketball. Dr. Allen is one of the best-known coaches; he has been head coach at the Uni-verversity of Kansas for many years.

All fundamentals, styles of offense and defense, subordinate plays are fully covered. Section on conditioning, training, first aid, bandaging, and taping is very complete. Basketball Tales is an interesting and unique feature. Book recommended for all coaches.

Allen, Forrest C., and others, *Rating Basketball Players; Their Batting and Fielding Averages Computed*. University of Kansas, Lawrence, Kansas: The Author, 1939. 25 pp.

Mimeographed publication of players' records at University of Kansas during seasons of 1937–38 and 1938–39. Attempts to rate players on shooting percentages and other fundamental statistics. Valuable and interesting study for all coaches.

Barbour, Ralph Henry, and LeMar Sarra, *How to Play Better Basketball.* New York: Appleton-Century Publishing Company, 1941. 111 pp.

Written for junior and senior high school boys. Fundamentals, offensive and defensive plays, team management, list of player hints, how to officiate. Play diagrams; glossary.

Bee, Clair F., *Drills and Fundamentals.* New York: A. S. Barnes and Company, 1942. 111 pp.

Clair Bee's idea of basketball fundamentals and how to teach them. Not complete in details. Illustrations and diagrams. No bibliography.

Bee, Clair F., *Man to Man Defense and Attack.* New York: A. S. Barnes and Company, 1942. 118 pp.

A complicated, detailed analysis of certain styles of man-to-man defense and offensive attacks for each. Recommended for the college coach. Diagrams are very complicated. Illustrations are interesting but do not always explain the subject. No bibliography.

Bee, Clair F., *The Science of Coaching.* New York: A. S. Barnes and Company, 1942. 101 pp.

A practical book for the basketball coach. Chapters on The Coach, The Player, Conditioning and Training, Practice and Coaching Methods, and Game Strategy and Tactics are all good. Offensive and defensive basketball covered rather generally but there are better sources for this material. Play diagrams and picture illustrations from actual games are used. No bibliography.

Bee, Clair F., *Zone Defense and Attack.* New York: A. S. Barnes and Company, 1942. 117 pp.

Probably the most complete analysis of the zone defense available. History, development, principles of zone covered; all styles explained with offensive attacks for each; diagrams and illustrations. Book not practical for the beginner in coaching or playing; recommended for the college coach. No bibliography.

Any of the above books by Clair Bee, coach for many years at Long Island University and later in professional basketball, would be good additions to a basketball library.

Bunn, John W., *Basketball Methods*. New York: The Macmillan Company, 1939. 327 pp.

Written after Mr. Bunn had enjoyed several highly successful seasons at Stanford University. A disciple of Dr. Allen, Kansas basketball coach, the author features zone defense. All parts of the game are well covered; one-hand shooting, made nationally popular through Hank Luisetti at Stanford, is explained in detail. Daily practice schedules and methods of instruction are valuable features.

Butler, George D., ed., *The New Play Areas; Their Design and Equipment*. New York: A. S. Barnes and Company, 1938, pp. 42, 70–72, 99, 101.

Important information on out-of-door basketball courts; type of material to be used, construction, dimensions; converting wading pools into basketball courts; popularity of the out-of-door basketball game. Of particular value to all physical educational directors and coaches. Present trends indicate great development of out-of-doors basketball.

Carlson, Harold Clifford, *Basketball: The American Game*. New York: Funk and Wagnalls Company, 1938. 189 pp.

A complete basketball book featuring continuity or Figure Eight basketball as used by Dr. Carlson for many years while coaching at the University of Pittsburgh. This popular style of offense is used in some variation by most coaches. Practical for classes as well as advanced teams. Illustrations and diagrams.

Chicago Park District. *Basketball Fundamentals Fully Illustrated*. Chicago: Chicago Park District, 1938. 92 pp.

Pamphlet published on basketball as a part of recreational series; valuable for any elementary instructor of basketball or for players. Covers fundamentals only.

Cordell, Christobel M., *Basketball Assemblies*. Portland, Maine: Platform News Publishing Company, 1942. 45 pp.

Reference in basketball administration.

Daher, Joseph G., and Clair F. Bee, *Fundamentals of Basketball*. Charleston, West Virginia: Morris Harvey College, 1941. 146 pp.

Other books by Clair Bee cover same material and are more complete.

Gee, Ernest Richard, compiler, *The Sportsman's Library: Being a Descriptive List of the Most Important Books on Sport*. New York: Bowker Company, 1940. 158 pp.

Includes a list of basketball books.

Gullion, Blair, *Basketball Offensive Fundamentals Analyzed.* Washington University, St. Louis: The Author, 1938.   88 pp.

A basketball monograph that explains the offensive fundamentals mainly through the use of individual pictures taken from slow action moving pictures.

Healey, William A., *High School Basketball.*   Minneapolis: Burgess Publishing Company, 1940.   68 pp.

A book for high school coaches; practical and easy to read. Duplicated pretty much in author's latter book: *Coaching and Managing High School Basketball.*

Hillas, Marjorie, and Marian Knighton, *An Athletic Program for High School and College Women.*   New York: A. S. Barnes and Company, 1938, Chapter VI.

Achievement tests in basketball; basketball squad practice; basketball relays; variety of basketball games.   One of the better references for women's basketball.

Holman, Nathan, *Championship Basketball.*   Chicago: Ziff-Davis Publishing Company, 1942.   155 pp.

The various fundamentals and team plays that make a championship team when properly executed.   Fundamentals are well illustrated; man-to-man defense is very good.   One of better books for coaches.   Film under same title also available through author.

Mr. Holman has coached at College of the City of New York for many years and was one of the outstanding professional players of all time.

Holman, Nathan, *Winning Basketball.*   New York: C. Scribner's Sons, 1935.   215 pp.

A good basketball book.   A more general treatment than Mr. Holman's later publication: *Championship Basketball.*   Various features of offensive and defensive styles of basketball are well covered.   The two-hand set shot is explained well.

Howard, Glenn W., *A Measurement of the Achievement in Motor Skills of College Men in the Game Situation of Basketball.*   New York: Teachers College, Columbia University, 1937 (Teachers College, Columbia University.   Contributions to Education, No. 733).   109 pp.

A scientific measurement of skills executed by college players in games.   Observation of each player for a specified length of time by expert judge; subjective methods and results not entirely satisfactory, but this is a study that should be examined by all coaches; should be an inspiration for much needed testing in basketball.

Dr. Howard is not a basketball coach but is professor of physical education at Queens College, New York. His dissertation is probably the first one ever done specifically in the field of basketball.

Hughes, William L., ed., *The Book of Major Sports*. New York: A. S. Barnes and Company, 1938, pp. 139–209.

Devotes a section to each major sport written by an expert in each sport. The basketball section is written by Charles C. Murphy, who duplicates this section in his book, *Basketball*. A rather ordinary treatment of the fundamentals of basketball. Questions for discussion and test questions on various phases of basketball are valuable.

Dr. Hughes was coach at DePauw University prior to his appointment as professor of physical education at Temple University.

Jourdet, Lon W., and Kenneth A. Hashagen, *Modern Basketball*. Philadelphia: W. B. Saunders Company, 1939. 165 pp.

A very complete book with excellent illustrations and diagrams. Section on set shooting excellent; all fundamentals; mainly eastern styles of offense and defense; coaching problems.

Mr. Jourdet was coach of University of Pennsylvania.

Miller, Ben W., and Karl W. Bookwalter and George E. Schlafer, *Physical Fitness for Boys; A Manual for the Instructor of the Service Program*. New York: A. S. Barnes and Company, 1943, Chapter VIII.

Team and group games of basketball; basketball for large classes; basketball tournaments; variations of basketball activities. Valuable for all physical education instructors.

Miller, William H., *Basketball of Tomorrow*. Tulsa, Oklahoma: The Jordon Company, 1938. 110 pp.

Mr. Miller was a veteran coach of Amateur Athletic Union teams. The Tulsa D. X. Oilers won the national championship under his coaching.

Mitchell, Elmer D., *Intramural Sports*. New York: A. S. Barnes and Company, 1939. 113 pp.

Details of arranging and managing college intramural tournaments; basketball tournaments covered thoroughly; basketball as most popular tournament game. Valuable for high school as well as college instructors.

Murphy, Charles C., *Basketball*. New York: A. S. Barnes and Company, 1939. 94 pp.

Printed from plates of *The Book of Major Sports*, edited by William L. Hughes, except photographic illustrations, which are supplied by Scholastic Coach.

A rather ordinary treatment of the fundamentals of basketball. Questions for discussion and test questions at the end of each chapter are valuable features.

Naismith, James A., *Basketball: Its Origin and Development.* New York: Association Press, 1941. 198 pp.

The last book by the inventor of basketball; how the game started; basketball in the earlier periods; present-day basketball; the future of the game. Interesting for general public; essential for all coaches and instructors for knowledge of game.

Neilson, Neils P., and Frederick W. Cozens, *Achievement Scales in Physical Education Activities for Boys and Girls in Elementary and Junior High School.* New York: A. S. Barnes and Company, 1939, pp. 18–19, 46–48, 112–114.

Tests on basketball throwing for girls and boys; test procedure. Should be valuable inspiration to coaches for more testing in basketball.

Peterman, Mark A., *Secrets of Winning Basketball*, rev. ed. Danville, Illinois: Interstate Printing Company, 1941. 96 pp.

Recommended for the high school coach. Distributed by National Federation of High School Athletic Associations, Chicago, and by A. S. Barnes and Company, New York.

Tobin, James F., ed., *Spalding's Official Basketball Rules for 1940–1941 as Adopted by the Amateur Athletic Union of the United States.* New York: American Sports Publishing Company, 1940.

A.A.U. rules written when A.A.U. was not a member of National Basketball Board.

Tobey, Dave, *Basketball Officiating.* New York: A. S. Barnes and Company, 1943. 73 pp.

Conditioning of the official; equipment, duties, officiating systems, single and double; game situations; ethics and relationships of the official, are all well covered. Chapter called Do's and Don't's is an added feature. Illustrations and diagrams. Recommended for officials and coaches.

Dave Tobey has been a prominent basketball official for over twenty-five years. He was coach at Savage College.

Tower, Oswald, ed., *Spalding's Official Basketball Guide for 1940–1941.* New York: American Sports Publishing Company, 1940.

Last publication of the guide by A. G. Spalding Brothers. This and all back copies of annual guide should be in library of the coach for reference. Divided into sections on college and high school records; official ratings; rules and interpretations.

United States Bureau of Aeronautics, Navy Department, *Basketball*. Washington, D. C.: United States Naval Institute, 1943. 257 pp.

One of several books on major sports written by expert coaches while in United States Navy. Intended for use in schools of all levels, including colleges; also playground and recreation centers. Stress is on mass participation.

Naval aviation basketball program reviewed; team defense and team offense; court facilities; the out-of-doors possibilities of basketball; equipment, safety precautions, ground school foundations; class organization and instruction.

Group III—prior to 1935

All books we know about published in this period are listed and recommended as historical references.

Allen, Forrest C., *My Basketball Bible*, 7th ed. Kansas City: Smith-Grieves Company, 1928.

An earlier book on all phases of basketball. Has been duplicated in Dr. Allen's later book: *Better Basketball*. Valuable now only as a historical reference on basketball.

Andersen, Leonora E., Basketball for Women. New York: The Macmillan Company, 1929.

Author has edited Basketball Guide for Women and is prominent teacher of basketball. Good general reference for women's basketball. Needs revision.

Andersen, Leonora E., *An Athletic Program for Elementary Schools*. New York: A. S. Barnes and Company, 1934, Chapters IV, V, VI.

Skill tests in basketball for elementary children; lead-up games to basketball. One of the more complete sources of information on basketball for grades one to twelve.

Angell, Emmett D., *Basketball for Coach, Player and Spectator*. Chicago: Wilson Western Sporting Goods Company, 1918.

One of the earlier pamphlets on basketball written for Wilson. An advertising feature, but very useful in its day. Valuable now only as a historical reference.

Barry, Justin M., *Basketball; Individual Play and Team Play.* Iowa City: The Clio Press, 1926. 123 pp.

  Written by Sam Barry while coaching basketball at University of Iowa. The late Mr. Barry also coached at University of Southern California for many years and was considered an expert on basketball.

Bickley, G., *Handbook of Athletics for Coaches and Players.* New York: A. S. Barnes and Company, 1929. 151 pp.

  Twenty-five diagrams on basketball are given, pp. 59 to 87. Material is out of date for current use.

Bliss, James G., *Basketball.* Philadelphia: Lea and Febiger Publishing Company, 1926.

  Included as historical reference.

Bocker, D., *Basketball for Women.* New York: T. E. Wilson and Company, 1920. 109 pp.

  Girls' basketball fundamentals, rules, plays, officiating. More modern treatment of the game is available.

Bowen, W. P., and Elmer D. Mitchell, *The Practice of Organized Play.* New York: A. S. Barnes and Company, 1929. 238 pp.

  Section of book is devoted to woman's basketball. See pp. 166–178 on related games. Material is old.

Carlson, Harold C., *You and Basketball.* Braddock: Brown Publishing Company, 1928. 173 pp.

Chandler, William A., and George F. Miller, *Basketball Technique.* Menomonie, Wisconsin: Dunn County *News*, 1922.

  The late Mr. Chandler coached many years at Marquette University. Included as historical reference.

Cummins, Robert A., *A Study of the Effect of Basketball Practice on Motor Reaction, Attention and Suggestibility.* Princeton, New Jersey: Psychological Review, 1914. 21:356–359.

  Important reference in research and testing in basketball.

Dudley, G., and F. A. Kellor, *Athletic Games in the Education of Women.* New York: Henry Holt and Company, 1909. 268 pp.

  Diagrams on women's basketball are on pp. 179–211. Good now for historical reference.

Fish, Marjorie E., *Theory and Technique of Women's Basketball.* Boston, New York: D. C. Heath and Company, 1929. 137 pp.

  Fundamentals are well illustrated. Later books are more complete.

Frost, Helen, and Charles D. Wardlaw, *Basketball and Indoor Baseball for Women.* New York: C. Scribner's Sons, 1920. 154 pp.

252 APPENDIX—BIBLIOGRAPHY

Excellent book in its day. Fundamentals of basketball well explained. Still valuable as reference for basketball during that period. Both authors were experts on basketball.

Frymir, Alice W., *Basketball for Women; How to Play and Coach the Game*. New York: A. S. Barnes and Company, 1928. 259 pp.

History and development of basketball; qualifications of the coach; basketball courts and equipment; all basketball fundamentals explained in detail; offensive and defensive basketball covered; how to play positions, healthful living habits and diet, competition for girls. Has limited number of diagrams and illustrations.

Gregg, Abel J., ed., *Basketball and Character*. New York: Association Press. Date not listed by C.B.I.

A pamphlet published between 1933 and 1937 by the Association Press (National Council of Y.M.C.A.).

Griffith, John L., and George P. Clark, *Basketball Plays and Attack; Fundamentals of Basketball; Fundamentals of Basketball Defense; Training the Basketball Team*. Chicago: Wilson Western Sporting Goods Company. Date not listed by C.B.I.

Four separate pamphlets published prior to 1928 for Wilson. Sold for fifty cents each and contain advertising material. Out of date now but useful as historical reference on basketball.

Gulick, Luther, *How to Play Basketball*. London: British Sports Publishing Company, 1907. 89 pp.

Mr. Gulick worked with Dr. Naismith in originating basketball. Book should be very valuable historical reference. One of original Spalding Athletic Library books, Group 7, No. 27.

Gulick, Luther, *A Symposium on Basketball*. Springfield, Massachusetts: American Physical Education Review, 1909. 14:376–389.

Another historical reference by one of the originators of basketball.

Hager, Robert H., *Percentage Basketball*. Oregon State College, Corvallis, Oregon: The Author, 1926. 112 pp.

Mr. Hager was coach at Oregon State College when book was written, but is no longer coaching.

An offensive style of basketball explained thoroughly; still used in some degree by many coaches; still a valuable reference. Fundamentals and defensive play also covered.

Hinkle, Paul, *Basketball's Assistant Coach*. Tiffin, Ohio: Saygers Sport Syndicate, 1933. Not listed in C.B.I.

Hepbron, George T., *How to Play Basketball*. New York: American Sports Publishing Company, 1904. 76 pp.

One of first books on basketball. Included for historical reference. One of Spalding's Athletic Library books, Vol. 17, No. 193.

Holman, Nathan, *Scientific Basketball*. New York: Incra Publishing Company, 1922. 123 pp.

This early book has been adequately replaced in all phases by Mr. Holman's more recent publications.

Hood Rubber Products Company. *Basketball Hints*. New York: Hood Rubber Products Company.

Booklets published by Hood between 1933 and 1937. Were distributed each year for advertising purposes but were very valuable; still good for references on fundamental notes. Include list of do's and don't's on offense and defense; plays and articles by leading coaches.

Indiana University, *King Basketball*. Bloomington, Indiana: The Author.

In print in 1928 and is distributed by Indiana University Book Store, Bloomington, Indiana. Included as historical reference.

Jones, Ralph R., *Basketball from a Coaching Standpoint*. University of Illinois, Urbana, Illinois: The Author, 1916. Not listed in C.B.I.

Included as historical reference.

Kennard, Ada B., *Tips on Girls' Basketball*. Detroit: *Sport Tips and Teaching Aids*, 1914. Not listed in C.B.I.

Practical for both players and teachers. A minimum of reading material and maximum of good diagrams. Wall charts also available.

Lambert, Ward Lewis, *Practical Basketball*. Chicago: Athletic Journal Publishing Company, 1932. 243 pp.

One of most complete publications on basketball. Short and long passing fast break; simple fundamentals properly applied; man-to-man defense, are features. Conditioning and training, coaching principles and suggestions very good. Revision necessary.

Ward Lambert was coach at Purdue University for over twenty-five years and was one of the best coaches in the country.

Martin, Warren L., *Shifting Basketball Defense*. Winfield, Kansas. Not listed in C.B.I.

Included as historical reference.

Mather, Edwin J., and Elmer D. Mitchell, *Basketball; How to Coach the Game*. New York: A. S. Barnes and Company, 1925. 109 pp.

An early illustrated book on basketball. Some fundamentals still apply but more recent books are better. Valuable only as a reference for basketball twenty years ago.

Meanwell, Walter E., *Science of Basketball for Men*. Madison, Wisconsin: H. D. Gath, 1924. 382 pp.

Explains the Meanwell short pass game in detail. Also covers all fundamentals well; particularly good on man-to-man defense. Probably best of earlier books and still quite practical except for team plays. Published in 1922 under title, *Basketball for Men*.

Dr. Meanwell was coach for many years at University of Wisconsin and was one of the leading coaches twenty-five years ago.

Meanwell, W. E., and K. K. Rockne, *Training, Conditioning and the Care of Injuries*. Madison, Wisconsin: H. D. Gath Publishing Company, 1930.

Part II is devoted to the training of a basketball team. Some of the suggestions are still helpful.

Messer, Guerdon N., *How to Play Basketball*. New York: American Sports Publishing Company, 1921. 101 pp.

A thesis in pamphlet form on the techniques of the game. Earlier edition published in 1911. One of Spalding's Athletic Library books, Group 5, No. 193. Valuable for historical reference.

Naismith, James A., and Luther H. Gulick, *Basketball*. New York: American Sports Publishing Co., 1896. 30 pp.

The first book on basketball. Authors originated the game. Explains how the game is played; general rules of the game; coaching suggestions. Valuable as historical reference. One of Spalding's Athletic Library books, Volume 2, No. 17.

Neilson, Neils P., and Winifred Von Hagen, *Physical Education for Elementary Schools*. New York: A. S. Barnes and Company, 1930, Part II.

A graded program of basketball for elementary schools. Games that lead up to basketball and other basketball activities are explained for each grade level. Useful for the elementary school teacher.

Nicholas, James R., *Technique of Basketball Officiating*. [1926]. 122 pp.

Included as historical reference.

Olsen, Harold, *Offensive Systems*. Tiffin, Ohio: Saygers Syndicate. Not listed in C.B.I.

The late Mr. Olsen was coach for many years at Ohio State University and also coached professional basketball.

Ruby, James C., *Team Play in Basketball*. Champaign, Illinois: Basketball Book Company, 1931. 157 pp.

A separate book dealing with team plays of various kinds, both offensive and defensive; value of team work in games; selection of squad. Duplicated in Part III of author's book: *Coaching Basketball*.

Ruby, James C., *Coaching Basketball*. Champaign, Illinois: Basketball Book Company, 1931. 307 pp.

Published in 1926 under title: *How to Coach and Play Basketball*. Mr. Ruby wrote these books when coach at University of Illinois. He is no longer coaching.

One of the best sources on fundamentals. Other sections need revision. Good reference for middlewestern basketball during earlier period.

Ruby, J. Craig, and G. C. Lipe, *How to Coach and Play Basketball*. Champaign, Illinois: Bailey and Himes, 1926. 268 pp. Illustrated.

One of the good early books on basketball coaching. Much of the material is duplicated in the author's later publications.

Smith, Hubert H., *Administration and Educational Values of a District Basketball Tournament*. New York: Teachers College, Columbia University, 1926. 7 pp.

A Phi Delta Kappa Thesis at Teachers College, Columbia University.

Veenker, George F., *Basketball for Coaches and Players*. New York: A. S. Barnes and Company, 1930. 234 pp.

Very complete book that is still practical. Fundamentals explained with illustrations. Simple plays diagrammed; particularly good on man-to-man defense and attacks against it.

Wardlaw, Charles Digby and Whitelaw R. Morrison, *Basketball: A Handbook for Coaches and Players*. New York: C. Scribner's Sons, 1921. 231 pp.

Fundamentals of basketball explained; training suggestions; administrational duties of the coach; how the game is played. Illustrations and diagrams. A very useful book in its day and valuable now as a history reference of basketball. Not recommended for the coach of present-day basketball.

Group IV—fiction and other non-technical books—all years to 1954

This is a miscellaneous list of picture and story books of a non-technical nature, including books for juveniles.

Allen, Forrest C., *Coach Phog Allen's Sports Stories for You and Youth*. Lawrence, Kansas: Allen Press, 1947. 223 pp. Illustrated.

This is a fine book of very interesting stories based on experiences of Coach Allen over the years. High quality.

Ayars, James Sterling, *Basketball Comes to Lonesome Point*. New York: Viking, 1952. Toronto: McMillan, 1952. 192 pp.

A story of boys starting a basketball team in their high school and their experiences. A young teen-age book.

Basloe, Frank J., *I Grew Up With Basketball*. New York: Greenberg, 1952. Toronto, Canada: Ambassador Books, Ltd., 1952. 210 pp.

How basketball started in Herkimer, New York. Interesting stories of games played more than fifty years ago. Barnstorming trips of that era described. In conclusion the author offers a controversial suggestion that a return to the old rules might aid the game. He prefers the game with the center jump after each goal, open baskets with no backboards; the game played in a cage and with limited substitution.

Bee, Clair F., *Backboard Fever*. New York: Grossett and Dunlap, Inc., 1953. 210 pp. Illustrated.

A Chip Hilton sports story for teen-agers.

Bee, Clair F., *Basketball Annual*. New York: Universal Publishing and Distributing Corporation, 1948. 128 pp.

Articles and stories of basketball written by college and professional coaches and others. Good entertainment.

Bee, Clair F., *Basketball Quiz Book*. New York: Greenberg, 1950.

Bee, Clair F., *Championship Ball*. New York: Grossett and Dunlap, Inc., 1948. 210 pp. Illustrated.

Another Chip Hilton sports story for teen-agers.

Bee, Clair F., *Hoop Crazy*. New York: Grossett and Dunlap, Inc., 1950. 215 pp. Illustrated.

A Chip Hilton sports story for teen-agers.

Burgoyne, Leon, *Jack Davis—Forward*. Philadelphia: Winston, 1954.

A Junior Literary Guild book.

Burgoyne, Leon, *State Champs*. Philadelphia: Winston, 1951. 210 pp.

Another book for juveniles. Illustrated by Joseph Balden.

Coombs, Charles, *Young Readers' Basketball Stories*. New York: Lantern Press, 1951. 191 pp.

A teen-age book (Young Readers' Bookshelf). Illustrated by Charles H. Geer.

Fishel, Richard Mark, and Clair Hare, *Terry and Bunky Play Basketball*. New York: Putnam, 1945. 80 pp.

A story book for the very young; elementary school level. Listed as a "how to play" book with some instructions in fundamentals.

Jackson, Carry Paul [pseudos. Colin Lochlons and Jack Paulson], *Tournament Forward*. New York: Crowell, 1948. Toronto, Canada: Ambassador Books, Ltd., 1948. 179 pp.

Recommended for ages twelve to sixteen. A story of high school basketball.

Keith, Harold, *A Pair of Captains*. New York: Crowell, 1951. Toronto, Canada: Ambassador Books, Ltd., 1951. 160 pp.

For ages ten to fourteen. The reactions of a young basketball captain to a newcomer. Another story of high school basketball. Simple vocabulary; large type. Illustrated by Mabel Woodbury.

Knapp, Sally Elizabeth, *Sink the Basket*. New York: Crowell, 1953. 186 pp.

For ages twelve to sixteen. A story of a girl whose love for the game led her into an experience which gave new meaning to her life. Illustrated by Dorothy Bayley Morse.

Lochlons, Colin [pseudos. Carry Paul Jackson and Jack Paulson], *Stretch Smith Makes a Basket*. New York: Crowell, 1949. Toronto, Canada: Ambassador Books, Ltd., 1949. 194 pp.

For ages ten to fourteen. A story of junior high school basketball. Stories and incidents with some coaching hints.

Mikan, George Lawrence, *Mr. Basketball*. New York: Greenberg, 1951. Toronto, Canada: Ambassador Books, Ltd., 1951. 80 pp.

George Mikan's own story as told to Bill Carlson. A very interesting, well illustrated book about the life and basketball experiences of one of the games' greatest stars. George Mikan has enjoyed top All America rating in both college and professional basketball. Closing chapter has valuable hints and tips for players.

Waldman, Frank [pseudo. Joe Webster], *Basketball Scandal*. New York: Pellegrini and Cudahy, 1953. 152 pp.

A book for juveniles. A story of high school basketball which includes an attempted bribe—successfully averted. Illustrated by Thomas G. Arthur.

Walton, Luke, *Basketball's Fabulous Five, The Indianapolis Olympians*. New York: Greenberg, 1950. Toronto, Canada: Ambassador Books, Ltd., 1950. 144 pp.

Biography, illustrations, and stories of five players who made national championship history at University of Kentucky. Gives later stories of these players while participating in the 1948 Olympic games and still later as professionals with Indianapolis. Not a coaching text.

Warner, Glenn S., and Lawton Wright, *Pop Warner's Book for Boys*. Toronto: Dodd, Revised Editions 1945, 1949.

Parts of book devoted to basketball. Illustrated by Richard Stevens.

Yarnell, Duane Leroy, *The Winning Basket*. New York: World Publishers, 1948. 217 pp.

A story for juveniles. "Ben Mason Comes Through for Clearview Academy."

Zinkoff, Dave, and Edgar Williams, *Around the World with the Harlem Globetrotters*. Philadelphia: Macrae Smith Company, 1953. 218 pp.

A very interesting, well illustrated book about the origin, development and travels of the Harlem Globetrotters. The author, secretary of the Globetrotters, assisted by Edgar Williams, does a fine job in bringing to the reader the fabulous travels of this team in the United States, and later to nearly every foreign country. Foreword by the astute originator, owner, coach, and manager of the Globetrotters, Abe Saperstein.

INDEX

Index